● ● ●

THE MEDIA ARCHIVE
WORLD EDITION

• • •

ADILKNO

[THE FOUNDATION
FOR THE ADVANCEMENT
OF ILLEGAL KNOWLEDGE]

• • •

Autonomedia

The Foundation for the Advancement of Illegal Knowledge/Adilkno: *The Media Archive. World Edition.*
Originally published as Stichting ter Bevordering van de Illegale Wetenschap: *BILWET Media-Archief,* Amsterdam: Ravijn, 1992; and Agentur Bilwet: *Medien-Archiv,* Mannheim: Bollmann, 1993.
Translated from the Dutch by Laura Martz, Washington, D.C., and Sakhra-l'Assal/Ziekend Zoeltjes Produkties, Amsterdam, 1997. Designed by Dave Mandl, Brooklyn, NY.

Adilkno (Dutch: "Bilwet"), The Foundation for the Advancement of Illegal Knowledge, was established in Amsterdam in 1983. It is a free association of authors and researchers.

In 1985 Adilkno published *The Empire of Images: Radiation Fear and Space Desire,* with analyses of *Paris, Texas, The Day After,* and *The Right Stuff.* In 1987 it translated into Dutch a book of essays by the German critic Wolfgang Pohrt. *Cracking the Movement: Squatting beyond the Media* was published in Dutch by Ravijn Books in 1990, in German in 1991 by Edition ID-Archiv (Berlin), and in 1994 in English by Autonomedia. *The Data Dandy,* a collection of essays on technoculture, appeared in German (Bollmann Verlag) and Dutch (De Balie) in 1994. Since 1989, in collaboration with the Academy of Ambulatory Sciences, Adilkno has edited the yearbook *Arcade.*

Many pieces in *The Media Archive* were originally written for the Dutch media art magazine *Mediamatic* and the Belgian film magazine *Andere Sinema (Other Cinema).*

Autonomedia
POB 568 Williamsburgh Station
Brooklyn, NY 11211-0568 USA
Phone & Fax: 718-963-2603
e-mail: autonobook@aol.com
http://www.autonomedia.org

Adilkno
POB 10591, 1001 EN Amsterdam
The Netherlands
Phone & Fax: (+31) 20 620-3207
e-mail: geert@xs4all.nl
http://thing.desk.nl/bilwet

Printed in the United States of America

Table of Contents

STYLIZED DESPAIR

GO BEYOND

SELF-RECEPTION

WRITING IN THE MEDIA

*"The archive! It cannot count on my wholehearted sup-
port. The A. is a philological and dusty thing, that interests
no-one; even the Nietzsche-A.:—who knows of it, who ever
visited it, whom has it impressed?"*
—Gottfried Benn

To write about media is to raise the question of what gives writing the presumption to speak for other media. Language presents itself as the
metamedium to contain all past and future media. In Western textual culture,
phenomena are only considered understood once they have been included
in a final story. Theory is believed to possess an extraordinary gift, lacking in
audio and video, to solve the mysteries that drive the phenomenal universe.
Whereas the word still maintains that the question of the world is in writing,
the symbol has long since assumed it is a geometrically representable master plan. Once, the harmony of the spheres was a musical program.

Preaching, drama, cinema, television, museum, sports, and concerts all
unite their audience in a collective ceremony. Conversely, solitary reading
creates a distance from the receptive ritual's shared experience, so that the
reader feels as if he or she were the only one receiving this medial transmission. The immanent silence in reading creates an imaginary space where
language appears to soar above the immediate tumult of the mass media.
The idea of order, which gives language its charm, is a medial effect that is
abruptly disturbed when someone reads over your shoulder. Insight is as
much the technological circuit's noise as it is an authentic source of information unique to primates. Writing is no exception to the rule. Media constitute
a closed system which sends off sparks into the cosmic void every once in a
while. Amidst the media landscape, we are never more than tourists who
keep stubbornly looking for landmarks.

Media writing ought to situate itself within the media network. Even
those who believe they can place themselves outside it in some heroic gesture and deny the omnipotence of the media remain just one among many
media figures. This puritanical, old-fashioned ambition, as surely as any
other, will result in an end product to be included in the universal media
archives. The consistent response to this is to destroy one's complete oeuvre,
which will serve to create not only a legend but a mountain of waste as well,

at the disposal of many an inquisitive generation to come. The halfway approach—to merely shut down all links to normality for a time, in order to lead the personal medium to ecstasy within an artificial desert—is to dream of conquering all other modes of expression on one's return. All that the outsiders ever notice of this totalitarian claim by certain media tribes is a brilliant book, a good film, or a pleasant evening. No matter how one-dimensional the talented presentation, in the media sphere the unique commodity is always and instantly classifiable as part of a genre, period, or development. The figure of the alien who grazes on history and deposits its droppings in it may be real enough—at the end of the day, it's just another modern artist who realizes the state of its art and acts accordingly.

The media text is not concerned with the secret intentions lurking behind an information transmission. Media are not carriers of cultural or ideological values. Rather than transporting messages from A to B, they form a parallel world of their own which never touches on classical reality. Media see the world as raw material for their own project, nothing else. Writing in the media does not seek the media's internal logic within their processed material, but within their ecstatic strategies. Media are forced to constant development, since all their ecstatic routes can be taken only once, after which the technique used becomes obsolete. Media never mature past the trial stage. Every medium must, time and again, discover its own dynamics in order to bring itself to a new conclusion.

The path followed by the various media thus far is the subject of textual-materialist media theory. The way in which media suck up material from reality is the theme of communication studies, while the field of cultural studies sides with the viewers. The media text, on the other hand, forgets about dialectics and strives for ecstasy, having understood itself to be part of the media. The media text, like the media themselves, can never produce a final understanding that might be established in a dissertation or magnum opus. Caught in the stage of experiment, it carries on in its own irresponsible but methodical way. The media text looks for trajectories, models of thought, tactical maneuvers, and magic words that will help it spell itself out to the point of exhaustion.

The media text describes no reality or ideas beyond the text. Its material are the media themselves—not their equipment or programs, but their possibilities. The electrosphere is full of potential media and media forms. Their present or future being is uncertain, but nonetheless open to examination. The media text offers an irresponsibly rash insight into them. It speculates on chance, danger, dream, nightmare. It challenges potential media to get real, starting with the media text itself. It provokes language to take on these forms. Potential media exist only as options, but once they are described, you run into them everywhere.

Liquid theory does not aim at an overall text, to be constructed chapter by chapter. The media text is no rhizomatic elaboration on schizoid currents, nor is it about stretching difference yet further. It focuses on the vaguest possible contours with the utmost sharpness. In its compelling will to text, it treats any concept or info that breezes by with systematic arbitrariness. It does not need to categorize its subjects—the magic words just cling to the media text, refusing to let go until they've crystallized. A media overview is by definition infeasible. The media text enables the potential media field to download on the level of language, so as to condense the mega data package which scrolls by as the limited, but (to us) comprehensible, Compact Text format.

Generation, manipulation, and recording are no longer sequential stages in data handling, but always take place simultaneously. Preservation does not take place after the fact, in the service of history, but is a technological a priori (F10). The unlocking of the media archives does not take place in the post-medial world, though they anticipate it will. The archives wish neither to raise an ode to transience and its traces nor to unleash protest against it. The construction of a new freeway attracts previously immobile traffic. To switch on a medium is to conjure up previously unregistered data. To establish a media archive is to attract files that would otherwise never have been compiled. To compile is no less to generate, than to generate is to compel to compilation; simultaneity works both ways. Starting an archive is sufficient to have it fill up with new material. There exists no more gratifying task than to write for the desk drawer.

Passive storage is not enough; data must be retrievable as quickly and efficiently as possible. While it is relatively easy to optimize access to one's personal archives, the real trouble starts with visits to other people's datasheds. On the other hand, this inaccessibility is an essential condition for amazing discoveries. Permanence is the hallmark of all structured attempts at preservation. The media archives will prove to be modernity's Alexandria, and likewise go up in smoke. Once the bookshelf has fallen over, it may be a small disaster to the author, but a giant step for the readers. The greater the gibberish beheld by the writer, the more clarity is gained by the audience. The media archives are open to any unsuspected cross-connections, and generously invite misreadings. They do not strive for the ultimate aha-experience, but anticipate the metamorphosis of their own content. To read books = to destroy books.

The Media Archive presents computer-aided theory (CAT) from the era of word processing (WP 4.2). The empty screen is an essential feature of word perfection, an electronic *tabula rasa* whose only known factors are the coordinates of the theory-to-come (Doc Pg Ln Pos). The soft page has not yet supplanted the letter-size thinking of the typewriting era ("to the end of the page and no further"), a poor use of computing capacity that shifts the computer into suspension gear: The PC processes nothing; the LCD screen's restricted parking area leaves all options open. Menu bars, sidekicks, windows next to or behind the text, even simple subscreens: They either were missing or remained unused. CAT is as flat as a pancake. No hidden codes, no footnotes, no registers. The keyboard's greatest literary achievement is the DELETE key. The computer serves as an unprecedented text-compression tool, and this is where it comes in handy in media archiving.

Compact hermeneutics rears its head as a compressed file, unzipped by the reader when requesting a book into an overall text, suddenly rich in slanted distinctions. The theoretical signal has been divested of its superfluous profundity. Even with 70 percent of the argument omitted, discourse still comes through loud and clear. There is no question of clandestine advertising for other registered authors. Our subliminal discomfort, which would like to have the diagonal text related to something at least, is not rewarded with specific clues.

Those in dataland who believe they have the hang of pattern recognition soon embark on a quest for the exclusive keyword to disclose new universes. Such magic words, however, may also settle in from outside, and start to suck up charged particles of theory, factoids, and semi-quotes. The massive assault on keywords continues until the inevitable overload occurs: time to reset. Unidentified Theoretical Objects (UTOs) are chance theoretical field compressions. Their vocabulary is discovered on desert islands in the web of scanned-in text. UTOs are crystal balls gleaming with the dim light of a yet-nonexistent theorem.

The peremptory essay ends the discussion before it has even begun. The arguments surrounding a given problem area are surveyable and refutable from the start. This fact lies at the basis of theoretical modesty, of its hope that all existing problems seem so familiar because they are never more than extensions of the twentieth century. To take debates never held to their logical conclusion holds a promise that beyond every existing issue there lies a hinterland, the "world after the media," in which the eve of destruction will not be repeated again, but we will end up way beyond World War IV instead.

Deconstruction, like semiotics, is a traditional method of reading. It is not an intellectual project to dismantle culture as a whole, but a faculty which—provided it is exercised a little—enables you to get your own show on the road. Once everything has been analyzed, it's time to think through the non-deconstructible remainder. Text destruction launches word processing. Critical casuistry test-drills a promising topos, taking a maniacal interest in paradigmatic splinters. It tries to say as much as it can about the smallest imaginable clues, without paying much attention to the entire exegetic field that surrounds them. It provides precision arguments about the how, not the why, of phenomena breezing by. By contrast, the study of disciplines—with its expanded-theory toolkit—carries out full-time research of the overall outline and places miscellaneous partial issues within a framework that provides insight as to why things are experienced as problematic in the first place. It seeks an arbitrary methodology that will suggest hitherto nonexistent relations. Since it claims no truths, it is dismissed as pseudo-science by the schools of thought analyzed by it. A negative thinking which denies all claims to unicity and the universality of actually existing attempts to interpret the world, is itself the gay science par excellence. Media theory cracks up over the determination whereby movie theory, art history, or dramaturgy defend their specific "extensions of man" and challenge their rivals by accusing them of cultural deterioration.

The media archives contain all the data in the world. The Adilkno branch is a scant and paltry thing; all this archive contains is instructions on the impressionability of the media, and proposals as to how to get rid of them. It was unpremeditatedly compiled in the period between 1988 and 1995, in response to the short summer of the media. Now that autumn is on its way and permanent tourism is likewise coming to an end, the question of the media is becoming more urgent. Both the global and alternative use of media have become stuck in perfect professionalism. Even without a Gulf War, infotainment is just no fun. The reality effects are superseded more quickly than technology can produce them. Now that it becomes clear that the media have no answer to their own global questions; we see a revival of premedial affairs, so that after a period of liberating breakdown and decline there threatens a dismal stage of reconstruction. The archives, on the other hand, stumble blindly into the postmedial world's state of uncertainty. It is only from that future that they can look back with pleasure on the media, without bitterness or nostalgia.

SOVEREIGN MEDIA

"I cue you."

—DFM

In this age of media overproduction, information immunity is a question of life or death. When the defense mechanism fails and the consumer is overwhelmed by strange impressions, doom seems near. To call a halt to crippling indifference, a media diet is prescribed. The pressure exerted on world citizens to constantly adapt their own image of the world and put technological innovations into practice puts them into a permanent state of insecurity. The urge to create disappears, and we are merely able to react to the overwhelming array of choices. Data are no longer stimuli to interest, but an inimical barrage constituting a physical threat. From exchange to effacement: communication is preying on naked existence.

Sovereign media insulate themselves against hyperculture. They seek no connection; they disconnect. This is their point of departure; we have a liftoff. They leave the media surface and orbit the multimedia network as satellites. These do-it-yourselfers shut themselves up inside a self-built monad, an "indivisible unit" of introverted technologies which, like a room without doors or windows, wishes to deny the existence of the world. This act is a denial of the maxim "I am connected, therefore I am." It conceals no longing for a return to nature. They do not criticize the baroque data environments or experience them as threats, but consider them material to use as they please. They operate beyond clean and dirty, in the waste system ruled by chaos *pur sang*.

Their carefree rummaging in the universal media archive is not a management strategy for jogging jammed creativity. These negative media refuse to be positively defined and are good for nothing. They demand no attention and constitute no enrichment of the existing media landscape. Once detached from every meaningful context, they switch over in fits and starts from one audio/video collection to the next. The autonomously multiplying connections generate a sensory space which is relaxing as well as nerve-racking. This tangle can never be exploited as a trend-sensitive genre again. All the data in the world alternately make up one lovely big amusement park and a five-star survival trek in the paranoid category, where humor descends on awkward moments like an angel of salvation and lifts the program up out of the muck.

Unlike the antimedia, which are based on a radical critique of capitalist (art) production, sovereign media have alienated themselves from the entire business of politics and the art scene. An advanced mutual disinterest hampers any interaction. They move in parallel worlds which do not interfere with each other. No anti-information or criticism of politics or art is given in order to start up a dialogue with the authorities. Once sovereign, media are no longer attacked, but tolerated and, of course, ignored. But this lack of interest is not a result of disdain for the hobbyist amateur or political infantilism; it is the contemporary attitude toward any image or sound that is bestowed on the world anyway.

Sovereign media are equipped with their own starters and do not need to push off from any possible predecessors or other media. They are different from the post-'68 concept of alternative media and from the autonomous "inside" media of the eighties. The alternative media work on the principle of antipublicity and mirror the mainstream media, which they feel needs to be corrected and supplemented. This strategy aims to make individuals aware of their behavior as well as opinions. This process will ultimately be seen in a changed public opinion. These little media have no general claims but work with a positive variant of the cancer model, which assumes that in the long term everyone, whether indirectly or through the big media, will become informed about the problem being broached. They presuppose a tight network stretched around and through society, so that in the end the activism of a few will unleash a chain reaction by the many. Until that time, they direct themselves at a relatively small group, in the certainty that their info will not stay stuck in a ghetto or start feeding back in the form of internal debates. This "megaphone model" aims in particular at liberal-leftist opinion leaders, who have no time to accumulate information or invent arguments and get politically motivated specialists to do this thankless work. Movements in the sixties and seventies gave themes like feminism, the third world and the environment a great range this way. Professionalization and market conformism in those circles, however, have caused people to switch to the "real" media. The laboratories where information and argumentation get tested are currently an inseparable part of the media manufacturing process, now that their movements have become just as virtual as the media they figure in.

At the end of the seventies, radicals who had gotten tired of waiting for the other's change of consciousness founded the so-called "inside media." At precisely the moment that the official media started emancipating themselves and terms like "press" and "public opinion" vanished from the scene, a group of activists gave up the belief in their deaf fellow citizens and got to work themselves. Although to unknowing outsiders they seemed a continuation of the alternative media activity, they let go of the cancer model and, like the official media, went gliding. The mirror of the alternative media was

13

shattered. It had become pointless to keep appealing to public responsibility; they needed to look for a different imaginary quantity to concentrate on: "the movement."

Although they were only locally available, they had no concern for the regional restrictions which the ascending local media impose upon themselves. They no longer wanted to be alternative city papers. In form as well as content they became transnational, like their global peers. They wanted nothing to do with growth. Their brilliant dilettantism turned out to be not a childhood illness, but an essential component. As a leftover product of vanished radical movements, which flare up every now and then, their continuity and unchangingness remain breathtaking to this day. It cannot be reduced to their dogma. They turn away from the short media time and create their own space-time continuum.

Sovereign media are the cream of all the missionary work performed in the media galaxy. They have cut all surviving imaginary ties with truth, reality, and representation. They no longer concentrate on the wishes of a specific target group, as the "inside" media still do. They have emancipated themselves from any potential audience, and thus they do not approach their audience as a moldable market segment, but offer it the "royal space" the other deserves. Their goal and legitimacy lie not outside the media, but in practicable "total decontrol." Their apparently narcissistic behavior bears witness to their being sure of themselves, which is not broadcast. The signal is there; you only have to pick it up. Sovereign media invite us to hop right onto the media bus. They have a secret pact with noise, the father of all information. And time is not a problem; there is room for the extended version as well as the sampled quotation.

This is only possible through the grace of no-profile. Without being otherwise secretive about their own existence, the sovereigns remain unnoticed, since they stay in the blind spot that the bright media radiation creates in the eye. And that is the reason they need not be noticed as an avant-garde trend and expected to provide art with a new impetus. The reason sovereign media are difficult to distinguish as a separate category is because the shape in which they appear can never shine in its full luster. The program producers do not show themselves; we see only their masks, in the formats familiar to us. Every successful experiment that can possibly be pointed to as an artistic or political statement is immediately exposed to contamination. The mixers inherently do not provoke, but infect chance passersby with corrupted banalities which present themselves in all their friendly triviality. An inextricable tangle of meaning and irony makes it impossible for the experienced media reader to make sense of this.

The atmosphere inside the sealed cabin conflicts with the ideology of networking. As a central coordination machine, the computer subjects all old media to the digital regime. The sovereign media, conversely, make their own kind of connections, which are untranslatable into one universal code. High-tech is put to the test and turned inside out. But this trip to the interior of the machine does not result in a total multimedia artwork. Disbelief in the total engagement of the senses and technically perfect representation is too great for that. The required energy is simply generated by short-circuits, confusion of tongues, atmospheric disturbances and clashing cultures. Only when computer-driven networks begin to break their own connections, and scare off their potential users, will it be time for the sovereigns to log in.

NORMAL MEDIA

In the long run, everything becomes interesting; such is the fate of normal media. The only surviving Mayan text may reveal the deepest mysteries to us or turn out a department store ad: neither would make it any less fascinating. Normal media are characterized by the fact that they cannot be interpreted as cultural expressions during their time of appearance. It is only after they become a collection with the appropriate chronology or an object of study for the science of normal history that they acquire that little extra of a misaddressed letter or conversation at the next table. Only through such annexations can the imagination be stimulated to practice the hermeneutics of everyday life.

Normal media, when planted into their natural environment, are so obvious that they exclude all metalevels. They are so much a part of their own space-time that they do not allow for the necessary distance to observe them in an anthropological sense, or simply for pleasure. They are like the tiny bone from which the whole dinosaur is deduced, or the one scene through which the entire movie can be reconstructed. As long as they remain submerged in everyday life, they are of minimal information value. But as paradigmatic splinters, they reveal the entire landscape in which they once figured. Untimely normal media can only be conceived of as the inconceivable.

Normal media require no advertising. They are handed out uninvited in inescapable editions. Waste is a precondition. Direct mail has achieved its goal if three percent of the recipients react. Normal media institutions abuse the statutory obligation to receive mail. Thus, we find descriptions of stray cats, announcements for next-door parties, Scientology leaflets about Hubbard's latest, an invitation to the official opening of Harry's Butcher's, interior design catalogues, respectable students seeking apartments, a salsa dance class, supermarket special offers, various local papers, a book club catalogue, Chinese takeout and Italian delivery menus, the neighborhood newsletter, a personal message "to all those at the designated address," political flyers, and cultural teasers. A similar category survives in the news sphere in the form of personal ads and obituaries, personal announcements and readers' letters. The white and yellow pages, too, enjoy regular contact with average folks.

Normal Media

Uninvited media ignore the contemporary consumer habit to compile one's own, personal media package. The classic unilateral model in which recipient B had no choice but to accept the message from source A has been renounced as undemocratic. The adage of "choose your own message" has turned reception into an act of volition. The media for the millions cut right through this conscious selection, sovereign to the extent that they are uninterested in market penetration or spiritual incorporation. They feel at home in a stack of old newspapers, down the hallway, out in the street, on top of a garbage can.

Normal media design requires a certain period of incubation before it can be recognized as such. In their layout, normal media neither plunder the work of risqué avant-gardists nor make an appeal to nostalgia. They inadvertently succeed in short-circuiting the field of tension between folk and mass culture. Their problem is how to draw attention without becoming interesting. They must avoid their instant degradation into a message for a single market sector at all costs. They combine the amateurish clumsiness of the anniversary and marriage song with the professional charisma of the quizmaster and reyue artist. Desktop publishing, handycamcorders and autozoom see to it that neither level is ever attained. They reveal a carefully edited normality in which there is room for everyone. This is where contempt fails. Average media may be copied, but they cannot be parodied. Letters by the city council or local industries may be a standard weapon in the Spaßguerrilla repertoire, but the first ironic mail order catalogue has yet to be written.

To turn to normal media for innovative content is useless. They have turned McLuhan's brilliant analysis—that the content of the media consists of the preceding media—into their editorial policy. They are shopwindows in print, visual radio shows, screen adaptations of myth, digitized town criers, neighbors by phone, motorized billboards. Whereas sovereign media still manage to produce some alienating effects by broadcasting movies on radio, filming novels by the page, screening radio plays or word processing in cyberspace, watching the radio on television has become common practice, what with talk shows, game shows, and the news. Tolerant media aren't necessarily conservative, just because they elaborate on the preceding situation. They do not long for the return of God, country, and the family, but offer a new security. Vegetarians are not upset by horsemeat mailings. On the other hand, racist propaganda is instantly exposed by its display of prewar typography and Nazi palette. Normal media merely annoy us because of their overwhelming numbers and the certainty that this particular stream will never dry up.

Dominant images may be scratched, stilled, or sampled, but they cannot be turned into camp. Normal media are distributed far beyond the reaches of kitsch. The only way to increase banality is through outdated pictures. For instance, there are no recorded instances yet of an ironic use of laptops or other mobile immaterials. Meanwhile, the solid wares that gave consumer society its material charm give one plenty to go on. Normal media are always one step ahead of the banality fans. Their emptiness is so much a product of its age that even the artistic avant-garde of durability radically overlooks it. Only as foundered cultural values can the maxima normalia become discourse carriers, and thus fit for artistic recycling.

Vague Media

*"The magna of culture: confused traditions, mono-opin-
ions, inconsequent discourses and quasi-argumentations."*
—Alex in *Xuxem*

Vague media do not respond to success. They do not achieve their goals. Their models are not argumentative, but contaminative. Once you tune in to them, you get the attitude. But that was never their intention; their vagueness is not an ideal, it is the ultimate degree of abstraction. The ability to avoid specific questions is combined with answers which lack any depth of field. This is why vague media still manage to appear diplomatic and polite. Their social critique is troubled by an unsteady worldview. For them, crisis does not lead to a new beginning, but to a gradual evaporation of the problem area. Doubt doesn't merely arise; it's a sixth sense. The senselessness of existence renders everything a sensible activity which can be given up whenever desired, so that nothing ever gets finished. Here, no one works; rather, one devotes oneself to taking apart and putting back together undefined objects and projects. The liquid being of vague-media adherents never crystallizes into definite forms. When beginning and endpoint have disappeared from view, existence can be experienced in peace. Having obliterated the factor of time, the vague ones distribute their concentration over n years and transmit their broadcasts only on homeopathic frequencies. They are no less present for that.

Vague media do not depend on any network requiring construction or maintenance. The lines of the net are dissolved in an astral mist. In lieu of distribution decisions, a random selection is offered, and eagerly snapped up. In this post-atomic business culture, uncertainty is the foundation of efficiency. The untrustworthiness of agreements is not a result of other activities, but a sign of good will. The field of possibilities is left open at all times. There is a willingness to get caught up in anything, be it a meeting, party, or accident. Parallel to transparent society, there unfolds a cloud of vague structures through which the subject moves in Brownian motion. This nonlinearity defies the rhizomatic dogma that prescribes endless switching. These hard-luck pilots do not wander, but stumble from one discontinuity to the next. Nor is it a case of trees or roots. With vague media, a veiled belief in progressive bifurcation gives way to mist on the window to eternity.

The Media Archive

Undirected recreations form temporary compressions in the random distribution of particles that roam the vague ether. Whatever order may be discovered in this chaos, it fails to impress the insiders. The brilliant conspiracy will be heard out for a while, then forgotten.

Vague media are impossible to follow. Their fuzzy logic frustrates signifiers in search of uni- or multivocality. The result is a fluffy sign (information value 0.34 or 2.74). Nothing is concealed or intentionally distorted. One simply does not know exactly, and this message comes through. In spite of it all, the other gets plenty of room to voice its revolutionary message. There is no fear of data here. The historical excursion is a strenuous exertion gladly undertaken, though the history of vagueness has yet to be written. There are still plenty of shadowy Greek philosophers and not-so-lucid theologians to be discovered who didn't quite get around to making their statements, or brilliant Renaissance painters who never came into their own. The B movie rose above pulp and started being taken seriously a long time ago; there is no reason why the same fate should not befall B thinkers (e.g., Russell), B literature, and the rest of illegible culture. Certain historical figures have found their natural habitat in vague media: Mao, Gysin, Manson, Reich, Jesus, Debord, Meinhof, Fromm, Hitler, Hendrix, Castaneda, Goldman, Marley, Pippi Longstocking; furthermore, cookbooks, weapons, children's drawings, witches, blood, skulls and crossbones, and animals (by all means, animals). As long as it's cut up, overloaded with text, dark and intense, with heavy black-and-white illustrations.

The vague medium as object and the vague one as determinant subject are inseparable. Their shared foggy concept of barriers prevents man & media from growing apart. Comprehensibility arises only when the subject succeeds in extracting an object, thus rendering himself obsolete. Vagueness is not so much a strategy as it is a style of media. The matching design, as rugged as it is blurred, does not signify a lack of concept, but something like an essentialist approach. Media are not used as homes or garments, but as durable nutrition that will last for years. Media, housing and clothing become interesting only after they've lost all practical or exchange value and any hope of ever becoming youthful, nice, hip, or risqué—in short, modern— again. Because the vague ones lack the team spirit that distinguishes most fashionable trends and movements, they immediately recognize the foreign as their own, whereas the normal is alien to them. They have passed through the doors of perception without realizing it and are incapable of finding anything normal in normality. This explains their immense rage against anything or anyone who tries to force things on them that are "only part of the complex society we live in." Far from profound, their indignation lashes out unreservedly, to be as quickly forgotten again—until the next clash. Not wishing to be irresponsible, they reject all responsibility. Johnsons in a mediascape full of shitheads, they subscribe to the slogan, "Mind your own business and let other people mind theirs." Their only means of attack is the boycott, the active denial of the enemy: Don't smoke, don't buy, don't go, don't drink, don't refuel. The achievement of the campaigns is to burden activists with impossible standards.

Vague media are not out of focus, badly printed, or amateurishly edited—or are they? Their technological presumption is unshakable. Their appearance has been carefully prepared. But these nebulous media do not consider themselves products, but atmospheres. It's much harder to generate a cloud than it is to cover up in the hype blown up by fleeting contacts. All information is admitted to a dimension where the whole is not distinguished from the obsolete detail. Overload does not occur, as time knows no bounds and chaos is part of the mystery of the world. Information and noise only differ when you're in a hurry. The issue of hazy media results from a spring cleaning of the personal archive. In contradiction to Third World scrap collectors who scrutinize garbage dumps in search of recyclable goods, the transmitters of crap patiently comb the public domain for material to embellish their private dumps with. Another example of Grassmuck-Unverzagt's Law: Waste can be transferred but not destroyed.

Ongoing research in the semi-scientific domain consists exclusively of sources, and is not concerned with such trivia as surveys, summaries, or final conclusions. Vague media adhere to the teachings of Claude Shannon, who holds that views and opinions can be deciphered only as information. The preference for torn-out newspaper photographs does not mean they see them as illustrations or works of art; instead they are a collection of possible meanings, none of which takes preference over the others. Even the more powerful signs and symbols (such as the star or swastika) that keep popping up on their pages and frequencies are blessed with this charm. Like crystal-ball media, they are simultaneously maximally and minimally abstract. From the viewpoint of vague media, meaning is a matter best left to users. To them, the blurred relationship between sign and meaning is a social achievement.

Far from being particularly obsessive or passionate, vague media harp forever on the same subject. Whereas sovereign media are on a perpetual journey of discovery, the vague channels pitch their tents for an indefinite time or stick around forever. The universe is all around, so why mobilize? For vague media, the greatest mystery is their own functioning. This existential moment sees to it that individual expressions never take on a definite or immutable form, yet make a point. The travelers of the *"terrain vague"* find their way in wastelands where even the hot-spot *tourists du moment* get lost. Vague media are not concerned with forms, but with the empty spaces in between, which are timeless. This is why they will long outlive the rising and setting of other media.

TOPICAL MEDIA

"Real time means less than three seconds, so that anything giving news within five goes under the umbrella of historical information."

—Reuter

Information as such radiates such availability that it evokes only pure revulsion. As being per se, it is just a little more than life can handle. Data can never be taken for granted. They must be made to resonate and processed through state-of-the-art equipment. Processing technology must be continually updated to prevent data from escaping and regaining their obstinate parasitical silence. Decay and erosion are major issues in the world of the recording and processing industries. Data recorded on magnetic tapes or CDs instantly cover themselves up in soothing static, soon giving up all legibility in terms of significance, listening pleasure, or other methods of pacification. It is only when the smooth generators have brought them to life that data become amusing. No recreation without creation. Watching the telephone or listening to movie reels is no longer a form of entertainment, but a sign of real obsession.

Back in the days when messages were still carried by sailing vessels, they were allowed to ripen into reports. Data developed into news because they had a chance to mature. Only when accompanied by opinions and commentaries could the message escape such crushing remarks as, "What business is that of mine?" By consolidating and concentrating the mixture of incoming messages, editors could impart their daily coherent worldviews. The substantialist presentation of ephemeral sensation enabled citizens to absorb the news as a segment of the daily package. It successfully provoked a general interest by appearing as a regulated encroachment on the ritual of personal existence. News originated outside. Inside, it caused the necessary reactions, spreading through the national community as the topics that gave it the required solidarity.

The notion of topicality originates with the acceleration of transport. The significance of the event was increasingly determined by absolute time. The interval left for the message to parade itself as today's item was reduced ever further. For example, on January 23, 1766, the *Amsterdamsche Courant* reports that the King of Denmark has fallen seriously ill. On January 28, it informs us that "Copenhagen is plunged into bitter mourning over the passing of its beloved Monarch," even though in fact he had already died on January 14. In other words, the moment of the monarch's death lasted two weeks. In telematics, this regime of the interval is utterly defeated, while reports of tales from elsewhere become never-ending stories. Reports are no longer delivered in segments, but as part of a continuous flow centered around local time. News no longer reaches you, but is permanently present. Instead of occupying a fixed place within daily routine, it can be consumed whenever desired.

Until recently, obstinate personal timetables were still curbed by the programmed media. They managed to lend an aura of news to info by selecting, saving, and dressing it so that the ritual digestion of international titbits regained its air of collectivity. News reports became platforms for local nationalities. The dictates of time imposed by the programmers and their television guides gave one the comfortable feeling of having made a personal choice by switching on the set. Programmed media presumed that the consumer as subject would naturally collaborate with the makers in giving a meaningful context to the presentation. It is when data succeed in escaping such dictates and television becomes a piece of furniture like sideboard family pictures that topical media are introduced.

Topical media appear as an interruption of the program. The fatal topicality of traffic (traffic information broadcasts, ghost drivers) is used as a means of coercion to stay tuned, even at home. Life itself is conceived of as a traffic flow that must never be interrupted. One unexpected result of the capacity of topicality to suggest relevant hierarchies that justify jumping the queue was the media users' fragmentation as subjects: As far as topical media were concerned, they no longer had a say. The equality between news and entertainment was restored by settling topical media on a wavelength of their own. At first, news still interrupted the regular program, but this invasion was soon allotted its own channel. But at the same time this eliminated the pretense that topical media have a universal right to all those aged eight to 88. Every minority was delivered its own message. Thus, the notion of conquerable markets became an integrated part of the medial and the liberal proliferation of channels could commence.

The secret of topical media is that they present themselves as separate media to the point where all programmed media are temporarily switched off or banished to tiny subscreens. Topicality's now-or-never is incompatible with lasting ratings. To everybody's surprise, the inflammatory character of spontaneous news bursts soon turns out to be the ultimate stage-managed affair. Those who are looking for in-depth information are better off having a chat with the neighbors or reading a book. Topicality and news are mutually exclusive. Once topical media start broadcasting live press conferences so that journalists will have something to write about, the interval in which events can turn into news is destroyed, as we watch the reporters on screen get up to report what we've just been watching. Long before the cameras arrive at the scene, we have already videotaped the stills of the camcorder witness.

When we can watch Nobel Prize writers write their award-winning novels via bulletin boards, or witness the shooting of a Hollywood feature to be released next spring via movie channels, or listen to live broadcasts of telephone conversations between world leaders, or follow the studio takes of a world-famous musician's CD live on radio, and when the only reports we see are about the production process of special reports: then the end product lags so much behind topicality that it can only be appreciated as waste. Why bother to buy the disc at all, when all of us have just spent months listening to the new track's recordings, minutely evaluating the various takes? The public is placed into the position of permanent journalists, while the viewers must keep on switching to get the message. Thus, the period of reception is given an active interpretation.

Waste has always been a pure object. One promising consequence of the silly urge to consolidate collected data into an end product screaming for a cool design is that all it does is attract more waste. Nobody needs to read the magazines, because everybody knows what graphic programs they were made with. But that which loses its meaning regains its secret. Obsolete media have successfully restored their silence. By nature, data evoke suspicions that they are not alone. They are always found in groups. Data may operate but cannot be received as such. Every single bit of data counts; data never lose their obstinate character. One cannot simply address data, one must know which language to speak. To look at data is to objectify them—as waste.

Topical media are media in progress. No longer able to produce instant documents, they roam the regions of raw material forever. At present, the avant-gardes of hard info study the next phase, in which the redundancy of end products will go without saying. They frantically test the data–vacuum cleaners developed in their own laboratories. The collection, attraction, gathering, tapping, clipping, copying, categorizing, storing, restructuring, and, above all, saving of data is their life fulfillment. In perfect keeping with sovereign media, they no longer require an audience to tackle their chosen subject. They are more and more amazed at the inexhaustibility of their data sources. Like traditional computerized societies, they perform a ritual to exorcise the social data surplus. But this anthropological approach to archaic modes of reconciliation ignores the fact that the problem of waste concerns all of society. There is a great danger of the amount of data exceeding its critical limit and exploding. A handful of priests wielding their data–vacuum cleaners can do little to avert the threat of crucial data carriers going up in flames: the incident as event.

Even the miniaturization of data storage cannot prevent the impending overload, but merely contributes to its amplification. Compressed nanodata are still objects, with all the power to strike back. Just like material waste, data can only be relocated, not destroyed. The ecological answer consists of data prevention ("Prevention is better than storage"). But this magic formula inevitably creates Gulag-style media-free zones and an educational censorship to erase data-intensive periods from history, for example. These solutions are as conceivable as they are outdated. Only the strategy of data recycling—to compost information as the manure for fresh events and phenomena so that they in turn may revolve through the wheel of mythical history as data—offers some hope of an effective reduction of immanent data accretion.

Incorrect Media

"Conceivably, the departing train will carry only a few passengers—just the ones who made it in time. But perhaps most of them prefer to miss it, because they find the railway station more pleasant, more comfortable, more intimate than the journey."

—Ernst Jünger

Incorrect media are found to have defected to the enemy. They prescribe set courses, forcing our protracted stay on a single channel. They're nondemocratic in that they prohibit independent rambles through the mediascape. They demand absolute reception. People who get on halfway down the line are quickly rejected, often resulting in a grudge held for life. Incorrect media ignore the immediate availability that characterizes accessible society, giving rise to suspicion concerning the intentions that preceded reproduction. But no positive response is forthcoming. Incorrect media refuse to discuss the discomfort they cause; they're masters of concealment when it comes to hidden agendas. Behind these media lurks a world which is continually copied through the successive stages of the technological era, but is never brought to light. There exists a terrible suspicion that these media not only contain but have long since analyzed technological consciousness, while the innocent observer is still trying to come to terms with it.

Contemporary media are always on. So, by definition, the program has been running for a long time before we come in. We are visitors in a world that will keep transmitting with or without us. Loyal media keep resetting, explaining their function and usage every half hour. But with incorrect media, the point of entry—our possible point of initiation—is nowhere to be found. If we'd understood what they were about, their complexity might have been acceptable. If we begin at their moment of conception, with much study, we might still grasp their deeper knowledge. But we are so far in arrears and have so little time, there can be no question of catching up. The walls that have been erected can only hide the secrets of some evil genius. But the subject behind this medium demonstrates no tyrannical urge to control the democratic media. It guards a spiritual treasure, and refuses to share it with us. Then why does it share our reproductive impulses? Is it the agent of extramedial forces, a sorcerer perhaps? Whatever caused this work to appear in the first place?

The modern phenomenon of the introductory chapter cannot come to grips with incorrect media. This is where all education fails. Incorrect media annoy us because they appear either too soon or too late. Too small to offer an alternative, they're too big to be ignored. They force themselves on us like some mysterious oeuvre or magnum opus. Their potential is enormous, but never finds room to unfold. Their works remain miserably limited to a circle of adept initiates. They contain possible solutions or events that never took place or may offer relief tomorrow. They're manuals to the wrong universe.

Incorrect media carefully distinguish between themselves and transmitters of the wrong information. The latter rest assured of their animated interaction with the medial environment. Once they make their dubious statement, communication can commence. The miscue fuels public discourse. Misguided content is not an attack on those who think differently; it is an application for membership in the media sphere. Prior to coming out as renegades, the incorrect could still speak freely in the cozy premedial climate. Generation after generation, on street corners, in coffeehouses and in pubs, the disaffected have vented their unpopular views on religion, revolution, and race. But once they enter the media, all fuses blow. Collaboration in the age of technological reproduction: Let the shit hit the fan, the microphones are wide open. For a moment, a lack of opinions seems averted, as the nation turns to face the question of media collaboration. Now the opinion leaders and their info-brokers face the task of swiftly eliminating the threat of all those personal opinions by making them the subject of public debate.

Attempts to establish communication with the impervious incorrect media commonly use the trick of pointing out the dubious statements they contain. This is based on the presumption that all writers and artists are collaborators, except those who haven't had the chance yet. The further we are removed from the twentieth century, the more obvious it becomes that the era has known nothing but traitors. Those who did nothing should have gotten involved; the ones who did should have shut up. Refugees should have stayed put; the people who stayed home should have scrammed. Artists should have explored the nature of technology; technologists should have left art well alone. Communists should have manipulated sexual desire; Fascists should have looked toward the other. Democrats should have woken up; the rich should have looked beyond their class interests. The colonies should have been liberated sooner so blacks would have stayed in their homelands. The Reformed, Catholics, and Protestants shouldn't have bitched, since they all turned Christian Democrat anyway. Instead of allowing its non-normative abuse, science should have founded a world government of experts to solve problems, of which the century saw plenty. The ones who caused them were given free play, while the little rational intellect that remained sat morosely aside. What on earth did those twentieth-century folks do with all the energy and resources they wasted?

Incorrect media are never of this age. Untimeliness is their central feature. Attempts to extract anything from them might prove fatal. It's when the makers of incorrect media try to put their ideas into practice that things really get out of hand. The art of incorrect thinking is to ignore any invitations by the Zeitgeist. It takes a lot of alertness and flexibility to be consistently off the mark. Means to this end are polemical silence or radical naiveté, undeterring perseverance on one's own set course (even if it intersects with modernity), ruthless negativism or willful amnesia, thinking modernity through to its most radical conclusions, carefree escapism into history or a touristic self-image, an alienating view of personal screw-ups or an anthropological approach to local rituals, regular contact with extraterrestrials, spurious use of philosophies and women's magazines, mixing up lines of incompatible thought, and incoming phone calls—you always get called.

Incorrect media are never springboards; they are ladders ascending to black holes. They painfully transcend their condition of being always in the right. Up there, the view of the moral landscape fascinates. All is seen, and none of it is of any use. This experience is what incorrect media are all about.

OLD MEDIA

Old media are back in force. Authenticists claim they have rediscovered the tools to call forth the spirit from matter once more: delicate shades of grey that flow from a pencil, the relief conjured up by oil paint, the magic of decaying nitrate films, the perennial eloquence of world literature, the astonishing relevance of ancient symbols, the sheer beauty of Bakelite phones, the elasticity of organic textiles, the ultimate poetry of typewriters, the stained-glass window's magical display of interweaving light rays.

All these techniques are thought to inform us about the true nature of human life, pointing to the emptiness of the modern media world. The old tools are thought to lead us back to a universe that predates industrial media, a place where sense still made sense. In this Golden Age, in which consciousness had not yet been eroded by the blur of images or the cacophony of radio and people still awoke each day to tune in to their cultures, pure reception observed a world of vivid forms and acoustic space was filled by the song and warble of birds (by all means worthy of rerecording). In this primeval era, there was still ample room for the message to contain secrets, not interpretations. Although contact with the gods had been lost after Homer, one could still profess faith in the deceased geniuses as a longing for the most ancient of media. Furthermore, there remained the possible miracle of spirit merging with matter to produce the perfect work of art.

To be misunderstood by one's contemporaries was not a case of failed marketing strategies or of mala fide agents taking the loot, but a quintessential feature of genius. One could still be unrecognized instead of just uninteresting. Today Manhattan harbors 100,000 painters, more than the entire globe had back then. In those days, there was still room for artisanship, for masters and apprentices, lunatic rulers dishing out ducats, bishops requesting new opuses by the week. Flourishing cultures produced masterpieces, masterpieces caused cultures to flourish; who wouldn't like to set their time machines for such space-time coordinates?

The authentic artist's charge against pulp culture is that civilization gets the art it deserves. Artists who exploit this state of affairs are celebrated as enlightened thinkers. Authenticists with an ironic understanding of contemporary profundities transform their cultural discomfort into works of artisanal banality, and are liberally rewarded for their efforts by investors. Others use their authentic reappraisal of outdated techniques as a sales technique. Their convincing presentations offer welcome relief from the collection of post-modern curiosities, which owes its existence to overinterpretation. The most inaccessible regions of the sublime have been democratized, yet our artists succeed in reactivating an exalted remainder. Deconstructed fragments are spontaneously shattered in their hands, revealing a landscape of true images. All those French reflections on language, signs, simulations, fractal power, result in the conservation of forgotten or lost destinies as truth and labor.

Old media are not aware of their purity. They are here to stay. Once the media, always the media. Ornate instruments have no quarrel with wax cylinders or CDs. It would be more consistent of the authentic performers if they would render their historical timbre only within the old medium of the parlor, and tried to convince us that microphones cause their viola da gambas and hammer dulcimers to go out of tune. Even if medial disruption of the instruments could be scientifically proven, and this knowledge converted into a truly authentic sound, the essence of the thing would never penetrate the ear molded to media. Even authentic art performances cannot exist without recording and reproduction. The old-music circles lack the will to dissociate themselves from the media. Since contemporary concert halls no longer regulate admission (unlike European squatters' bars, which have banned recording equipment), they are deprived of premedial ambiance. By reproducing ancient charisma through state-of-the-art techniques, the authenticists automatically end up as folklorists; the end point of all culture, the repository of old media, out of which they can celebrate their comeback in the new.

By nature, media seek to associate with their peers. Old media will not be forced back into a historical village, like cute old handicrafts, wielding the same brief power of nostalgia as a spinning wheel in action. The old media are as intoxicating and empty as the new playthings. Their age is no guarantee of wisdom. Nor can we accuse the old media of dull or demented behavior. Their chronicling continues; they perceive with the one sense to which they have been doomed. With a little exercise, old media may serve us just fine, amid all the contemporary telematic machinery.

The hybrid character of media means that anything can be linked to anything. In post-history, the opposite is equally true. The cinema has always shown great interest in the dressed-up past. Visconti's extras were not just required to wear original attire; he forced them to wear corresponding underwear, supposedly conducive to the old ways of moving. Likewise, Stanley Kubrick thought it necessary to shoot *Barry Lyndon* using late eighteenth-century candlelight, for which he had to develop a special kind of highly sensitive film. Techno artists also exhibit a persistent urge to prove they can make real music on stage. The latest trend is movie adaptations of computer games. Soundtracks often far exceed actual movie popularity, and may even lead to the rerelease of pictures that were otherwise complete failures. Any major picture worth its salt appears as a novel soon after. Due to overwhelming response, the video clip is now available on compact disc. Now all we have to wait for is a video game adaptation of Rilke's *Neue Gedichte*. Have you read *Cyberspace: The Manual* yet?

To say that interactive CDs are making world literature more accessible is stating the obvious. Great literature has always been interactive. Only those who failed to comprehend it ever thought of it in terms of CD-ROM. This memory-only attitude considers the past a closed area, inaccessible to data input. Things only get going once media are falsely hooked up. Only misconnections can produce sparks. Old media should be treated as RAM and accessed at random.

Data processing is unthinkable without the use of old media. They supply the materials to be processed. Computer peripherals are meant to absorb this material. There's a whole world waiting to be scanned. Only when the computer world has liberated itself of all its peripheral equipment, and the central processing unit functions autonomously, will the status of old media ever change. Only then will the computer create an intractable data world in which the human archive has been fully assimilated. At present, integrated circuits still need TV screens to communicate progress, and printouts on their performance are still available. Only when computers refuse to tell us what data manipulations have been carried out will they have become a pure metamedium. The possibility informs fears about the artificial intelligence of neural networks.

The question remains, however, to what extent the recording frenzy that underlies the construction of this giga-databank can ever be exhausted. The ideal of a comprehensive archive dates back to the eighteenth century at least. The twentieth century needed a world war to keep up with the pace of worldly dynamics in an open archive. War was the ideal condition for the brutal introduction of revolutionary recording techniques. But we do not have to follow this military storage strategy in order to maintain the status quo. The old media archives may continue to exist (or perish) freely, unabsorbed by cyberspace.

A more subtle option is to have the media do as they please, forming multirational links as they see fit in a "personal network" of old and new media, not necessarily interlacing but possibly compatible. The user as a disturbance variable occasionally interferes with the sublime operations of the autonomous matrix. Only technocrats dream of perfectly integrated media systems, of ISDN as the generator of absolute transparency. Deficient conversion techniques guarantee that the mystery of technology will remain, even for the most brilliant of cybernauts. Malfunction is their only food for thought. It's when the control panel flares red that the console prankster comes to life.

TOTAL MEDIA

"To hear more and to see more is to shorten one's life."
—Luis de Gongora

As long as the extramedial exists, the media cannot be total. Even if we take the technological trends of multimedia, telepresence and interactivity to their logical conclusions and beyond, there will always remain doubt that not all ground has been covered. There have always been items that didn't make the news, consumers who accidentally switched off, unused takes, near-data, one-way recording devices trained on the wrong side at the critical moment, leaky ideological grids. The Gulf War not only taught us that media can control an event on all fronts, it also brought us Hussein's Law: One can always remain invisible. Even if satellites confine one's freedom of movement to a twelve-inch margin, it is still possible to find adequate media camouflage.

The nice thing about operations like Desert Storm is that the concentration of extensions on a single focus creates a proportionate medial cast shadow. Thus, antiwar actions are allotted their own Temporary Autonomous Zones (Hakim Bey) where they are free to discover their own trajectories, unhampered by the obligation to be unequivocal and without the make-up of images. Saddam Hussein's gift to the West was the joyful experience of a few weeks in the background, out of sight of the media. The mobilized medials fought their New World War still influenced by the global philosophy of the eighties—namely, that the whole world must be fed the same images. They ignored local developments, as they were ruthlessly made to understand during the subsequent massacres in Yugoslavia where the media didn't stand a chance.

As the planet disintegrates and local populations become obsessed with their defrosting forebears and the genius of their locale, the media get the uncomfortable sensation that they're just going over the same old show. Ever since man first set foot on the moon, all their resources have gone to lending credibility to the slogan, "The sun is always rising somewhere." But consumer confidence in the 24-hour marketplace is now dwindling. The nonsense attitude of the nineties calls for a different appreciation of media, in which a local omnipresence is to guarantee that the brilliant transience of instances gets celebrated only in front of one, two, many cameras. The irresistible inertia of being shatters the one eye of God. The severity of classical

32

universal themes such as the ozone layer, greenhouse effect, AIDS, refugees, drugs, recession, the Mafia, and the communist legacy is intended to suck up the user into the media. The viewers' attention fuels the media engine. Still, it is in permanent conflict with the twentieth-century yen for touristic experience. Whereas media demand absolute participation, the tourist's desire is to break out completely for a while. This oppositional constellation not only feeds the medial discomfort about John or Jane Doe, it also induces media resentment of their incredulous masses.

Material media are no more than technological switches. Short-lived extramedial islands will always arise within the networks. God's great asset was his immateriality, his power always to be everywhere and to interfere even with the most local of events, down to the congregational conscience. The question of attitude is to be appreciated as a contemporary sacralization; it shares with the historical religions their aspect of immanence. If the media are to keep their sources of public devotion from becoming exhausted, they will have to move hearts and souls. Total media rule by physical absence; they owe their existence to the collective sensation that everybody is always in the picture. Theme parks represent the educational project that promotes this mentality. Here, touristic desire is eroded from within.

The project carried out by total media is to re-create the outside world according to its immaculate image, such as only the media can present it (after the necessary information adjustments). No matter how sublime the upgrading of European inner cities, some human excrement always remains on screen. The profound disappointment with the image pollution that is inseparable from classical reality demands a mecha-approach of superhuman proportions. The theme park not only summarizes a given culture, it demands that the surrounding nonpark follow its example. Once outside the gates, the visitor is expected to read the old surroundings as a precursor to true civilization as solidified behind the counter. Second-rate reality is redefined as the input supplier of total media.

"Do you want a total world peace?" There's no need for Americans to explore the States or their illustrious history anymore; they've been exhaustively covered in the Disney-Galaxy. Europeans don't have to cross the ocean to study the imaginary aspect of the New World. In Paris, Eurodisney offers Baudrillard all the excitement of "indomitable vigor" and "orgiastic elasticity" he can handle. Instead of the original, the Japanese prefer to stay in a 1:1 copy of the Dutch "Huis ten Bosch" or in the Deutsche Märchenstadt, Hokkaido. In this age of frenzied stagnation, there is no longer a need for corporeal confrontations with the uncomfortable world. No more notorious pickpockets, grumpy waiters, sagging hotel beds, 24-hour strikes, jet lag, or dingy restaurants. The enterprising home entrepreneur is delivered from all ecological and anthropological guilt. The disturbing and oppressive sensation of being an outsider is replaced by the comfortable feeling of having truly understood a foreign civilization. Aboriginals elsewhere seem unable to value their own cultures nowadays, what with their noisy mopeds, garish souvenirs, ghetto blasters, public drunkenness, and unrestricted demolition schemes that amount to crimes against humanity.

The tourist industry crisis generated by this new trend will be parried by the managers of State and Capital with relentless representational frenzy. The exclusive mechanism of this plot against the unreasonable nations is obvious. All nations will demand a park of their own, to be located on the rich nations' territory on the principle that you "get it where the money is." With development aid withdrawn, national debts frozen, and the abandoned territories having lost their exotic charm forever owing to desertification, overpopulation, civil war, and epidemics, the wretched of the earth now turn to us. While the depraved dress up as refugees and try their hardest to hide their origins with false identity papers, the elites opt for safe cash flows and open "reality parks" to further exploit their indigenous cultures over here.

Visit Euro Machu Picchu Park near Cologne for the ultimate Peruvian experience. After forming a vigilante committee using handmade wooden rifles and meeting with liberation theologists and professional revolutionaries, you will camp outside in the freezing cold, but not until after you've seen Los Incas perform at Lambada Discotheque, of course. Witness an authentic skirmish between drunken Sendero guerrillas and the cocaine mafia over conflicting participation interests. Get struck by cholera after eating potatoes in the street; you may even get cured by an elderly Aztec herbalist. In our simulation area, witness the lack of oxygen at 13,200 feet or a case of severe air pollution; after, make a human sacrifice on top of an old Inca pyramid. Of course you won't leave without attending our make-your-own-panpipes course in Von Däniken Parlor, or a bribery workshop. To top off our three-day, all-inclusive stay, you get to participate in a real coup d'état. This park is the dream of nations!

Disneyland is mere fantasy; there is so much more to enjoy. Take "Tiranacitta," Tuscany's Albanian Park, built with Italian assistance, or the Zairean park constructed south of Brussels at a cost of 600 million Belgian francs. For a change, visit theme park Katastrophia, a 1:1 replica of the twentieth century. With parks popping up everywhere, the demand for global information is swiftly dwindling. Why take in information, when the real experience is readily at hand? That is the question the twenty-first century will have to face. "More speed means less time for boredom." It remains to be seen whether the extramedial will succeed in motivating coming generations of troubleshooters to spoil the positive ambience that reigns within the ramparts of total media.

INTELLIGENT MEDIA

"ITV will let you massage the medium AND the message."
—Mike Saenz and Michael Synergy

The medium of the media has been universally installed and has successfully completed its stage of acceptance. The final reaches of satellite orbits are being colonized, and intramedial growth occurs exclusively within the channel package. But on reaching their adult phase, the media already face a mid-life crisis. From the beginning, the couch potato's passive indifference has been acknowledged and radically reversed through the acceleration of images and the generation of participation, the sense of oneness with the medium. The media fear that this indifference will spread like an epidemic and lead to inscrutable situations in tomorrow's boundless world. In accordance with the old-fashioned notion of marketing, the answer consists of maximum product differentiation to keep every niche in the market involved: the Stalinist channel for elderly communists, Toddler TV, pet television for free-range pigs, etc., and all of them twenty-four hours a day, of course.

But this offers no solution to the far greater threat of a massive defection to reality. The increasing urge to make a little history of your own on a hobbyist/touristic level other than work represents a conscious effort to place the media in the shadow of the event. For an instant, people have no time for the media. The generators of experience skillfully refer the media to the worn-out historical symbols that belong to the visual repertory of the mediatists and tend to suggest that something is about to happen. Through these media traps, the busy daytrippers clear their own field to instigate the right thing somewhere else.

In the museological cities of the West, this has produced a company of handiworkers: the antimedial movement, which puts an end to all connections inspired by the slogan, "Smash up a medium for breakfast." Through actions of disappearance it creates local and temporary media-free spaces, to the point of terrorism with its own harmless anti-satellite laserguns. It represents the ultimate secret movement, because it is carefully kept out of the news and only makes itself heard as interference and sabotage. It claims every event that does not make the media as a victory and leaks them to the whole extramedial circuit it identifies with. Stirred up by this violence, along with the alarming increase of public indifference and fragmentation of the ratings, the attitude police will have no option but to initiate a broad public debate on the future of the media. Meanwhile the media lobby, impatient of the final outcome, has already begun R&D of the inevitable answer: The intelligent media.

Whereas interactive media take the point of view of the subject and render reality obsolete, intelligent media (IM) take the point of view of the object and would like to determine what happens in front of the screen. The fragmentation of viewing behavior during the previous, rigid media age was a result of remote control. Television producers either ignored the practice of zapping altogether, or tried to prevent it by compiling even catchier programs or simultaneously broadcasting different versions of the same story on various channels. Moreover, the media spread out the diversified package during the day, a relic from the juvenile phase when the nation still used to watch a single channel all through the evening. Now that the ratings lose their commercial value due to endless switching, attention shifts to the registration of channel time—the number of minutes the user spends on a given channel. This is accomplished by introducing an extra chip into the remote control.

Digital IM go one step further. They receive permanent viewing behavior feedback and establish certain threshold values above which the product reaches the screen unaltered. If average channel time threatens to drop below such levels, the IM conduct subliminal testing to find out what programmatic elements need to be introduced or altered (news, sex, personalities, setting, dialogue, music, colour). Producers merely deliver potential programs; the chances of integrated screenings of old blockbusters are minimal. Competing channels are constantly scanned for more attractive bits. The classic sequential edit of sound and image has been replaced by the central computer's synchronized mix. Contributions are judged according to the discreetness of the applied manipulations. If, in spite of it all, attention drops to a minimum, we imperceptibly slip to a completely different program segment. Fragmentation will remain, if only because public taste is an erratic affair, and there are early adopters and followers. But from being a threat, it has become a first condition of existence.

Still, IM cannot remove the disaffection for the media. Intelligent media lead to a universal relativity of information. Uninteresting news items gradually take on a different content. The fellowship of true democrats freaks out and demands an alternative to save information from its destruction, strengthened by the outcome of its broad media debate. Since the TV image of the last of the politicians is increasingly dependent on the media, they are out for revenge. Because with their state-monopoly broadcasting systems they are in no position to compete with the dynamic media, they come up with reasonable proposals. They suggest showing a logo as a warranty of reality in the upper left corner of the screen. IM, who will never agree to this, compensate by releasing specified zones where the community can set up its own media-passive reality districts. At the same time, these are meant to split the antimedial movement into a radical wing and a faction willing to negotiate.

The democrats proceed by saying that healthy social conduct depends on a media diet. Some patients will have to decrease their intake, others increase it. IM are required to build in an ecological principle: if the number of viewers drops below an absolute minimum, the channel must switch off; if it rises too high, the information level must be increased to establish the proper infotainment balance. At first, channels may be canceled for a day or a week, but for the IM tycoons it is far more attractive to shut them down for good, because this makes viewing far more exciting and thus increases the channel time of the worst stations. Besides, media politics demands that the excess of redundant information be controlled so that the essential may be brought back to the historical surface. Again, IM can make no promises because, after all, information is just noise. The proposal to sidetrack politics to a channel of its own is rejected because it wouldn't last for a week. Democrats will always remain an intolerant minority in an utterly democratized media order. But these ecological restrictions will in turn be used by IM to legitimize their permanent control of media use, and consequently of every movement that takes place within range of the sensors. The common denominator remains that there has to be media participation at all costs.

The intelligent response to IM is given by the IM themselves: PTV. Personal television does not depend exclusively on material offered by IM for its visual intake, but uses sovereign images to produce its own samples and remixes. PTV lifts the video·game from its infant stage and offers a central visual pool to the interactivist. Besides file footage and latest reports, one gains unlimited access to scenes from security cameras, satellites, camcorder clubs and survival treks. Naturally, participants immediately relay their personal versions of events to the pool for further processing by others. Thus, these do-it-yourself media are to save the ideology of creativity. The only viable media survival strategy is to stay more interesting than reality at all times. PTV is an attempt to replace the individual bid for history with a final techno fix.

With PTV, the media enter their third life stage. But reality cannot be locked away in a park as a tourist attraction forever: it will always lurk around, ready to jump any media maker sooner or later. The extramedial circuit is already among us, but stays out of reach of touristic experience because it refuses to give the game away. It quietly awaits the death of the media.

PROBING McLUHAN

"Properly, we shd. read for power. Man reading shd. be man intensely alive. The book shd. be a ball of light in one's hand."

—Ezra Pound

The opening up of the new paradigm of media theory took place in a literary milieu at the beginning of the Cold War. In the 1930's Marshall McLuhan became aware that literature should not be appreciated on its aesthetic merits, but that it was to be understood as a scientific method. The analysis of poetry and prose according to the principle of "practical criticism" focused on the link between their social consequences and stylistic features. In the 1940's McLuhan applied his insights to written advertisements, expecting that future audiences would find these more interesting than the literature produced by his contemporaries.

According to Robert Anton Wilson, the "most important idea ever presented by McLuhan" can be found on the first pages of *The Mechanical Bride*, McLuhan's 1951 debut. These are dedicated to the collage aspect of *The New York Times*'s front page, which McLuhan calls "a collective work of art." Newspapers are a "daily 'book' of industrial man, an Arabian Night's Entertainment." McLuhan defends the use of discontinuity as a basic concept against his contemporary critics, who saw incoherence as irrationality. "To the alerted eye, the front page of a newspaper is a superficial chaos which can lead the mind to attend to cosmic harmonies of a very high order." But people remain unaware of the newspaper page's rich symbolism. "Industrial man is not unlike the turtle that is quite blind to the beauty of the shell which it has grown on his back." It is only several decades later, after the historical view gains depth of field, that we discover the beauty in advertisements, book covers, jukeboxes, the 1949 Buick Roadmaster with Dynaflow Drive, the comics in *Crime Does Not Pay* ("More than 6,000,000 readers monthly!"), the careless but equally helpless "Men of Distinction" sporting their "rare, smooth, mellow, blended Lord Calvert Whiskey," or the August 1947 *Reader's Digest* table of contents ("Marriage Control: A New Answer to Divorce," "What Price Socialism?," "Laughter, the Best Medicine").

Probing McLuhan

The Mechanical Bride consists of crossovers between *Blondie,* *Superman,* Coca-Cola ("a kind of rabbit's foot"), Emily Post, *Tarzan* (an amalgam of noble savage and aristocratic detective), and horse operas, with John Wayne at one end and Margaret Mead, Sigfried Giedion, Le Corbusier, Gertrude Stein, Wyndham Lewis, Toynbee, and Kinsey at the other. McLuhan is the one-liner's philosopher. Eventually, this worked to his disadvantage, because hordes of people never progressed much beyond stammering the slogan, "The medium is the message." "Have you had your literary hypodermic today?" Most of the slogans are questions: "How much behaviorism is needed to make a big mental proletariat behave?" In the "How to iron shirts without hating your husband" department, he wonders "if there is any known gadget for controlling a rampant Know-How." "In the beginning was montage"; "How often do you change your mind, your politics, your clothes?"; "Superman or subman?"; "You little culture vulture, you!" Finally, in the "Understanding America" section, he remarks: "Don't run but look again, Reader. Find the Mechanical Bride."

Simultaneously with the publication of *The Mechanical Bride,* his book on advertising, television was introduced and he was forced to admit that he had written a review of a historical era, rather than a critique of his own age. He decided he could only keep up with technological advancement by treating the "communications media" as a scientific method, much the same way he had done with literature.

Art, to McLuhan, was an "early warning system"; he defined art briskly as a powerful style with powerful results ("Literature is news that STAYS news"—Pound). The technique of, say, Eliot or Joyce was to use the old medium of the written word as though it were already part of the new electronic age. The accelerated circuits made possible by electricity opened up a new environment to humanity, which till now had been caught in typographic settings. In the eyes of McLuhan, art consisted of "special artifacts for enhancing human perception." Like human antennae, artists were in the best position to develop an insight into the impact of technology and the media because they allowed for and tested its effects in their own literary styles. The function of art was to make humanity realize the psychological and social consequences of technological advancements.

"Joyce is, in *Finnegans Wake,* making his own Altamira cave drawings of the entire history of the human mind, in terms of its basic gestures and postures during all phases of human culture and technology. Joyce could see no advantage in our remaining locked up in each cultural circle as in a trance or dream. He discovered the means of living simultaneously in all cultural modes while quite conscious."

In 1953, in his article "Culture without Literacy," McLuhan for the first time summarizes Western history in terms of media. In it, he also introduces historical tripartition, which he will elaborate on and diversify in all of his later works. The first stage he terms that of "preliterate man," who lived without a script in an acoustic environment that had no set points of reference. Preliterate man was completely and universally connected to his surroundings, in a mythological and unfragmented world. He translated his entire body into outward form: that of a ship, a home, or a roller ("the Incas did not know the wheel").

The second stage is that of "literate man," who connected to the surrounding world by renouncing certain bodily functions, which were transferred to technological devices. The spoken word represented the first fragmentary guideline in acoustic space. Next came written/printed language, which visualized acoustic space ("an eye for an ear"). The act of joining sentences produced linear logic, which came to its own in the book, filled with linear lines. McLuhan considers the book an extension of the eye, while all the printed works in the world together make up the comprehensive milieu of the "Gutenberg galaxy." The distance between man and the world expanded as more of his bodily functions were emancipated as tools.

The third stage is the present one, that of electrical/electronic man, "manthefactfinder," who, like the man in stage one, is without script and externalizes and amputates his very being: The information network is his nervous system. He has regained a mythical understanding of the world; he has once more become tribal, all involved; and he does not require sequenced fragments in order to feel that he knows what he's doing. Man connected to electronic media is in a new acoustic space, where he is bombarded by signals.

With this first and tentative proposition, McLuhan opened up the field of media theory. From then on, his own way of writing would enable him to remain enthusiastic regarding the effects of modern media. "Nothing ever printed is as important as the medium of print." There followed one book after another. As for media theory itself, McLuhan's universe is all it needs to fathom every artistic and technological revolution.

Media theory is a Theory of Everything. As the medial terrain is by definition interminable, McLuhan prefers to step right in the middle of it. "There is no longer a single item that is not interesting." Media theory is a way of looking at the universal data archives with pleasure, without having to doggedly chase after some idea of an overview: What you see is what you get. Thus, McLuhan stumbles from one brilliant insight to the next. Since everything is related to everything, the important thing is to construct one's own quotation-magnet which, as a strange attractor, will cause the right sort of bifurcation on every occasion. Media theory establishes a temporary local center of global civilization in the form of an obscure collection of points. Now, take your scissors and cut out all the texts featuring pine trees, Doberman pinschers, Formica tables, Inuit, tobacco, Stevenson and war babies. Combine these with a selected number of favorite authors, and presto: your very own full-fledged theory, something millennia to come will be able to sink their teeth into.

Media are artificial extensions of sensory existence. Language was the first outering of the central nervous system. In language we put all of ourselves outside. Then we retracted and began to hedge our bets by putting out single senses like wheel (feet), hammer (fist), knife (teeth-nail), drum (ear), writing (eye). But when an organ goes out, it goes numb. The central nervous system has gone numb, for survival, i.e., we enter the age of the unconscious with electronics, and consciousness with shifts into the physical organs, even in the body politic. There is a great stepping up of physical awareness and a big drop in mental awareness when the central nervous system goes outward. The one area which is numb and unconscious is the area which receives the impact.

Organs moved out of man and into the world as technological devices go numb within man himself. Through this defensive reaction, the individual prevents the amputated organ within from being crushed by the onslaught of impressions suddenly released upon it. "Each extension alters both private and corporate images, creating great pain and alienation." Every new technology is a medium that topples man's former worldview. Everything is changed in relation to the central nervous system's new technological possibilities.

In this sense, media are new art forms: They enable new modes of perception. This led McLuhan to formulate his set of media definitions: "All media are fragments of ourselves extended into the public domain"; "A new medium is like the trumpet at the battle of Jericho"; "The new media are not bridges between man and nature, they are nature"; "Any understanding of social and cultural change is impossible without a knowledge of the way media work as environments."

> Europeans cannot master the new powers of technology because they take themselves too seriously and too sentimentally. Europeans cannot imagine the Earth City. They have occupied old city spaces too long to be able to sense the new spaces created by the new media.

Media can be understood in their relation to the body, private or social. That is, not in terms of the transfer of messages but from an ecological perspective: they create a new environment. To McLuhan, the question was "how the medium affects the person, not how people affect media." The introduction of new media exposes the environment which would otherwise remain "virtually invisible and unnoticeable, subliminal." The environment exposes its characteristics during the transition from one medium to the next. The only one capable of perceiving environments is the artist who connects an old medium to a new environment: Joyce's stream of consciousness was already television.

Art, like a sense of humor, is "anti-environmental": both liberate man momentarily from an invulnerable environment that imposes its restrictions as a matter of course. And that is precisely the point. "Professionalism is environmental. Amateurism is anti-environmental. Professionalism merges the individual into patterns of total environment. Amateurism seeks the development of the total awareness of the individual and the critical awareness of the ground rules of society. The amateur can afford to lose." Media theory will be critical or not at all.

> The children of technological man respond with untaught delight to the poetry of trains, ships, planes, and to the beauty of machine products. In the school room officialdom suppresses all their natural experience; children are divorced from their culture. They are not permitted to approach the traditional heritage of mankind through the door of technological awareness; this only possible door for them is slammed in their faces.

McLuhan labeled the methodical part of his scientific method "pattern recognition." Typographical man, in need of chronological accounts and argumentation to understand certain processes, has been succeeded in the electronic age by enthusiastic youth whose thinking no longer follows trajectories such as "in for a penny, in for a pound." *Homo electricus* follows a nonlinear logic which seeks to grasp the pattern in a series of facts and events. Instead of shifting from one fragment to another, processes are now seen to be an aggregate of imperative combinations, links, collisions, repetitions, intersections, and manifestations. Pattern recognition is like that of preliterate man: mythical, tribal, all-involving. It is based on trial and rejection and yet more experimenting, rather than de- and induction.

"Suspended judgment," in short—don't start all over, but consider the possible outcome instead. Until the nineteenth century, to discover meant to discover things. Nowadays, one discovers methods. Once the method has been found, there follows a series of inventions. "The method of invention is simply to begin with the solution of the problem." McLuhan, like Elias Canetti, wrote satirical theory. He described his texts as "observation minus ideas": Deduct your moral judgments from your insights and look again with what's left; ideas are sure to follow. "I grope, I listen, I test, I accept and discard; I try out different sequences—until the tumblers fall and the doors spring open." The word used by McLuhan to sum up his intellectual activities was "probe."

> My work is designed for the pragmatic purpose of trying to understand our technological environment and its psychic and social consequences. But my books constitute the process rather than the completed product of discovery; my purpose is to employ facts as tentative probes, as means of insight, of pattern recognition . . . I want to map new terrain rather than chart old landmarks. I'm trying to get my audience involved in perceptions. I expect my readers to do more work than I did. I am offering opportunities, roles of initiative.

Whenever McLuhan got hold of a book, the first thing he did was to read page 69. If it managed to raise his attention he would continue by reading all the left pages. This way he hoped to avoid the redundancy in books. He took an "Evelyn Wood reading dynamics" course in speed-reading. This, he said, "revealed patterns, not data." Applied to writing, this library-surfing provided a "redundant scattering of samples," a "wholesale use of quotations"—a mosaic. Which is exactly what McLuhan's books are: "Clear prose indicates the absence of thought." Time and again, McLuhan succeeds in reducing the patterns he discovers to a single brilliant slogan, so admired by him in advertisements and poetry, to mythical formulae, the somersault by which thinking suddenly breaks to a new level of insights (as he himself had experienced while working on "Culture without Literacy"). "Forcing thoughts into abrupt interface with each other." Media-conscious poets and ad makers try first of all to cause a reaction in their audience. Both work according to the brainstorm method, "serendipity through association." Advertising slogans are haiku, and the aphorism's modern equivalent is the headline.

McLuhan's gay science aims to beat the media men at their own game, by inciting his readers to stop ignoring the environment which commands their lives in every detail without their ever realizing it. Time and again, he stresses that "literacy [was] a brief phase," that literacy belongs to the Gutenberg galaxy, but that we are now "beyond Jupiter." We are free to treat literary texts as casually as we are to take advertising texts seriously. Every "breakdown is a breakthrough." By leaving the past behind, we enter the present, where we can begin to charter the unknown, the "hidden dimension," so obviously close it remains invisible. "I predict only what has already happened. Anyone who truly perceives the present can also see the future, since all possible futures are contained in the present."

Media theory is not looking for feedback, it's looking for feedforward. The present is a network of past analogies; the past is a toolbox open for plunder by those who wish to think further. Burglarize all the books in the Gutenberg nebula if you will; don't stop to wonder whether the present "tribal situation" is better or worse than the (il)literacy of past generations. "Help beautify junkyards—throw something lovely away every day." The secret rule of media theory discovered by McLuhan was the capacity to write with enthusiasm about everything one opposes. "Blast the Canadian beaver—apt symbol of our dammed-up creativity. Bless culture shock as dislocation of mind into meaning." Historical data are no more than material in which patterns may be discerned; they do not provide imperative conclusions concerning the question "What to do?" In the network of the media, we are past such linearity. According to McLuhan, one had to proceed with utmost caution when dealing with the media; therefore, one must understand media. The only chance of disarming the media was—and is—to understand their laws.

After extensive investigations, McLuhan had discovered four media laws and could find no more. He pictured them in the shape of a tetrad. All media cause four simultaneous processes: a medium enhances a given human function, restores lost practices, renders still others obsolete, and turns into a new function itself. McLuhan places this quadruplicity within a graphic image: a circle surrounding a cross, with each of the four parts of the circle representing one of the media laws. Thus, for example, the pipe as a "human artifact" enhances "group participation via environmental smell," brings back the "contemplative inner trip," renders the "individual nervous haste" outmoded, and may turn into the "solitary smoker; need for consideration of audience." In his series of "simple quadruplets" we find liquor, brothel, cigarette, mass, medicine, hermeneutics, high-rise buildings, kinetic space, microphone/PA system, perspective painting, refrigerator, semiotics, tactile space, and xeroxes. Amid these quadruple condensations, the page still has plenty of room left for brilliant ideas and quotes. All of this can be found in *Understanding Media's* successor, *Laws of Media*, published by McLuhan's son Eric in 1988.

We now move to the higher tetrads. Here we find Aristotelian causality, cubism, the clock, the law of the jungle, washing machines, TV, cars, electric light, and new genetics. Thus, the satellite enhances the planet, brings back ecology, renders nature redundant, and turns into implosion: "The population as participating in their own audience participation." Under "the pollster" we read: "Who am I? Let's take a poll." And: "Does the president really have 17 per cent more charisma than Campbell's soup?" Under the "slang" entry, McLuhan observes that "our current technologies are slang—tetrads explore their verbal character." Slang enhances new possibilities of perception and brings back "unconventional feeling." McLuhan uses this to indicate how language can raise the media to understanding—for every technology is lingual by nature and offers its own percepts: the outlook that enables obstinate perception.

"I would prefer a stable, changeless environment of modest surfaces and human scale. I find most pop culture monstrous and sickening. I study it for my own survival. The effect of the new media on human society has never aroused the slightest enthusiasm in me. Only by understanding change can I ease the burden of experiencing it—and therefore the only extension of man I desire is that of awareness. I wish none of these technologies ever happened. They impress me as nothing but a disaster. They are for dissatisfied people. Why is man so unhappy he wants to change his world?"

MEDIA OR BARBARISM

There is increasing talk about "media or barbarism." Is this a choice, an alternative, a threat, a slogan, a questionnaire, a luxury, an advertisement for opinions perhaps? If it's a matter of choice, we must examine the pros and cons of each option; we must make an assessment of the merits of medial barbarism and the use of media by barbarians—or of barbarians by the media—in order to arrive at a sound and balanced judgment. Let the experts provide the arguments and analyses, and let a public discussion draw the conclusions.

If "media or barbarism" is seen as an alternative, then we see the media as the most powerful psychotherapeutic means to cure the last of the disconnected barbarians—from the illiterate to the Muslims—as though watching *Dallas* and *Twin Peaks* might save them from the dead weight of their premedial history and finally include them in the civilization of market democracy. The coming of the media is always accompanied by the threat of impending armed intervention or humanitarian aid campaigns. Increasingly, disaster areas will refuse access to the media in order to avoid the catastrophic arrival of international aid organizations. If, on the other hand, the battle scenes and environmental calamities do get extensive coverage, the information offered attains such a complex scale that even the most sympathetic of citizens find it impossible to keep up. Media have no civilizing impact on either those in the pictures or the viewers. If the barbarians refuse to see media as multipliers of complexity, but instead as archives full of evidence, they proceed to treat the question of media in their own way—by shooting as many media carriers as possible. Every dead journalist is a victory in the media war.

The fear underlying the question of media-or-barbarism is that without mediation humanity quickly loses control of itself, that it starts acting like a beast as soon as it is deprived of images to distract it. On the one hand, the media are expected to keep the masses off the street; they've a long record as the people's opiate. On the other hand, the media are thought to corrupt the people and incite them to violence, satanism, ecocide, and cultural devastation. Once again, the relationship between cause and effect is completely forgotten. The practice of relativism has led to a rampant revaluation of values. The middle classes come up with the wildest proposals: censorship, freezing government subsidies, rescheduling, self-regulation, educational categorization, age discrimination, the scrambling and encoding of naked images, the dubbing of bold statements, and other methods to conceal harmful data. The moral terror of other people's consciences is given free play to frustrate the evil schemes of one's fellow humans, from incest, fraud, corruption, child pornography, drug abuse, and serial killings to car theft, adultery, nationalism, and racist remarks. The media are credited with the power of turning people into either barbarians or civilized participants. Bad media must be made good, the question being how many cubic meters of public information it takes. The point of political correctness is not to behave correctly yourself, but to have the others corrected.

As a slogan of the antimedial movement, "media or barbarism" reflects a real 1980's attitude: the dream of destroying a communicative global empire. Those who demolish teleports and MediaParcs claim that a bit of negative energy can only serve to strengthen democracy. Recently, their slogan has been taken hostage by the emerging media ecologists and transformed into the equation "media = barbarism." All the shit that flows through societies we owe to media. A reduced emission of i-smog would result in a manifest reduction of multicultural abuse. The route followed is from the outside in: Violence and crime are seen as mental disorders that are containable through a correct and balanced data diet. Information turns people on, and frequent encounters with multimedia have a titillating effect that is ultimately released upon the others. The only way to prevent this is through the implantation of inner peace. Nudist data don't dress themselves up through design, but strive for a natural representation within a sheltered environment. Data dietitians prefer to be left to their own creations, without the constant interruption of someone else's tragedies and monstrosities.

Our hot and central question gains real stamina once it is seen as a call for "decision." But where is this sovereign? Is it the editor-in-chief? Is it the tycoons? Should we wait for a world government to decide on the urgent matter of whether Russia should be allowed more media, or that we arm ourselves pending a second Cold War? The consequences of a massive import of media are as unpredictable as those of the interruption of media. Every conceivable question of power is up in the air, where it remains without consequence. Only on the local level do we still find some self-made sovereigns who take pride in the control they have acquired over the remote. Only within the self-defined private reality are fatal nanodecisons still being made. Within this reserve, decision becomes a fashionable gesture, intended to provide oneself with the necessary individuality. It is the coming-out of the will to decision; not a postponement but a proposed conclusion.

The puking-out of the twentieth century is well under way, though there's still plenty to look forward to in this dynamic age of ours. The question arises: Will the unbeaten record of '39–'45 be improved upon or not? It remains to be seen whether we will achieve the necessary escape velocity to leave the twentieth century and continue on our way, or instead end up in the eternal return of the same twentieth century (or, perhaps, witness the crash of spaceship Earth). The marshes having been drained and converted into farmlands, the latter are now being reflooded to create neo-swamps. According to Hans Peter Duerr, the last barbarian became civilized at least twenty thousand years ago. Terror and joy are both products of Civilization & Progress, Inc. Nothing could possibly ever enter civilization from outside again. The fear and the desire that civilization can be corrupted and eroded from within represents a cultural high point, presented with massive technological support. The ancient Greeks understood tragedy as an exquisite dramatic genre. No Dionysus without Apollo, no Sarajevo without Dallas. The crisis is a must you can afford to miss. The question is not whether the barbarians are at the gates, but what to do with all the technology at hand. Once the crisis is taken seriously, you lose track and can only internalize it as the next personal experience of the end of ideology, history, international aggression, and the subject. Add the twentieth century to your media archives, free to flick through it on weekends. Those who prolong their artificial existence in personal opinions cater for a lost cause which was undesirable to begin with. The world after the media is not made up of barbarians; more likely it is full of businessmen. It is their stockjobbing that poses the next challenge.

MEDIA IN THE
NEW WORLD ORDER

On leaving the twentieth century, the world has acquired a sixth continent that encompasses and dwarfs the previous five. Communication technologies have created an autonomous field which, though evident in all four corners of the globe, never touches the regional civilizations into which the world population is still organized. The relentless fascination with the media environment results from its ability to make familiar issues appear forever and totally alien. The pleasure of uncommitted sharing in someone else's joy and misery produces a state of euphoria that lasts as long as one is on line. No sooner do we turn our backs to the media than our awareness of local duties and diversions reemerges unaltered to detail. Just after having donated your savings to the victims of some Bangladeshi flood disaster, you may well blow your top over the neighbors' leaking washing machine.

The global consciousness created in the media never leaves its medial surroundings. Awareness of the surrounding world occupies its own, separate level within the collective unconscious. Archetypes generated by the news somehow never find their way into the civilized mindset. Compassion for African victims of starvation is easily coupled with indifference concerning one's countrymen. Predictions of how the media would cause a shift in social attitudes have proved more than prophetic. Media teach us not to aim our actions at our immediate surroundings, but rather to subject them to the information at hand.

The media's educational scheme aims only to initiate users in the rules of immateriality and show them an individual approach to global virtual reality. The contemporary potlatch of the game show proves how viewers may be abundantly rewarded for their concentrated participation—a pastime to instruct us in the casual attitude necessary to market one's own personality. The slick promotion of personal identity represents a code of behavior so far removed from workplace and bedroom bungling, it's simply amusing to watch.

Whereas hi-tech is taking traditional progress to unheard-of extremes, local populations reorientate on civilizational models or cultural ideals quite immune to advancement. The current resentment of rebellion and extremism does not result from some reactionary scheme to implement bourgeois values; rather, it represents a victory by the emancipation and liberation movements. A normal existence is now viewed as a universal human right, no longer to be abruptly impeded by outside forces. The clearing of bigotry and prejudice concerning the social identity of labor and sex has led to the disarmament of social critics. Where gays embrace marriage, feminists advocate motherhood, and the notion of "jack of all trades and master of none" denotes a flexible attitude toward employment, the beckoning option of uncertain expeditions into experimental modes of living has become unthinkable. Lifestyles that attempt to shed light on their intentions via the medial environment are merely providing meaningful contributions to democratic citizenship. Multicultural society proudly advocates its tolerance of distinct identities, no matter how odd. Bag ladies have the same existential right as do ethnic butchers or lesbian pornophiliacs.

In this legible society, there no longer exists any beyond to tempt us. The other, for want of comprehensible proofs of identity, is persuaded it must either integrate or be banished. Finally, those who refuse their social emancipation or liberation can only be relegated to the posthistorical through military or colonial measures. Parliamentary democracy, the free market economy; they're not values advocated by the Free West, but conditions to be realized by the individual lest he falls under direct attack by the New World Order. They comprise a formalized model, open to covert rule by political/economic elites as long as they respect their own national borders and the rules laid out by the world economy. The nation-state is a prerequisite for full participation in the World Order. The rise in nationalist movements represents a misinterpretation of this fact, carried away by the remnants of local history; those who have thus missed out on the capture of economic markets easily take to the market of capture.

The implosion of communist regimes and Third World dictatorships must take place in an orderly fashion, dictated by New World Order patterns . . . for we are mere spectators. It's all right for the media to keep us posted on upheavals, but don't expect us to interfere. The greater the media attention on former Warsaw Pact countries or the Middle East, the deeper our stupefaction and the lesser chance of people here ever taking to the streets. High ratings during live registration of conflicts denote fascination with the power of modern communication technologies, not concern through the awareness that "we are all in the same fight together." In fact, all those liberation movements just threaten our own positions. Both refugees and cheap products endanger individual citizens' work and welfare. The one political factor to which bourgeois awareness remains sensitive is defensive by nature: preservation—of benefits packages, the virgin environment, and multicultural society. All other themes for action are, by virtue of their unintended air of masochism, unfit for the calculating citizenry. No matter what radical discourse may be mounted, all lines of argumentation must end up in some Gulag or Auschwitz.

The study of the two parallel worlds of media and classical reality teaches that anything taken from the local environment to the field of hi-tech is instantly incapacitated. On the other hand, it is clear that all positive action taken on the level of everyday life can only reinforce the desire to leave everything as it is. Tolerance and indifference both reflect the same urge, that is, to shut out the outside world from that level of consciousness where insights must be acted upon. Information no longer is a weapon, but an arsenal in which we permanently find ourselves.

Those who refuse to accept this state of affairs can take three possible courses of action: inside, against, or outside the media. If, in the first instance, we enter media reality, our purpose would be to erode the media by charging them with an explosive topicality. The patronizing notion that bourgeois media need to be rectified by counterinformation has been abandoned. Mediumistic actions discard all well-intentioned content and lines of argumentation, employing semio-artillery discharging pure signs. Even if all the action's intentions are fleeced, distorted, or omitted, it will generate images so powerful their significance cannot be devalued. To paraphrase a Dutch squatters' slogan, "You can tear down our ideas, but our images will always be ours." A guerrilla based on the presumption that the emancipated citizen has no faith in whatever the media churn out to begin with, privately chuckling away at the destructions on display. Negative images are still images. Disguised as issues, they force themselves on the media in order to gain maximum circulation. Their assault on the dogma of PR, which effectively blocks any true intervention in classical reality, turns the media on themselves, thus clearing the field for an autonomous abuse of media and the obstinate defiance of their reality potential. A radical version of this strategy is to be found in the workings of sovereign media. They no longer view the media as channels for the transmission of information about events, but as material to be freely adapted by all and sundry. The purpose of sovereign media is not to invade recent media, but rather to encapsulate them so they can subject them to their own homemade rules.

The second option is the domain of the antimedial movement. Convinced that all information is disinformation, this democratic movement seeks to reinstate the twin categories of truth and falsehood. It aims at the radical short-circuiting of the parallel worlds so that the planet's unity may be restored, if only for a few moments. Through its antimedial acts of sabotage, it temporarily eliminates "media-related communications," thus giving way to time and space for direct encounters on the local level. These Temporary Autonomous Zones challenge events to unfold in the present, based on an awareness that democracy thrives on real conflicts—not stage-managed, but spontaneously erupting, under no one's direction.

It remains to be seen whether the event will respond to these actions based on media critique. Demolishing the tentacles of the electricity grid; disrupting telephone communications, electronic banking, terminals, cameras, and other tools of everyday repression; and sneaking viruses and worms into mainframes and networks were all part of an experimental stage in media renunciation. They were an expression of a will to reality, relic of a pre-Nietzschean, nineteenth-century paradigm. Romanticism from a tourist perspective. However, even in the case of unforeseen events and all-out rioting, the mob is still democratically obliged to inform the rest of the community concerning the upheaval's nature and development. This forces the antimedial to invent tactics for the willful takeover of the media, in order to prevent distorted reports from causing confusion. The final dilemma of any antimedial strategy lies in the fact that it must maintain the media if it is to save democracy.

The problem of the antimedial movement is how to employ the media without becoming a part of them. Perhaps the media never possessed either transmitters or receivers to begin with. It requires little effort to imagine a network that functions to perfection, unaided by operators or users, free of input or output. Images have no meaning whatsoever to start with—they merely exist. They do not require our concern; we do not have to charge them with our attention or disinterest. To them, it's all shit and onions. The antimedial gesture intends to establish contact with others; it is not aimed at the media and their existentiality, but at ourselves—the human remainder. Still, the continuing broadcast of signals remains a persistent source of annoyance and aggression. The antimedial movement is the media's ultimate issue. The media implode through their reports on the antimedial movement; it, in turn, disappears through its exposure to media.

The third option, that of extramedial acts, is based on the presumption that all positive activist goals are ultimately defensive, and can only reinforce the conservative climate. Any medially discernable goals served by extramedial actions are utterly negative. Extramedial operations frustrate media attention by being simply indescribable. As soon as the media appear, they disappear. All that remains is fits of laughter, astonishment, and terror. They claim no attention, but are satisfied to occupy their own worlds. Contrary to the antimedial movement, they do not wish to restore society. Most likely, they've been a part of it all along, though it's hard to tell. From our medial point of view, they are in a state of uncertainty, immeasurable, not open to comment. They are forever transmutating, in defiance of destiny; they may be the medium of the event.

Virilio Calling

"Time is a resource and we're running out of time. It is necessary to travel. It is not necessary and becoming increasingly difficult to live."

—William Burroughs

To Paul Virilio, the Gulf War acted as a watershed. He had proved right before in some of his minor predictions. His conclusion that any state that submits to its inner urge toward total control will end up exterminating its own people came true in Pol Pot's Cambodia, much to his own horror. But it was not until the early 1990's that he was forced to admit to the global accuracy of his military/technological analyses. A few years before, the French intervention in Chad had already led to his observation that from now on, world wars could only be fought in the desert. As the espionage satellites were maneuvered over Iraq and the cruise missiles set to new coordinates, Virilio knew what was about to happen. Still, the renewed correctness of his thrilling tales on the development of state-of-the-art weapon systems was not what shocked him most about the events.

In his published books since 1976 (some ten in all), Virilio developed his position that if in the past speed was the essence of war (cf. Sun Tzu), today it equals war. The latter is no longer directed at the enemy, however, but against the world's material existence. The greater the acceleration, the quicker does reality evaporate. Light has absolute speed; technologies that make use of it are absolute weapons. Therefore, too, instant communication technologies are apocalyptic by nature: "I spy with my little eye—who is seen will have to die." But if before, media merely unhinged space-time awareness and immaterialized the human body by transforming it into transmissible light waves, during the Gulf War, apart from the devastation of derealized land, information as such became incredible.

In Virilio's chronology, Desert Shield and Desert Storm were followed up by Desert Screen. The same strategic developments that helped visualize the Gulf War in the Arabian Desert are also occurring in the public sector. Just as generals can direct field campaigns without ever leaving their bunkers, so the viewers can do their jobs without leaving their homes. All information converges on, and radiates from, the screen, the pole of inertia. Distant viewing—yesterday's television—has been replaced by distant action, today's and tomorrow's teleperformance; from teleshopping and home banking to telepresence and teletourism in virtual reality. Only, as Virilio adds in *L'écran du Désert* (*Desert Screen*), his war chronicle, we now know what the communication weapons are after. Who is seen will no longer have to die; rather, it is the observer who will be struck blind. Whereas, time and again, Virilio has described the history of control over the external world as an acceleration and refinement of observation techniques and their logistics, with data transmission acquiring the speed of light total fascination turns out to converge with absolute disbelief.

What's left of information when it reaches journalists and the public simultaneously, without there remaining a second for verification, analysis, or double-checks? The news that reaches us as information through the media-communication weapons can always be disinformation. If information is a weapon, disinformation is the shield. The viewers can no longer believe their eyes. But if they cannot, the world as we know it will disappear, as Virilio has warned us for years. Distrust of the media means the end of the world. The central and final question in *L'écran du Désert* is thus: "Can omnipresence and instantaneity be democratized; that is to say, can inertia be democratized?" According to Virilio, democracy is impossible without the categories of truth and falsehood, which have currently been replaced by the "actual" and the "virtual."

Paul Virilio represents a critical, antimedial stance. Live connections must be interrupted in order to restore democracy. To him, media coincide with observation technologies, all of which are the products of military intelligence. He sees the development of the logistics of observation—hilltop, watchtower, hot air balloon, reconnaissance flight, satellite, field glass, photo camera, film camera, video—taking place analogously to the development of infrastructure—road, railway, freeway, cable television, air corridor, orbit. Now that the industrial traffic revolution has succeeded, Virilio finds it impossible to distinguish between the military and the civil. Both institutions are characterized by acceleration; both turn classical space-time inside out in their respective ways. Both culminate in the speed of light (laser) and both turn the world's natural environment into a desert ("glacis"). The media, viewed as a global network produced by observation machinery, are the greatest obstacle to our (re)cognizance of humanity and the world.

Although the media remain the object of Virilio's concern, his absolute disaffection never results in a hostile attitude towards technology. Salvation may well come from within, and is impossible if we turn our backs to techné. "There would be hope in our careful study of disaster." To Virilio, the unlocking of creation takes place through a sequence of shipwreck, collision, car crash, derailment, plane crash, explosion, short-circuit, malfunction, jam, breakdown. As with the computer hackers, his method combines resistance against the technological control strategies with a vast knowledge of, and open fascination with, apparatuses. Unlike the Foucauldians, his resistance does not necessarily reinforce the system, but is a necessary attitude to arrive at post-science. The latter understands "that it is developing a way of not-knowing, and that all development of understanding can only expand the unknown." The non-military science and technology envisioned by Virilio use the media as information vacuum cleaners that remove data from the world and emphasize how much non-knowledge there is actually circulating. Media show us that there is nothing to be seen; all else is disinformation. Cases of data void are like accidents that prompt reconsideration; they are revelations of relativity.

Virilio, too, knew the antimedial dilemma that democracy must break all its ties with the media, but that it cannot exist without data transmission. If all information is distorted and the media can only communicate not-knowing, the inevitable question arises what democracy is to be based on. Virilio answers that it must be based on physical perception. His vision is not confined to some Parisian study. Since the end of the Cold War the figure of the political observer appears in every area of conflict, where it has become synonymous with the concept of democracy. After a trial period attending dubious elections in Third World nations, the observer was sent to NATO/Warsaw Pact military exercises, arms depots, nuclear power plants, civil wars, nuclear laboratories, and chemical arms factories. If the observers are refused entrance, one is de facto at war with the world. The physical presence of independent experts guarantees the democratic quality of intentions and practices. Satellites can record everything except democracy and human rights. This technological limitation indicates where classical politics may yet be situated, now that the military perception has become transpolitical.

Virilio discards the notion that democracy owes its existence to political observers as naive. The world's visibility suffers less from camouflage and concealment than it does from problems of perception on the part of the subject. Humans, according to Virilio, are not lingual beings, but are controlled in their thoughts and actions by the force of implanted images. Mental images are "fragments of the public domain extended into ourselves." "It is unnecessary to visit the National Gallery or the Louvre to watch eighteenth-century scenes. We only have to open our eyes in the morning, and already we find ourselves in a museum of outlived modes and styles of observation." Perception is occupied territory.

Negative perception discovers a space as-yet uncolonized. If the image of material objects is necessarily predetermined, then new things can be made visible only by looking at the void in between things. To see nothing is to maintain sight. In the void we may yet observe the disappearance of our culture. The disappearance of the natural contours of landscape, city, national borders, political adversaries, bodies, time, the interval, and the decision comprises a story that Virilio tries to come to terms with over and over again, and that takes up a considerable part of his works. By turning perception inside out it becomes possible to visualize disappearance, even if it is by definition invisible.

Virilio Calling

Time and again, Virilio's paradox resurfaces: everything he warns against he simultaneously considers indispensable. With him, thinking in terms of and/or escalates both ways, clearing a field of unsuspected concourses of thought. At the same time he denounces disappearance as a political and social disaster, he praises it as a principle of knowledge and aesthetical method. Virilio sees both unbridled imagination and restrictive common sense created during those brief moments of mental absence which all of us experience daily. The disappearance of conscious presence stimulates the creative or prescribed interpretation of lacking fragments. Virilio himself uses this picoleptic faculty like no one else does.

To read Virilio is to see the invisible, to interpret the unwritten. The voids, the interspaces, the black between the images—Virilio is the thinker of absence, of disappearance, of negativity, of the future. Only those who recognize the invisible, hidden from sight by the visible, are able to see the world. Virilio's is the gift of clairvoyance in the age of total transparency. The invisible is the material he researches, the challenge he poses, the question he imposes on thought: find that world.

If everything is visible, scientifically visible, permanently veri- or falsifiable, then it becomes impossible to form a coherent worldview. Coherence becomes possible only through the absence of information, through the need to form one's own links beyond the absences, interspaces, and intervals. Virilio is against disinformation, but is a supporter of temporary uninformed zones. Understanding can only derive from seeing nothing occasionally.

Negative thinking remains close to the body. It translates the prospect of death into the strategy of taking every social development to its logical conclusion. It is not a case of the extrapolation of the present into the future, but of the happy recognition that even what is to come is already past. Doom does not await us, and the signs of the apocalypse are all around. As a thinker of '77, radical negativism is Virilio's logical starting point. Back then, "no future" presented a way out of the Cold War, by stating that WW III had already come and gone and one should not be intimidated by the question of perspective. The physical condition became the new point of calibration: "the mysterious existence of living bodies who are curiously present in time." Negative thinking incorporates social processes in order to study their effect on personal well-being.

Since '89, the matter of whether the body will evaporate on the pole of inertia or rather backfire is once more completely out in the open. The astonishing conclusions in Virilio's books were suddenly surpassed by the chain reactions in military/political space. Current events went beyond dromology, forcing live theory to stop and reconsider. The old will never return, nor can the new be methodically implemented. Negativity's counterpoint has been set adrift. From the start, democracy has been the precondition for dubious thinking to vent its harsh criticism on the system. Now we find that democracy is impossible without screening and exclusion, revealing its moral bankruptcy. With this loss of a safe haven, negativism faces the task of finding a new point of calibration, without lapsing into positive proposals.

WHAT IS DATA CRITICISM?

*"The 'intellectual' has always said no, does always say no,
and will always say no. He says no to each and every thing,
as a matter of principle."*

—J. Goebbels

I.

Once upon a time there was critical theory. In 1937, the "Zeitschrift für Sozialforschung" (Vol. 5) defined the stakes of this critique as the need to expose the object value of traditional theory as being class-defined. Criticism was the precondition for emancipation, and thus of democracy. Adorno, Horkheimer, Marcuse, et al. had good grounds for making their statement. The totalitarian enemies of critique were doing everything they could to stamp out the "professional naysayers." To the Frankfurt school, criticism and theory were inseparable. Their power lay in the fact that they offered no alternative, only negation. Positive critique was alien to them; on the contrary, they launched an attack on the communist pair of criticism & self-criticism, supposed to solve all contradictions.

Although critical theory was not of this world, the social critics among the sixties generation were unconsciously solidarious with the latter. It was the heyday of criticism. But the negative critics' uncompromising nagging did not turn out to be the inner drive of the sixties after all. Criticism led to nothing. Everything had to be changed, to which end the alternative appeared more promising. Non-normative science was abandoned in favor of socially relevant research. People were no longer going to be passive observers, but were finally going to get the job done. Criticism thus succumbed to the ego trip of a better world that starts and ends with oneself. Ever since, a critical attitude has been a standard social skill, indispensible to get your career going. Unemancipated workers no longer make for loyal employees but have become obstacles to the dynamics of democratized business. In cynical thought, criticism is the hub of permanent reorganization.

Thus, film criticism was once part of a comprehensive social critique. The intellectual workers, engaged in class war within the ideological body, followed the alternative as well, in admiration of the "politique d'auteur" of the likes of Godard, Resnais, Truffaut, and Rohmer. Authors like Fassbinder, Wenders, and Herzog, and women filmmakers such as Dumas and Akerman were read as critical cineasts who offered a broader European alternative to Hollywood. The genre of the review was opened up to make cinema a weapon that would arouse the critical awareness of the masses. Profound sobriety was to exorcise the casual entertainment of spaghetti westerns, love stories, teeny movies, and James Bond. To sketch the poetry of everyday boredom was to take political action. The spiritual slowness of Soviet film-makers like Tarkovsky or Paradyanov and the subtle sense of humor of the Czechs and Poles were hailed as good news from another world. Their very incomprehensibility was the hallmark of quality.

The next step in critical cinema was to dismantle traditional film institutions from within. No genre was left undisturbed; there were constant proclamations of the end of some unwholesome form of entertainment or other. Analogous to this development, academic film theory was founded. After taking on the whole of cinema, television was labeled the new enemy, whereupon all the old movies could be rediscovered as masterpieces. Once film was upgraded as the superior visual medium for both elitist and popular culture, the cinematographic museum represented the divestment of film criticism and critical filmmakers.

II.

In the eighties, criticism was found to have lost its subject and object ages ago. Criticasters turned into losers who had missed out completely. Opinions were rapidly becoming exhausted, and yesteryear's absolute negation was degraded into today's critical note, a load of bull used by columnists to fill their dailies and weeklies. Postmodernism, much against its own free will, was upgraded by opinion leaders from serial to dominant discourse. The dash of PoMo thought currently in vogue would say that the overall stories have lost out to deconstruction and that criticism has lost its Archimedean point. All ideas are equal (but some are more equal than others). Critique is true only if well written and in newspaper format. The fascination with the fluctuation of exciting viewpoints may have stood its ground for a while, but the free-floating individualist's precision arguments never met with resistance. The unbearable lightness of personal differentiation reactivated cultural discomfort. Nostalgia arose for an age in which critique had threatened the very fabric of society. The growing demand for engagement of the early nineties represents a revival of the quest for an opposable common denominator. In an era in which Marxism has been replaced by miscellaneous conspiracy theories, there can be no hope of convicting any one prime suspect on our increasing misery. Too many interconnections blur the big picture, no matter how hard we try to invoke this vision.

The ingenuity of the sixties generation lay in their ability to reveal the political in the private. Thus, criticism had something to go on derived from its immediate environment, which it did not shun but thoroughly turned over instead. The family wasn't rejected, but replaced by the psycho-drama of the commune and experimental lifestyles. What was somewhat neglected was to puke on the lot. Today's negation was avoidable in that the alternative was already on offer before the outrage could ever gain momentum. There existed a workable solution to everything. Instead of theory, establishment of a praxis was now the goal. I was OK, you were OK. Now that the alternative has come of New Age, negative theory has been replaced by the philosophy that will (in its new capacity of spirituality) save you from all moral dilemmas.

Again, film criticism faithfully keeps to the Zeitgeist, presenting itself as a special issue on visual culture in all its aspects. Pornography turns out to be just as entertaining as photography, cult movies, TV shows, found footage, religion, and the body. Even the review is back in style as a microstudy on the artisanal precision of editing, camera work, score, trackings, and the interplay of author and actor. It is no secret that all one writes is an ad for the movie pages, just as one is but one of many elements in the film distribution process.

Film criticism is just noise disturbing the formulation of the individual moviegoer's private reviews. The weekly verdicts have shriveled to attitudes of experts who spit out opinions at random. The audience has come to find the empty theaters after some scathing critique quite silly. The industry in turn exploits this by releasing movies without a press showing, or by staging "sneak previews" of movies not yet maimed by the press, in which the audience has no idea what to expect. The sensation of having outsmarted the dailies and weeklies is "totally addictive" (a sneaker). Even video stores stage their own premieres. Movie magazines are part of the motion-picture industry and are well aware of where the sponsors are. An option yet to be examined is to write about movies that will definitely never be released, or to review every Turkish or Hindi picture, old and new. More likely, criticism will play it safe by subscribing to the metalevel of cult.

III.

Under the rule of unhistorical immaterialism, only absolute data criticism is a feasible option. Even film is no more than information. Within the current media system, criticism of the programmatic arrangement is no longer conducive to discourse. Sad though it may be, the situation is far from hopeless. Why should beauty be harmless? Or ugliness, for that matter. Fiction and reality are both marginal in relation to the omnipotent media concept. It's no use criticizing individual media; the only targets left for negation are the entire boot and root sectors of the media disk. Data criticism is the art of the absolute negation of information. It is not a survival strategy, but a head-on attack. Data criticism is no easily avoidable attitude. It is the denial of all that exists, it starts where cynicism ends; it does not put down the world, but responds to the challenge posed by the unpredictable. There is no alternative to data. Like a Medusa, the only option is to meet them—face-to-face.

THE DEMAND FOR ENGAGEMENT

The demand for engagement is a demand for intoxicated politics. The medial supercooling of hot phenomena in the 1980's forced this classical connection back into the collective unconscious (or so it was in the Occident at any rate). Ever since the 1970's, the natural urge to collective uproar had been marginalized, privatized, and criminalized by the establishment. The idea that you can blow your fuses and call it politics was linked by resurgent antifascist and anti-Stalinist forces to the awkward experiences it resulted in during the first half of the twentieth century. Political awareness might still lead to concern, but should no longer result in fury. Meanwhile, the street as a stage for the thrilling absurdity of public life was being remodeled as the folkloric locale of commerce. Under the influence of the peace movement, demonstrations as a potential public disturbance were neutralized into a dignified affirmation of identity and citizenship. The bourgeois demonstration signaled the end of playful violence and directed destruction.

During the eighties, the natural combination of armed resistance and carefree drug use that had given the sixties so much spunk was removed from history by leftist ideologues, to be replaced by a reliable version of their own ten-year uproar. The arrogant assault on the authorities by shiftless longhairs was reprocessed, *mirabile dictu,* into a responsible contribution to the general public welfare. Thus, the disturbing element was reduced to a sensible phase of emancipation and awareness. The former enemies of humanity were miraculously transformed into protagonists of human rights, to be realized through politically feasible benefits packages. The notion of politics as the moment of destruction in the family of nations had been suppressed to the point where all criticism was forced to be constructive. The crass behavior of destructive idealists was pushed aside as an obstacle to subsidy negotiations.

Consequently, rapture retreated from the evil outside world into the circle of private life, where it became fragmented. If before, biological, chemical, and technological ecstasy had combined with the ideological high to produce a giant tangle of drives and urges, now they lost all connection. The "stoned in the street" happening gave way to weekend recreational drug use. The variety of drugs were no longer a dangerous concoction, but substances to be independently consumed within the leisure arena, as long as it didn't interfere with performance. The street junkie's public display of discomposure was beyond the limit of intoxicated ethics. Likewise, the abandon with which political dogma had been consumed as a psychedelic drug well into the seventies was erased in a suddenly emerging aversion to the neurotic and repressive character of the political impulse. The ideological institution was deregulated into a political enterprise, while the ritual stylization of the political was soon highlighted in the media as a form of entertainment.

In the period between punk and yuppie, passionate social optimism was converted into a game in which the remaining politicians were used to heighten the fun. The urban movements of the 1980's made impossible demands that had to be met immediately. Many a dazed administrator responded by sending in the riot squad. Although the activists succeeded in a temporary revival of bits and pieces of prewar street life, the ideological serum had already evaporated to the extent that it could no longer serve to fuel the action. The very concept of politics became clouded by such Babylonian confusion that even the classic "in for myself and no one else" might be cited as a protest statement. The recipe for debate, argument, and explanation had been lost, and with it the love of the hermeneutics of personal action. You don't need ideological hype to get high.

By now, the Dionysian aspects of this form of social change were light-years removed from the dominant bureaucratic arts. Whereas radical action still contained a trace of the link between radical negativity and the Red Dawn, the actors were fed up with coming on like the bona fide legators to Western Humiliation. At the end of the day, nobody felt affiliated with a Marx, Bakunin, or Sartre. Art had long ago succumbed to good taste, which demands that words or images, though possibly unsettling, never act disruptive. Government, in turn, transforms these artistic strategies into a program of soft deregulation of social relationships. This urge toward disorganization gave politics such speed that there was no more need for would-be artists and actors to keep the government alive through protest and resistance.

The shock of pleasure, of the new, the disruptive, and the astonishing traditionally evoked by art, was removed from the order of time in which it could be followed by an explosion of energy transforming indignation into politically significant confrontations. Any artistic attempt at outrage was drowned in the bottomless pit of medial amnesia. The social urge toward metamorphosis was too fixated on the next Mafiosi assembly of debutantes to remember the last wave of young talent. The belief in successive trends, generations and decades enabled the cultural planners to discover one cultural or political novelty after another. If there was any conflict at all in the field of small-scale maximality, it was considered nice material for another debate to cover up the dirt. This was all that remained of the good old cutting edge that wounded so easily and made the twentieth century what it was.

By the end of the 1980's the public, beginning to understand the workings of entertainment, decided it might amuse itself by becoming interactive. Causing the polls to rise and fall at random was great fun while it lasted, but things really got hilarious once the voters started to use elections as an anti-political action. With each election, a random number of voters gets the urge to show up (or not) in order to vote for the wrong candidate en masse. People who want to have a go at involvement and participation run the risk of being ruthlessly punished for their efforts by the allotment of a position on some congressional committee or in a provincial state. The expansion and collapse of parties every election gives the dilettantes a chance to develop their showmanship on a stage far too long dominated by timeworn vaude-ville. The commentators' frantic attempts to discover any meaning in voting behavior are themselves part of the fun. Exit the idea that the public can be won over for any ethical/moral scheme through political manipulation.

MEDIA OF DEATH, DEATH OF THE MEDIA

When the dead and the living still used to treat each other on equal terms, every person was a medium and the media fell outside of the event horizon. Contact with ancestors and future generations was established collectively. The tribe was complete; there was no need for telecommunication with absentees. It is only after the dead depart that there first appears a need for media to keep the lines to the disappeared open: without direct contact with its origins, humanity loses its vital powers.

Ritual is a medium, a synthetic channel which allows the living to die in order to regain their lives from the deceased who no longer need theirs. Without such a connection, the dead take revenge by sending uncontrollable cacodemons who can no longer be ritually exorcised. These are not the messengers of dreams but of traumas. By turning the dead into ancestors through careful ceremonies, future unpleasant surprises could be avoided. Rituals were great wild parties in which contact with the past was made in the meantime. The long bacchanal of the deathwatch gave people little time to produce much-needed surplus values, but at least it helped them to overcome their grief within a week or so.

When the deceased spirit could no longer be directly connected to, attention shifted to the dead body. After Christianization, the deceased becomes an individual corpse, whose image lingers on for a while in memories or in the little oval above the sideboard. The body has become an image, and promptly appears in the dark as a haunted spirit or phantom. The Christian deceased is a loner who is awarded the inner cinema of next of kin as a dwelling. The connection with origins has been disrupted. In the mass media, the dead even lose this final abode. Nowhere do there occur more deaths than on the personal screen. But the displayed corpses always remain anonymous: they are merely the dead of humankind. This universal community cannot live without them. Without images of death, people forget that they are survivors. If this awareness decreases, then the live report's magic power may well be lost forever.

The Media Archive

II.

The Gulf War distinguished itself from its Vietnam predecessor through the absence of images. The military deprived the media of their dead. Instead, the upset viewers had to derive their drama from the exciting question, "Is this a video game or a real bombing?" When the Iraqi soldiers finally appeared on screen, they turned out to be poor dupes who hailed General Schwarzkopf. The urgent demand for the image of death remained unfulfilled. Even the dying birds along oil-infested beaches turned out to be just file footage. All that remained were a few authentic arms industry ads—and commercials do not usually feature dead bodies. The war was less against Iraq or Saddam Hussein than it was a positive gesture toward the New World Order, in which there are only fellow players in the game of supply and demand, not enemies.

The topical media took terrible revenge on the military, as the Kurds in their mountain camps were soon to find out. While the international relief troops were nowhere to be seen yet, the media were already making up for their acute death shortages and instantly transmitting the distressful images worldwide. In order to present the item of genocide so as to reinforce humanity's awareness of being survivors, a few explosives were set off within the collective unconscious. The shocking images of dead babies and dying old ladies represented the destruction of the old cycle from ancestors to posterity. After the dead had not been allowed to appear during the war, they returned elsewhere as uncontrollable disrupters of the New Order. In war, death had found a meaningful context in the media, but Desert Storm's hundred thousand had remained invisible. Now, they reappeared elsewhere and were dying in numbers in a nameless and meaningless catastrophe. The live effect's power derives not from its immediacy, but from its fatal consequences.

III.

The structure of topicality is that of medieval death; the time of the item, that of the hourglass. Its suspense lies in the fact that its finiteness is predetermined. Every item has its own decisive moment. The announcement, "Charles Jacobs live in Riyadh" is the final drop, after which the sandglass can be turned around again for the next report. The cut is the scythe in the directors' hands, causing a sudden break in what might otherwise have been an endless data flow. It cuts fractions from reality and presents them as reality itself. In the autumn of the media, the dance of death is performed when the spectacle reaches its macabre stage and raises tension to the edge of exhaustion in an orgy of catastrophic moments. How and when we do not know yet, but we can be certain that the image will be extinguished for good after the twilight of the media. Perhaps the media will burn on for years after, as the warriors move on from one station to another. The global data network will disintegrate and the tribes will recover their own time, gathered around the campfires where ancestors, future generations and the living meet again in bewilderment.

But the dying age of the media has only just begun. As long as they have deaths to portray, they themselves live on, while not to portray them causes their catastrophic return elsewhere. The new technologies inevitably steer toward the physical experience of the other's death. First expressions of this are reality-TV shows about hospitals and police stations and speed sports like base jumping, sky surfing, and heliskiing. But the closer the media bring us to death, the closer we are to the death of the media. It will not be a patricide or suicidal performance, but a catastrophe the media themselves will never report. Now we are rehearsing the rituals to ensure that the media do not only die, but will become our ancestors as well. Only thus can we prevent the media from returning as cacodemons one day.

Warriors and Their Media

"Invisible warriors will turn out to have been a sign of the times."

—Christian Unverzagt

The Ramboids

The advent of the Rambo figure came with the disappearance of the locatable battle scene in favor of the virtual war of the disarmament race of the 1980's. In answer to the successful tactics of Ho Chi Minh's jungle commando, Rambo embodied the disintegration of the regular army. He declared war on the nineteenth-century command structure which survived into the twentieth century as electronics. He replaced the army (no longer able to wage war, since it existed purely as a deterrent) by becoming the war himself. After the combat soldier lost his corporeality in WW I's Materialschlacht and the primal electronics of the WW II Blitzkrieg, now he regained his image as a media consumer in the rippling anabolic steroids of the invincible Rambo-man.

The Rambo outfit assumed museological forms and habits purloined from the tristes tropiques by the colonialism of anthropological conservation. The popularity of his attire was inspired by TV pundits and book clubs. The Rambo figure combined the outfit of the premedial warrior with the efficiency of the latest compact weapons, but his location was the consciousness of the bargain-deal video consumer. Bound to the imaginary reality of the empire of the image he had no option but to remain a media warrior. Unlike the guerrilla, his task was not the liberation of oppressed peoples. He was simply concerned with the coming-out of his own individuality in which the viewers might reflect themselves. In order to shape his subjective identity he had to return to the front each time, without political or aggressive motives, to be reborn as a full-fledged individual. In the invisibility of permanent war, he acted as the disruptive element that gave vent to a fighting spirit which had become purely folkloric. But within the context of total world peace, he could be no more than the viewers' nostalgic identification with the actors they no longer were.

Warriors and Their Media

The Sign Masters

In the universe of media networks, there exists no vertical relationship between signs and reality, only horizontal ones between the signs themselves which create their own reality. Metarealists seek the passwords to penetrate this matrix. On the one hand, there are data producers; on the other, data travelers. Both are media warriors. Data producers launch their signs from an extramedial standpoint, in order to realize a public reality on the screen. Their objective is to change the world through the belief that information affects the mind. They fight racism, sexism, and pollution through data manipulation and image defacement, avoiding physical encounters with the police. They need the media for their blockades, raids, riots, and pop concerts. But they go one step further than the critical generation, which tried to challenge media power by means of discussion. Their oral culture has now been replaced by the spectacular images of media reality, and hence the activists have become the artists of signs.

Data travelers also depend on the media. Like tourists cruising at the speed of light, hackers can drop in on other parts of the world like greased lightning. In this sixth continent without geographical limitations, physical exertion is replaced by the sensation of gate-crashing security programs. Just as Grand Tour tourists carved their names into Florentine frescoes, these pioneers of the electronic midnight toil leave their numbers in forbidden regions of the planetary network. The transition from name to virus is the beginning of the emigration to this land of unlimited possibilities. Their Trojan horses are signs that produce a reality. As effects, they owe their existence to the disruption of the arbitrary order of the electronic realm. The future will see cyberpunks living as outlaws in data land. They will have become signs themselves, surviving their physical death as flatlines stored in the form of hidden files. Future generations of activist actors and apocalyptic cyberpunks will abandon extramedial objectives and enter to realize the great beyond: a total delete.

The Black Hand

Everything is recorded. Events are documented as evidence and used as weapons in the information war. This happens both at long range, amid military satellites and telezoom, and over short distances with amateurish photo and video cameras. But even in this age of total transparency, there still exist clans which act as if they want to safeguard their privacy as some sacrosanct privilege: the Mafia, special forces, rioting autonomists, royal families, and other secret societies. They surround themselves with bodyguards who act as antimedial warriors. Their function is that of black holes which suck up media matter so that the event may vanish altogether, although in reality they turn out to be press magnets who secretly enjoy having their privacy invaded while basking in the limelight. They put up a heroic fight in the no-man's-land between media and classical reality. We see them in the final reel where the hand pushes away the camera, the soldier takes aim at the viewer and fires or the order is given to stop filming.

This apparent form of antipublicity fails, because forbidden images command the highest market price for the information distributors since they show that on a global scale, Glasnost is simply work in progress, thus demonstrating the viability of the media. As long as there are people who suggest that the camera's omnipotence may be curbed, its omnipresence can only increase. "Avoiding publicity is the best publicity"; that is the motto on every front where the media can still capture unrecorded events. Until, due to lack of authentic regions, the media are forced to censor their own revelations and employ warriors to withhold certain images from the viewers.

The Absentees

There are rumors of a kind of blissful beings, who resort beyond the event-horizon and have hidden themselves behind history, observing the media like we watch the screen. Among them are the extramedial warriors. Their space-time runs parallel to our own and seldom touches it. Like the classical warriors, they have mastered the art of emptiness, to emerge on unexpected planes of reality. Their ways are invisible to the media eye because they act in a dimension which no more than cuts through the horizontal sign exchange. It is at these points of incision that disasters in media sign communications occur, appearing as terrorist actions by the other circuit. The goal of the media, after having rendered the universe visible, is to make these interfaces speak up. But warriors only reply to unasked questions that silence the media. They present themselves as the snow that dissolves the iconographic order. The static image is their ultimate information.

THE SOCIALIST'S MEDIA

"Who speaks of victory? To survive is everything."
—Rainer Maria Rilke

The socialist in his actually existing form—that of a government official—may have disappeared over the horizon like a shot, but as a potential figure he can look forward to an unbelievable future. Socialists were spoon-fed on programming (version 1.0 of the socialist program was out by 1830). Lacking suitable hardware, they were forced for 150 years to install their program onto society. The social question this raised caused a reaction which led to an extension of the original design and a formidable number of new applications. With each setback the socialists produced new plans, undaunted by illegal copiers like the Spartacists, revisionists, Leninists, and Christian socialists.

When Hitler and Stalin linked up socialism with incompatible software like nationalism and totalitarianism, the development of leftist programming stalled for quite a while. Of the many applications, only data storage and file management, for which historical socialism showed a true obsession, survived. Think of the spreadsheets with the production figures of the Five-Year plans, the intelligence services' miles of files, the Leaders' collected speeches, the endless series of forms and applications which had to be filled out at the drop of a hat. This was a social format that got entangled in paperwork, a Leviathan too big to be computerized. All the memory of the world could not have held the data overload that was heaped up in the archives.

Yet the urge to program reared its head again in the 1980's in the person of Gorbachev. He discovered that contemporary social programs require a different hardware than society. Planning is now merely PR material which presents a corporate image. When the investors had Gorby's chain investigated, the marketability of the Soviet Group was finished. But with the disappearance of communism, the socialists finally got another chance to vent their programming lust in the media which do it the most justice: computer games, media banks, and virtual realities.

In the West, the school of life has given up learning from the past a long time ago. Historiography has been completed, from the nano- to the cosmic level. All phenomena and objects have been fitted into a chronology which runs from the first attosecond after the Big Bang, the cigar, the bathroom and

69

bedroom, anorexia, teddy bears, the sublime, medieval cuisine, and going to the beach to the image of the vagina, death, and the fine nose of the nighthawk. All of history is reprocessed into information and made into news. In contemporary historiography, miscellaneous news items go hand in hand with world politics and stock market quotations; determining factors (sub- or superstructural) such as historical materialism knew them can no longer be distinguished. Ultimately, information is just information; Western historical consciousness has succumbed to an excessive availability of the past. Information never penetrates deeper than the main memory of the democratic citizen. Everything can be forgotten, because storage is always left to others (expert systems). Until we are forced to recognize with horror that virtually all episodes of the old TV series have been burnt.

Socialists have a good relationship with their own hard disks. Like the former Marxists, they learned the hard way, with mnemonics of steel. To them, history is not just one of the many possible areas to click onto, but the domain where the driving principles of recent data can be found. The socialists' relationship with the past has always been a technological connection. From birth, they were less revolutionaries or heretics than media engineers. Books, pamphlets, newspapers, proposals, manifestoes, interventions, polemic, criticism—socialism was a literary movement that believed in the word's persuasive power to maneuver the revolting hordes in the right direction. For the socialist, words, though not originating events, could still direct it because they discriminated between the chance circumstances of an uproar and the iron dynamics behind them.

For the socialists, an event is not a fait divers but an omen. Because they never erase files and always have more information storage capacity, their future is not a blank space and (unlike modern Westerners) they do not have to start from scratch at each turn. The Westerner is already tired before he's even begun from all the patient digging and searching that needs to be done. For the socialist, events are embedded in a universe of old and new writing. Whether a text discussed prerequisites or end results, it always resulted in yet more text. The goal was to fabricate one massive interactive hypertext out of socialism. Everybody thoroughly read the others, reviewing them over hundreds of pages. Paper was not just a mass of dead letters, but a stimulus for written reactions. Banned authors could always be reinterpreted, after which debate was energetically thrown open, resulting in a new supply of bulk text. Independent of technological innovations and new media like photography, film, and radio, the socialists constantly developed new connections, but always exclusively within their own media system. This practice makes them ideal candidates for the management and expansion of cyberspace, which also shirks parallel media and constructs rhizomes. The 1980's showed that retraining the scribes as programmers is a relatively small step. The absence of illustrations in soc.txt is no obstacle to the socialists' entry into the new pictorealm. They had been operating in a larger context than the single picture all along, since their medium had been 3-D society.

The Socialist's Media

As a storage specialist, the socialist has three options to preserve social-ism. First, the complete text edition will be available on CD-ROM. But the market is decidedly not waiting for this, especially now that the sugar dad-dies have left Moscow. The acidiferous textual tradition is yellowing and crumbling in the hands of desperate archivists. Only a Band Aid "Save the Archives" concert could still provide the necessary resources. Now that fur-ther writing on the socialist project is slowly taken over by historians who judge "objectively" with the academic eye of the outsider, the socialists, con-trary to nature, turn destructive and destroy their archive while they can. As the ex-socialists own up to their past mistakes, others act in an attempt to prevent socialism from degenerating into information. The soc.txt is approaching dark times of nostalgia and memoirs, while the ground texts have lost their medial potency. On the socialist diskette, the tab has been moved from "write data" to "read only." Storage of the entire socialist dis-course is not only impracticable but objectionable.

The second option consists of scanning actually existing socialism. With the trend to shed light on every pernicious side of the twentieth century in a museological context, the crimes, lies, and complete failures of the Eastern bloc will get all the (disk) space they need. At the same time there will arise a worldwide fascination with the strange fact that for decades, hundreds of millions of people acted as though another system besides democracy and market economy was possible. The aesthetics of socialism was that between a well-defined beginning and end point it managed to develop a whole sys-tem of own products, artistic movements, fashion and design, of stunning uniformity. Theme parks and sensory spaces will be installed to make this historical phenomenon understandable: a tour past collapsing housing developments, consumer queues, barking police officers, informers, military parades, moral dissidents. Ascetic, modernist nondesign will pass through the cycle of avant-garde, hype, and timeless fashions and include socialism in the fifties-sixties-punk-eighties sequence. This recycling ignores the great possibilities the socialist has in mind.

The third option is that of storing and managing socialist potential. Finally the medium is at hand whereby socialism can be instituted without troublesome side-effects like politics, management, environment, and mili-tarism. Socialism as a model is motivated by the realization of total leisure. The Soviet states were well underway with it. The worker's paradise knew many opportunities for getting away: you went to work to have breakfast in the people's kitchen, and then after a coffee to find some friends to have a beer with and catch a movie. Existence was of a relaxed idleness in which the dialectic of production and consumption had been transcended. The socialist work ethic can be understood as an early form of VR. In the data environment, too, there is nothing to do, and the aura of the goods is miss-ing. Pressure to perform can easily be avoided (by pretending you are work-ing). Socialism as a VR environment is an atopia where one may act or watch without consequence. For a socialist, VR is not an archive or a museum, but a parking lot for an ideal society in a period in which the New World Order imposes the same work pressure on the entire world population. The socialists recognize that this monopoly must not be fought, but endured. They do not wait for pauperization and its subsequent class consciousness, but keep on tinkering with their virtual model, as they used to keep writing at their textual galaxy. Until VR implodes in reality. The socialists will be ready.

SECRET SOCIALISM

"May God smite him who, himself blinded, seeks to show others the way."

—Mulla Nasrudin

The revolution is not of this world. It takes place in historical tomes, exotic landscapes, outdated political systems. From an attainable moment, achievable in the near future even by us, it has evolved into a touristic reading/viewing experience designed for consumption only. The unlikeliness of a revolution occurring in Western Europe's museological cities is matched by the unreality of images of street violence, coming from so far away that all they really broadcast is a certainty that the upheaval on display will never reach us.

It took the revolution twenty years to develop from future to perishable consumer product. The students of the sixties lost their naive revolutionary joy upon learning in Cuba, Vietnam, and China that revolutions are, by definition, unpleasant for the population at large. Much to their own surprise, this loss of perspective turned out to be a godsend. The activists, who had just come out as hegemonic intellectuals, found they could solidify their identity as independent leftist thinkers (ILTs) through the endless story concerning, and based on, the personal crisis. The preached revival never came about because, like any sermon, its only goal was to bind the flock together. Far from expressing existential questions, the leftist crisis was the success story of a generation that had spent the best years of its life looking for nuance, and became frightened by its own radicalism.

This narcissistic attitude led the ILTs to ignore the social changes that continued to unfold elsewhere as they celebrated their cult of dilemma. Then, midway through the eighties, they suddenly found themselves part of an information society governed by speed, efficiency, and marketing. As the long institutional march appeared to be in its final stages, the ILTs applied for retraining, only to be told they'd been reading the wrong books for twenty years. The ruthless reorganization of the now underprivileged leftists culminated in a dialectic reversal: re-education for the ideological class war generation! So they were the last of the Europeans to find out that power does not own the media, but that the media own power. Switched on to the screen, they consciously formatted their entire literacy and entered the world of pure topicality.

The ILTs cast off their nineteenth-century conceptual mindset with abandon, hoping to share in the media's permanent revolution. They themselves thought of this dogmatic reaction as a newly acquired flexibility. Instead of restyling themselves as Marxians, the ex-Marxists humbly converted to model democrats, saying of their repentance after the fall of communism that "the right was right." They failed to notice that right-wingers had been spectators just as they had, and by no means welcomed the enemy's surrender.

The latest ILT consensus holds that the left no longer exists, and that it's lost touch with the individualized media masses. Modern-day cultural society has disintegrated into a tangle of single issues to the point where the ILTs can no longer blend them into any one state-political scheme. They get the uncomfortable feeling that they're looking at the back of some patchwork quilt, while in front of it, the multicultural public shamelessly wallows in aesthetic fascination with one-dimensional, day-glo items. The cure propagated by the leading thinkers of the backward classes consists of the magic formula that "we have to connect to social changes." In other words, computers, soap operas, fashion, sports, and money are cool, while intellectual talk, labor unions, parties, and workers are passé. The ILT zines have assumed the rewarding task of transmitting the correct lifestyle instructions.

Where socialist perspective once beckoned, we now hear only Muzak. Although even the ILTs have long since settled comfortably within "technological culture," they habitually attempt to "influence public debate" with a bit-free jargon that masks self-importance as ironic self-criticism. In this masochistic consumption of personal crisis, all pleasure derives, not from playing with the media, but incorporation in the media. What is not seen is that the media are long past needing any help with their introduction (F3) but instead are on their way out (F7).

The history of revolution is characterized by accelerated gyration. The upheavals caused by the prehistoric introduction of fire, mushrooms, writing, grain, cattle, the horse, the wheel, and roads have retained their energy for thousands of years since. But with the ancient Greeks, revolution became politics, and hence a brief and fluctuating affair. After that, revolutions became moments of repeated historical revivification. Fire, blood, banners, barricades, and improvised weapons, versus helmets and rifles, became part of the arsenal of images in a collective memory that transcends the ages.

At the beginning of the nineteenth century, industry caused a revolution whose very goal was to revolve. After this turned the outside world upside down for a century and a half, the 1960's witnessed the beginning of the psychic revolution (along with the less significant sexual one). Here, chemistry and physics so expanded consciousness as to penetrate the outside world through the electronic and digital expansion of the mind: the audiovisual media and the world of computers.

Secret Socialism

The "media" replaced history with the artificial space-time of a satellite- and live connection–induced perpetual omnipresence. But this is even less self-sufficient than (political) history. It feeds on energy invested in its reality or released by it. Everything can be submitted to revolutionary change. Toothpaste, furniture, the brain, the city, love affairs, clothing, the universe, dogs, airplanes, perception: If all things are in a state of revolution, then the desire for a radical overthrow of society turns into panic and doubt. And even this doubt can be efficiently marketed as the scientific method of chaos and catastrophe—a paradigm fit for a millenarian age.

It was this same doubt that befell the ILTs during the seventies and inspired them to set up camp in the blind alley of historical faith for a decade. A double bind, from which they were released when Fukuyama, the poor man's Baudrillard, introduced them to the end of history. If one thing terrifies them in their new forgetfulness, it's the classical revolutionary images of blood, fire, and barricades. When these unfolded on their doorsteps in the early eighties, the ILTs at first still interpreted the new autonomists in the reassuring terms of history ("not another May '68") or anthropology ("ritual- ism")—thus siding with the law. In the early nineties, the same images were given a medial interpretation: "poor visual presentation." What the ILTs overlook is that the images are now being produced only for the media, and that extra-imaginary reality is elsewhere.

ILTs think media are great. With the end lost, the means justify them- selves. It is no longer in the streets or in parliament, but only through a "proper relationship to the media" that their "digital socialism" can be brought back on track. Power is what they want, and the road to it passes through the station of "media." The everlasting debates of conference cul- ture have been reduced to short statements that make the news media in uncut format. This roundabout construction results from a poor understand- ing of the way virtual forces like media function.

One seizes power not by sheepishly following the masses, but by bluntly claiming it and dumbfounding the public. There are currently two options to effect a takeover: Either the media are eliminated and one personally becomes the medium, or the media are ambushed and radically jacked in to one's own program. To become an item is lethal ("We don't want more air- play, we want the whole goddamn media").

The first option boils down to neutralizing current media power. This can be accomplished by giving every European, American, and Japanese commercial station access to the home. The overload will turn against the satellite giants as it shatters the ratings. The less transnational mediatization is accompanied by criticism and discussion, the less power the media will have. Once the whole of media politics has thus been suspended, there can be room once more for the medium of a socialism based on argumentation and decision-making.

The second option strives for hegemonic media power; that is, the max- imum exposure of socialist symbolism. The Christian Democrats are a good example. The systematic provocation of scandals, or making of decisions that nobody agrees with, results in prime-time media exposure. The old idea that media power can be either seized or democratized has been increasingly superseded by the spread of understanding of their operation: if the rules of the game are skillfully applied, the reporters will show up automatically.

The first option creates a media void where socialism can unfold. In the second, power itself has become void, having surrendered to the media, where the only spectacle left for it to stage is that of its own permanent decomposition. These options, intended to gain absolute parliamentary majorities, consider power as the end to which media are the means. But this is now an outdated view, and is only supported by the ILTs because they obviously don't want power and/or social developments at all, and are plagued by fears that the public will implicate them regardless to get its revenge.

The ILTs' fondness for images of political action free of revolutionary connotations comes from their own suppressed history. This further explains why it is impossible for them to realize that the media are already past their prime. The media are overwhelmed by all the topics that present themselves as political action. Too many people have figured it out. The media react defensively to both producers and consumers. Supplements and special sections are initiated to channel the users' pressure on the media. Viewing guidelines are handed out to prevent remote controllers from mixing up all the TV channels or not watching at all. All mutuality between transmitter and receiver is lost. One side is overcome with doubt, the other threatens to succumb to indifference. The media fear their users and wish they could do away with them altogether. They realize that their contribution to the abolition of the world has been marginal, and that their time is up. Any counteractions they launch are by definition medial, and can only serve to accelerate the current trend.

The question remains: How to bring socialism any nearer? It is not up to politics to control or direct social developments. The idea that they can be accelerated must be discarded. One cannot overtake the media (the speed of light), but one can let them pass by. Therefore, socialism, if it is to retain its seductive power, needs to slam on the brakes. The only future for socialism is to reject all social change from the start and freeze at the zero point of negativity. Or else it must learn to act in accordance with Bell's theorem, according to which events influence each other over great distances without necessarily bridging the space in between, thus leaving the speed of light behind.

The medial revolution caused and witnessed by 1980's activists will lead to the autodestruction of the media at our fin de siècle. After posthistory, it is time for the postmedial. In a media-free world, the energy sucked out of reality by the media will radically and gradually break free and start to gyrate. This actually existing revolution is going to hit the ILTs like an unprecedented, unheard-of disaster. Socialism will invade their lives like a truck crashing through the bedroom window. While outside a riotous celebration rages by, they'll heroically cling to their monitors. It is only when the bonfires have erased all their files at once that they will go into audiovisual blackout ("ILTs must exit"). The consequent outburst of panic will be their final hallucination. "Our socialism has no room for socialists."

The secret of socialism is that it's a story that has to appear in print. Mao was aware of this. In the strictly imageless, ceremonial universe of a post-medial age, writing can witness its eternal return. Through its initiation to textual life, humanity will enter the extrahistorical vacuum where socialism has resided ever since its conception. The text as object discloses a metahistorical space. That which has been transported as a spurious element from the nineteenth into the twentieth century—namely, the love of books—will soon become a constituent principle of the social order.

This is not to say that the ILTs are doomed. It is not their crisis but their past that offers hope. Their previous ritual treatment of the sacred scriptures of, say, Gramsci, Althusser, or young Marx will prove to be a recommendable quality in the cult of writing, whose contents are unimaginable and around which life organizes itself. At present, the best course for the ILTs to follow is to go underground immediately and re-emerge at some future point to serve as scribes for the republic of letters. Their hope lies in the classical observation that while media are perishable, writing will last forever. Those who still wish to render video service or communicate medially had best organize in gangs of pictorial thugs and roam the margins of literal socialism.

Already, secret socialism's virtual societies vehemently reject any emerging revolutionary subject, for nowadays no starry-eyed idealist exceeds the medial level. The refusal to implement socialism is the secret socialists' most powerful weapon. They strive to encourage thorough indifference, by announcing we will never arrive at socialism; not today nor tomorrow. Their radical negativity is sensational. Anti in the extreme, yet they do not propagate it. This frustrates the enemy, who is urgently waiting for dialogue. The hidden nature of its program produces a vast social demand which will never be met. Who but the socialist could possibly reverse the implosion of society? Yet the wealth of ready-made solutions remains untouched, never circulated as capital. What does socialism want?

LIVING IN THE MEDIA

I

Dutch squatters once proclaimed, "You can't live in tanks." But you can live in the media. Some people take the abolition of public and private a little too literally. Why should the abandoned carriers of the imaginary not be transformed into living rooms? Take the Victoria Theater on Amsterdam's Sloterkade canal, a monumental building in late Jugendstil style which stood empty for years. Two weeks before it was finally squatted, the public function of the building had been jeopardized for good when local hooligans in search of a hangout for those boring evenings set the screen on fire by way of an experiment. The day of the squat, the fire brigade paid the new residents a visit to congratulate them with their little palace, thinking the building's new function might contain the fire hazard. The enormous auditorium was so impressive that for the first few months, the ten squatters decided to camp out on the empty stage, where the loudspeakers still worked. The red plush foyer became a late-night bar almost by itself. The Pakistani who had last managed the building had taken the projectors but left the backup units, so that the atmospheric lighting could be turned on immediately. As movie theaters by nature have no windows, the residents' biological rhythms went totally haywire. They would wake up to find the shops already closed, which led to alternative shopping behavior as they learned to take the shop window rather than the front door.

To get through the long nights without light shows, people fell back on such primary vital functions as sex, drugs, booze, and rock 'n' roll. It was not until months later that the whole company moved to the upstairs offices, where the administrative records of seventy years of cultural industry were still stored in crates. A kitchen was built after rumors spread concerning a case of scurvy. The squat had been occupied in early autumn, and the squatters couldn't get the heat on because the gas company refused to provide service. The concerts they managed to organize never really got going because everyone was standing freezing around the hot-air blower under the balcony. Only the neighbors burned up with rage owing to the racket that lasted deep into the night.

The remarkable phenomenon occurred that every house hunter who hung out at the Victoria for more than three weeks became incommunicado to well-meaning outsiders. The Victoria's warriors even lost contact with the central monad of the neighborhood squatters' group. Groups constantly moved in and out over the years, each taking the same inevitable route from responsibility to a raging standstill.

It took survivors years to make the switch back to civilian life in the inhabited world. The intensity of the squatters' involvement in the permanent performance of the building's phantoms left them profoundly amazed, a state of mind which spanned the whole spectrum from myth to taboo. You cannot live in theaters, and those who transgress this rule will pay the price.

II.

A second group has discovered communication itself as its living quarters. Certain radiomakers and hackers end up in a studio or workshop and never leave again. Their work schedule is so much at sixes and sevens that they pass beyond the critical stage where a distinction between leisure and working for the cause can still be made. Their presence on the air or the network assumes such scopes that even others accept the fact that they are in permanent transmission. From then on, every coworker is merely one of their guests. Distinctions between the few personal belongings and the equipment can no longer be made. Only the mattress and a few clothes point to the secondary residential function of the space.

The work space is transformed into a cozy salon stuffed with found and donated electronics. Some discarded machines are beyond repair, while others, divested of their casings, are fully operational. The black-box myth of the media is shattered and technology stands unscrewed, in all its naked pride. Immune to user stress, this personal relationship with hardwares takes its time to explore the matrix in every detail for nights on end. Visitors are treated by the data doctors to an extensive tour of those parts of the jumbled collection that enjoy their current attention.

A prolonged stay in media space eases the burden of everyday time schedules. There is no more question of expensive broadcasting or programming time; each minute is priceless in its possibilities. Because every encounter is a personal broadcast for the studio residents, they can always put on a brilliant show, even without transmitting equipment. Always on the air, they are open to every guest on their live show. This distinguishes the armchair mediatists from their Japanese fellow-otakus, who seek the loneliness of the electronic monad to play their games with the others. What they have in common is that to both, classical reality is a black box, cast in eternal darkness.

III.

We have been living in the media for years now. Delocalization or detemporalization is a natural state of mind for large sections of the world population. Earthly wiring and stratospheric irradiation have created an infrastructure in which anything can happen anywhere and anyone can be present at any moment. The telecitizens of the global state are all in the same boat together, and they had better face up to it. We all row with the media we have.

The cold war ideal of the open society and its enemies finds its logical sequel in the telemonad of the smart building, where twenty-first-century cave dwellers sit staring at their electronic interiors. In emulation of the barricaded squat, the home regains the allure of the medieval castle. Buried in electronic security, people think they can keep junkies, refugees, Eastern Europeans, child molesters, art thieves, intruders, rapists, and other representatives of deviant behavior out the door.

The paranoid fear of robbery finds its counterpart in the fear of missing out on global events. People connect to every available channel, from the astral to the local. Fluctuations in the dollar rate are as absorbing as the length of the reported traffic jam. One reads at least four daily papers, a stack of newsmagazines with all the favorite contributors and every appropriate trade journal, from *Cosmopolitan* to *Semiotext(e)*. In short, those who have taken up residence in the media no longer know what is going on outside.

As long as the media fail to eliminate earth's biological time differences and synchronize every watch, the human remainder will keep muddling on with its private day and night rhythms. Designer drugs somewhat accelerate information processing. The new trend toward natural stimulation of the synapses of the human main processor serves no other purpose than to step up the speed of the internal clock so as to keep up with the frequency of visual alternations. To the data user, a stay in the media is an unequaled show. But to the nomadic mind that dwells outside the media strongholds, the media buzz is synonymous with total inertia. From this point of view, the info carriers' metapassengers are blind because they see too much, deaf because they hear too much, handicapped by their excessive mileage. From this perspective, the monads are sick to the bone, while, to those inside, the nomads are the criminal virus-carriers par excellence, and urgently need to be dragged through the DNA mills.

In this class struggle between teleworkers and the dataless, the latter will deploy matter itself in their offensive against digital omnipotence. As far as the opponents of data are concerned, there is little reason to fall back on the modern adage of light, air, and elasticity. They would rather reach out to a stranger in town and strike up a conversation. They join the Babel-like confusion with abandon. Teleworkers who have not yet been discharged into the data-sewers of the free flow of information will be dismissed, after which nothing will prevent the condemned media monads from being squatted. Leftover data will disappear through the hole in the ozone layer and dissolve into interstellar dark matter.

THE DOOR IN OUR CONSCIOUSNESS

The door is an obstacle, not an interface, and was never a means to promote contact between inside and outside. Nor did it wish to burden anyone, whether insiders or outsiders, with a secret. The door remains in the picture by transforming itself throughout subsequent cultures, maintaining those characteristics that appeal to it. Its position has always been that you cannot get around it. It demanded to be seen, and only allowed passage on the condition that it be touched. As an object with a vast malicious potential, it forced passersby to observe a complicated ritual of gestures and etiquette. Fond of human beings and animals, the door loved other objects as well: doorknobs, judas holes, locks, chains, keys, mailboxes, door checks, strings, knockers, Christmas bouquets, ironwork, metal strips and reinforcements, nameplates, and notices like "No Evangelists" or "No Hawkers—We've Got It All" or handwritten notes such as "Be Back Soon" or "Gone to the Pub." In its immediate environment it attracted doormats, stoops, hatracks and umbrella stands, doorsteps and doorposts, chimes, peepholes, and especially other doors, from the screens and bug curtains outside to the inner doors of the porch and hallway.

Western Christianity is the ultimate door culture. Its doors are massive, large, sacred, and often winged (as in the double door). Where else but in the Occident could the revolving door have been invented, having already converted bridges into doors (the fortresses' drawbridge)? The modern era began when Luther nailed his theses to a door. In the Arab world, except for the gate that separated the courtyard and women's quarters from the outside world, the door was usually a curtain (later copied in the West as kitchen or terrace bead curtains). Under Islam, the door found its most individual form in the shape of veils, while in Japan it maintained its original and most universal form, that of the sliding wall.

In the West, the door allowed itself to be used as a means to obstruct and control currents: city gate, garden fence, church door, entrance hall, or (emergency) exit, accompanied by the appropriate guards, lions, dogs, sextons, doorkeepers, janitors, warders, bouncers, videotists, and electronicians. This gave the door its dark side: burglars, bailiffs, death. Enter the little doors of resistance: the small gates in church and fortress walls, the hatches into subterranean tunnels, the bookcase-cum-door of Anne Frank and other dwellers at the back of the house, the barricaded and barricading doors, the mind-expanding door of psychedelics (the Doors of Perception), the cliché's open door, the creaking door in horror movies, the bullet-riddled door of the assassin. Where there's a door, the West finds its borderline experience. The groom carries his bride through the open door so that she may open hers, a stork's wreath on the door tells you she has, the bang of the door signals the premature end of the affair; finally, the deceased are carried to the grave on their own front doors: the last door before the gates of heaven.

World War II was the brutal crowbar with which the West forced its entry into the world, in order to bring earth under the sign of acceleration as the one true universal value. Everything was turned over and had to be permissible, debatable. The ideology of contact led to the communication ecstacy of an open society. The Eastern bloc soon called it a day, opting for an antimediumistic cult of deceleration behind the iron curtain's veil. The West decided to take the battle against its self-created secret to the bitter end: Everything must be brought to light, from psyche to globe. Obstacles were localized as centers of resistance and disarmed through freeways, airplanes, high-orbit satellites, and incentive social measures. This post-Western model of openness declared the door a relic of a stage of violence now considered taboo.

The door was reinterpreted as the medium of currents. Its traditional philanthropy was believed to reflect its ancient longing to effect open connections. The door was degraded into a connecting part, of the same glass used to replace the wall. The door became a window, unmysterious, transparent, and misunderstood. Armstrong made his giant step by proving that he could even open the door to the moon, and humanity stepped out live with him. This signaled the end of the Occident; the task of fascism had been completed: *Lebensraum* had become the universe, light, air, space. To deny the door is to leave the world.

When public life became saturated with anti-door-like transparency, the door decided on the combined strategy of retreating to prejudiced positions and launching sudden attacks. The front door witnessed a spectacular comeback. On the one hand, it raised early Western culture to the status of style with nostalgic bare-faced pomp (the heavy door). On the other, it launched a plot together with groups like the neo-social squatter's movement, which broke down disused front doors only to place them at the magic center of its cult of resistance. The squat door demanded oblations in the form of steel plates, garden fences, spring mattresses, props, and beams, reaffirming its former function as a magnet for objects. The squat door carried no nameplates and seemed to long for anonymity, though its real task was to create and guard a secret. Since this met with major objections in the justice and police departments, the squat doors were either sawn down and rammed in or socialized as communal doors and replaced by the nomenclative prefab of redevelopment.

The Door in Our Consciousness

In public life, the door has embarked on total war. The public door found itself stripped of all its attributes: doorhandles and doorsteps disappeared, the mailbox was removed, doorbells were replaced by closed-circuit TV, electronic buzzer, and intercom. The invisible door, initially the cause of brutal collisions and accidents, was disarmed by converting it into a self-closing entrance. The post-Western door has been utterly Japanized and turned into a sliding wall. It is no longer seen or touched, there is no room for rites of passage: it opens up before it is reached. Robbed of its favorite attributes, it has become its own caricature, condemned to a life of one among many media.

The door wants to be an object, not a means but an end, door per se; stoicism. It wants to be open, closed, or left ajar. But should it be misjudged, it will take revenge, reverting to terrorism and relapsing into the forbidden stage of violence. The door has chosen to be on the dark side of life. Everywhere at night we witness the return of the door as the iron curtain covering the glass fronts of the state of transparency. Mocking all the acceleration and unlimited openness, the shutters whisk down, cursing the turbulent city with desolation. Not even the little light beams that penetrate their tiny plastic windows can dispel the new dusk in the streets. Social bylaws to replace the massive steel with semi-open constructions and sliding doors hardly make shopping any more fun. Shutters are the mirror image of post-Western life: Openness without doors is like a desert without an oasis. The price we pay for a life without doors is death.

THE OCCULT TRAFFIC SIGN

If the traffic sign indicates the safety of deceleration, locomotion sides with the danger of acceleration. The red, white, and black of the prohibition sign derives from the pre-capitalist, absolutist power system, in which it was used to warn currents against the fatal other side of fast traffic participation. The traffic sign was introduced in the 1930's as a primary visual system of motion control. National motorization was systematically enforced as a means of combating the ongoing crisis in economic traffic. The Austrian highway designer A. Hitler (1889–1945) founded the European traffic initiative. However, he confused the need to accelerate motor traffic with his craving for geopolitical space. He assumed the red, white, and black as the symbol of a Movement which would ultimately founder on the outdated blood-and-soil coordinates of a static prehistory. Commuter Model 40/45 resulted from his confused attempts to both conquer space through acceleration and protect the race and the nation.

The tricolor reappeared on timeless-looking traffic signs during the postwar reconstruction period. Although these no longer designated blood, death, and purity, they successfully revived the traditional power over life and death in terms of fast traffic. If, during the preceding centuries, power had taken the form of impregnable fortresses and strongholds, in fast traffic it now reaffirmed itself through firmly fixed bollards and traffic signs. As the craving for space got obsessed with cosmic air during the cold war, the tricolor's dark side lost its natural influence in the mundane unconscious. Thus, the traffic sign could witness another baby boom, without the catastrophic consequences of earlier years.

Even today, the road sign's design is less inspired by its occult color scheme than by the postwar enthusiasm about the liberation of traffic: an élan undampened even by road casualties. There was simply a general, unshakable faith in the progressive disciplinary power of road signs, even if they reintroduced chance and fate upon, above, and along the thoroughfares. The insurgent act of demolishing or reversing road signs is an attempt to control this fate and turn it against the power system of mobilization. Bollards can be bent over or used as battering rams, street furniture can be converted into barricades or used as a shield, torn from the ground and paraded as a trophy or be equipped with a new message (-50° C). Resistance against traffic-control signs naturally appeals to the imagination and is a part of every action or riot. Penalties against such sign perversion are low, because even power considers them obstacles.

With the traffic boom of the 1960's, the visibility of road signs became a problem. In an information brochure entitled *Man-Road-Car*, Keesing's "Reflector Series" had already raised the issue of the disappearance of the prohibition sign under the heading of "The Human Animal": "Even in modern vehicles, with their infinitely superior view, drivers survey no more than one fifth of their total visual range and observe only a single object at a time. In effect, the options of drivers are so limited that traffic engineers had best assume they will fail to notice any traffic signs." But before its late twentieth-century confrontation with policy plans to impose a sign diet on the grounds that there are "too many traffic signs," the road sign was first to witness a democratic revival.

Prior to the road sign's removal from thoroughfares, it had already begun to infiltrate slow social traffic. In this intimate sphere of pedestrians, bicyclists, consumers, and nighthawks, prohibition stickers pay their moralistic respects in the public spaces of escalators, platforms, gates, street furniture, self-closing doors, crossings, street signs, and household goods. Annoying signs of proper conduct ("No Smoking," "No Snack Food") are meant to stimulate public awareness of cleanliness and safety. In the interests of public health and environmental protection, even blood is being reintroduced as a dangerous prohibition sign. "Doctor J. K. van Wijngaarden, head of the National AIDS Control Commission, pointed out that a wide reestablishment of the old adage that blood is a dangerous substance is imperative." The Stop AIDS Campaign compared the risk of participation in loose sexual intercourse with the unavoidable risk of tank trailers overturning in residential areas. Similarly, signs like "Stop Acid Rain" or "Stop Immigration" try to convince private political and environmental consumers that these traffic flows are in a state of crisis, not unlike that of motor traffic with its endless traffic jams.

Furthermore, road signs increasingly take on the form of an absolutely informal advice presented as information. The fascist red, white, and black is being replaced by the more stimulating and democratic blue, green, and yellow. The new pictograms fit into an endless variety of designs. Appropriated by the sign, masters of marketing, the road signs infinitely refer to each other, whereas the prohibition sign's power lay precisely in the fact that it managed to avoid all fashion codes.

Although the traffic sign's crisis can be solved by transplanting its iconographic system to the slow circuits of the social and political and of public health, this would render fast traffic directionless. In fast traffic, the tricolor is being overtaken by the blue and green, but as immobile obstacles even these "notifications" frustrate movement. Thus, road signs gain an air of nostalgic attraction. Drivers slam on the brakes to admire their timeless aesthetics or to add them to their collection of modernist objects as collector's items.

Because road traffic refuses to give up acceleration as the principle of motion, it copies the sign language of faster data communications. As the auto connects to the computer, national computerization becomes the issue at stake. Laser signs, suggested itineraries, and speed control are introduced to solve the problem of "responsible driving." At the same time, hacking offers a chance for digitized traffic to reestablish unprecedented, high-risk contacts. The tempting perspective promised to road users is full of virtual traffic signs that will communicate directly with the board computer, without bothering the driver with injunctions or instructions. The people's movement of fast traffic will coincide with automation and tourism and vanish down a fiber-optics cable.

One counterstrategy consists of delaying this development through raids or blockades. In practice, this can only lead to clever alternative routes. The collision of various means of transport is far more interesting. Power has always struggled to prevent the transition from one mode of traffic to the next. The ritual signs of financial, sexual, highway, and data communications had to be kept pure and separated at all times. Traditionally, the intermingling of currents has been condemned as the sin of incest which leads to death and destruction. But this warning is ignored by the dangerous life, which actively seeks out such fusions.

Beyond the
Public Screen

The movie audience typically forms a close mass. The cinema's layout delimits the audience's ability to grow. Only those who pay admission can join the elite. The darkness disciplines individuals to hide their presence. The event takes place on the silver screen; it has no place in the darkened theatre. This is what gives the mass direction. Even with open-air showings, there is such a strong association of movie with enclosed space that the audience feels itself surrounded by an imaginary architecture. The theatre produces the audience; the movie is the event that discharges this mass.

But the rabble, who are looking for cheap entertainment, manage to escape their duty to remain a purely imaginary mass by forming an actual mass through antisocial behavior at moments of release. Shouting, loud popcorn consumption, physical contact, bottles rolling across the floor, the odor of sweat and bare feet—noise drowns out the movie's content. Cinephilic and journalistic reception denounces this spurious use of cinema as mass-producer, demanding the absence of both other and theatre. It advocates inner experience and searches for significance, consuming the mass medium as though it were a book. Cinephilia owes its existence to the rejection of traditional movie characteristics. "The Ego and Its Own Film" is its credo. The cinephile lives on the suggestion of being the last viewer, a survivor of the death of film. This corresponds to the movie fan's unique habit of sitting through all the credits until the lights come on.

Television has settled into the cozy environment of living room and bedroom. Due to the honeycombed architecture of privacy, the silver screen could be turned into a piece of furniture to prevent all mass formation. But the only way to make lonely picture-screen consumption bearable was to assure the viewer at home of the presence of many fellow watchers. The user had to be convinced at all times that televisual space contained a mass with which one could communicate (at least in theory). Viewers felt part of this imaginary mass as long as they could imagine the others with whom they'd review the shows in the morning. Watching something different from everybody else raised serious doubts as to where your sympathies lay, or that maybe your tastes weren't too extravagant to even be discussed. The private screen owed its existence to the public space outside, which guaranteed the existence of fellow viewers. The contents of whatever was broadcast were quite irrelevant compared to the medium's ability to produce this imaginary mass. The only informative aspect of television was, and still is, the expansion of the group of participants until, at critical moments, it encompasses the entire world population.

We know the public screen from SF movies. In *Blade Runner* or *Until the End of the World* it still looks like a billboard with moving pictures on it, stuck high up on some skyscraper. *Blade Runner* even features a bulky spaceship with an enormous screen hovering over the city. However, the screens attract zero attention; they produce no mass. In accordance with Orwell's book, *1984* features telescreens everywhere, the population forced to react to Big Brother's commercials. This refers to the intellectualist fear that, with the introduction of television, the new medium would serve a totalizing or leveling function. With the decay of public space, the Orwellian city has been dismissed as a disciplining factor and replaced by the public screen. The actual mass is caught within an architecture replaced by screens, where it is permanently overloaded by inescapable untruths. Orwell's presumption was that public space could be replaced by television, which would thus effectively obliterate the imaginary space of individual emotions and fantasies.

In *The Running Man*, guerrillas try to seize the public screen in order to liberate the people through alternative news broadcasts. Amid the high-rise buildings, where wealth circulates within communication networks, the abandoned population is kept at bay with manipulated news footage and lethal game shows. These marginalized masses, subclass of the Fourth World, are constantly being brought to discharge through their participation as gamblers in the one event allowed to them: the spectacle on the screen. Again, there's the implicit notion that the public screen can force the actual mass into passive behavior—only not by repressing emotions this time, but by maximum stimulation of them.

The nightmares of classical science fiction are based on the fear that the public screen has the same disciplining effect on viewers as the movie should, according to the cinephile. But since the public screen is first of all an enlarged television screen, the mass effects it produces ought to be imaginary rather than actual. In fact, they are neither. This was proved by the live registration of a concert by David Bowie and his Tin Machine in Amsterdam's Paradiso on June 24, 1989. Five hundred meters away, on the Museumplein square, a public screen, five by four meters, had been erected, while Nescafé, the sponsor, had gathered some 30,000 spectators through newspaper and aerial advertising. The concert was broadcast only to this square. A TV event reserved for those present; no further transmission took place.

The program started with a well-known commercial from regular television. The show itself was so smoothly and professionally edited that it was impossible to tell it from a regular video clip. The masses were overcome with the feeling that they were just watching some pop television show; all it lacked was the matching homey intimacy. Nor was it compensated for by the suggestion of a self-imagined architecture—as with the open-air movie showing—since the mass was open by nature: the square was open to all, and admission was free.

Even the hope that nightfall would turn the square into a movie theatre remained unrewarded. By now, the audience had made an awkward discovery: the imaginary mass, always presumed present in TV consumption, was now actually present. Any possible link to viewers elsewhere was thus effectively obstructed, as the whole of the viewing public stood gathered in front of the screen: Though outside, there remained no imaginary Outside, beyond the screened event. The square-dwellers were nothing but a bunch of disconnected individuals, and they failed to arrive at their point of discharge.

While on screen the audience in the Paradiso went berserk, on the Museumplein the applause soon petered out completely. The viewing experiences of cinema and TV had intermingled and were now mutually extinguishing one another. Without warning, Bowie and his musicians disappeared from stage ("The artist has left the building") before the party had even begun, followed by credit titles and Nescafé commercials. Time to bugger off. The main sensation produced by the public screen had been that of being taken for a ride.

In the case of the Museumplein, all contact with the event had been cut off. The giant screens on stage, which have been used for ages to support mega-concerts, political rallies, and conferences, never lose their supportive function because the event itself remains visible, even if microscopically small in the eyes of the theatre or stadium audience. Through them, the close mass of festivalgoers goes into rapture and finds its point of discharge. The visible presence of the performer is the imaginary factor that brings the screens to life. The public screen alone can never launch an event; it would soon fall victim to indifference.

But the mass is not going to give up its inalienable right to the event without a fight. Soccer fans, if refused entrance to the stadium—and thus forced to watch the game on the public screen as an involuntary mass—inevitably turn their boredom into positive energy. The profound awe of video technology is rapidly dwindling. The classical intellectualist fear of the massifying power of television is checked by the equally classical and ancient mass strategy to make room for events, even against all odds: "Smash it up!" Here, the pleasure of recreation turns into the consumption of facilities.

First to go is the furniture closest at hand. Next in line are actual fellow spectators. Presently, slingshots are produced to eliminate each pixel one at a time. Paint bombs further brighten the mood, as a cluster bomb makes a first breach. This signals the moment to tear down the fences and haul down the screen, bringing the mass's full weight to bear. The one question in everybody's minds: Do video screens burn? Crackling sparks fill the field as the people celebrate their revolution amid the smoldering pictorial ashes.

It is uncertain whether things will ever go that far. Presumably, beams will fill the air to project virtual 3-D events almost impossible to distinguish from the real. But even these devices can be tracked down and eliminated, provided the necessary know-how. The custodians of the sedated masses traditionally suppress the universal right to the event by means of bread and circuses. The mob's tenacious ability to pirate space for its own game techniques forever guarantees the effective dismantling of all control strategies. In the end, management always stands between the ruins. Should its structures persist—simply because nobody could care less about them—it can be trusted to tear them down of its own accord.

BILLBOARD STUDIES

The billboard is a highly outdated medium. In Europe, the artificial use of the American industrial term "billboard" instead of the equally valid European phrases aims to include European trade and industry in the megatrend whereby the industrial production of commodities loses out in favor of the distribution of brand names. The commodity has become a sign; labor has become design. The concept of the billboard places outdoor advertising beyond Canetti's endpoint of history, at which the stage of commodity cancer turned into the timeless dimension of the post-historical. In this epilogue, all that remains is a festering growth of signs within medial networks.

King-size advertisement photos appeal to the youthful élan of our postwar American way of life, which has, in the U.S. itself, long since deteriorated into empty routine and facelift terror. Whereas, in said U.S. of A., the billboards are already being cleared away, Europe is busily erecting its own as proof that it has entered modernity and that the continent's final reconstruction can begin, from the Atlantic to the Urals.

The billboard as a frozen image is a Renaissance atavism. It simulates vitality by feeding on the principles of perspectivist illusion, whose center is the eye. By detaching advertisements from their commodity setting, the ironicist Warhol of the early 1960's turned ads, whose function was to transmit consumptive messages, into two-dimensional objects that required no fixed viewpoint. Now *that* was modern art. Urban advertising follows a similar trajectory, but in the opposite direction. Thirty years after Warhol, the European billboard appears as a senseless, detached message, but does so in order to make renewed appeals to the passerby as consumer. Warhol's principle of repetition (which he copied from advertising) is perverted by posting the same signs all over town, where they soon start to stage a system of their own. The intelligibility of such signposting does not result from its information value, but from its design's capacity to function as a lifestyle mirror for the city and its users. Billboards owe their existence to the third dimension that appears when they catch eyes and become part of a meaningful identity décor. Because stylized advertising stays in the place where future consumers will be born, it will never become modern art.

The billboard has always been part of the public picture, deriving its effect from the slowness of the passing masses. Its natural environment is the city, where it boasts a long record as proclamation, mobilization or liquidation order, placard, political poster, announcement, or advertisement. The street and square where it resides constitute political space ("Conquer the streets, and you will have conquered the state"). From the Place de la Bastille to Tiananmen Square, it is here that the people reaffirm their existence and instigate events. This coming-out is accompanied by the defacement of all signs of power; plastered over, torn up, burnt, pulled down, or commented upon. Nocturnal bill-stickers hang their own unauthorized posters in forbidden spots, scrawlers chalk their texts on pristine walls, rampant subversion defiles political purity: "The street has always been the bloodstream of popular life" (Eberhard Freiherr von Künszberg).

The police traditionally have the job of controlling sign traffic and protecting the public visual order. In the 1970's, as the social management of the welfare state and the repression of hooligans failed to guarantee the intended sign peace, the street scene was privatized. Where, before, there had been police, now there were billboards. The daily clean-and-run operations by parapolice commandos on glassed-in billboards on the pretext of "preventive maintenance" represent a tactical shift from criminalization to the elimination of popular vital signs. In this civilizational offensive, "bloodsucker propaganda" is now being used as "urban décor" to defend the spotless home of the nation against evil stains. Urban furniture becomes a purification plant that declares death on all city waste.

Resistance against this clearing of the streets is broken by billboard overkill, each of them instantly replaceable by the logistical management in case of destruction. This "stage of acceptance" of the billboard ends with an aesthetic discourse on its "appreciation." At first, the billboards were couch and end table in an urban home. Now we are suddenly expected to admire the art directors' posters as little paintings radiating the familiar intimacy of a Bambi. This is where iconoclasm fails. The only threat to these billboards is the indifference of passersby.

At the current stage, the public image resides on the TV screen; all other images are but folkloric relics. Even the city is a thing of the past. The "natural need for traffic" has shifted from the classical transport of passengers and goods to the transmission of data within global electronic networks. As a result, social wealth no longer accumulates in the city, but in the peripheral Byzantine high-rise buildings where the computers reside. Its loss of economic reality forced the city to redefine itself as theme park, as a result of which the tourist industry has become the largest in the world at the end of the 1900's. The inner city is rapidly being transformed into a museological environment to preserve the luster of local history.

At the same time, modern facilities are being introduced. People visit the city in order to convert income into personal experience. This release of purchasing power explains the use of billboards in the urban décor. But they must be carefully applied. The critical limit beyond which outdoor advertising begins to interfere with the nostalgia-productive quality of place is not to be exceeded. The billboards "have become fashionable"; they are "seen and

implemented as instruments to transmit the desired municipal identity."
Dutch research showed that the citizens of Maastricht were fed up with
"well-maintained outdoor advertising," whereas those in Rotterdam "simply
do not pay much attention to it." Until billboards can be placed along the
planetary data routes, the advertising designers ("We don't want the Belgian
situation, where they have one billboard after the other") will be stuck with
this subtle disordering of the polls by the Dutch population.

Since the billboard, to its own regret, has no part in new technologies, it
humbly refrains from any revolutionary or avant-garde role. Its posted noti-
fication is no more than a spin-off effect of advertising campaigns launched
in the real media behind its back. Its self-esteem has to be boosted by telling
it that it "offers more potential than the mere enlargement of advertisements." It finds itself stuck with a free-floating quotation, a grotesque sign
blown out of proportion like some HIV virus waiting to break the sign immunity induced by others, in order to infect and renovate lifestyle. It falls victim
to a plot of market artists and city governors scheming to promote themselves. Its will to banality is constantly repressed by its forced subjection to
artistic standards. Revalued as fast-art, receivable in four minutes, yet it
remains more of a fortress than the short-range weapon the ad strategists
would make of it. The billboard is preserved and trained to "raise its creative
and artistic level" and thus expand its fire-power, even though it more
closely resembles a dodo than a hawk. Its clumsiness feels most at home with
"Canned Beans $1.09." This is why it is looking for co-conspirators who will
take its ignorance to the extreme. In a technological culture where all objects
are subjected to an artistic special treatment, the only people it deems fit to
finish the job are dropout artistes.

With the acceleration of social transactions, the billboard is forced to
adapt to the transient nature of passersby. On exit roads it gains speed by
placing itself directly beside and above the flow of traffic, reversing speed as
it goes: It becomes careering oncoming traffic itself. Since it must expand to
remain visible, it may as well inflate as a pure sign and release its information value. Its goal is to distract attention, and to merge with the rippling
waves of subconscious sexual intercourse. There is no future for the further
acceleration of billboards. There is good reason for the freeway ban on bills.
The billboard is considered a ghost-driver from another circuit, leading to
devastating chain reactions within security thinking. In fascist billboard critique, it becomes a form of pollution that interferes with the natural relationship to the surrounding environment. The implication is that this connection
to cultural civilization may yet be reestablished through an automobile viewing experience. But fast traffic turns every landscape it traverses into a
large-screen television showing the in-flight movie. Thus, to erect billboards
along the highway would be an act of antifascism. Still, despite its history of
resistance, the Netherlands will never witness freeway advertising. At best,
the privatization of the airways will lead to the inclusion of acoustic advertising signs during traffic information broadcasts. The national billboard lives

on the city's deceleration, where commuter traffic has crystallized into a permanent traffic jam, with ample time left to gaze at the public images behind glass.

VIDEO SILENCES

In the autumn of the media, we celebrate absence. The invention of photography revealed that painting is so enchanting because reality does not appear on the canvas; the introduction of film, that the photograph derives its beauty from the absence of movement; that of the sound film, that the silent movie astonished us so because it made no noise. Color filmmakers were the brains behind the aestheticism of film noir. After that, television made it clear that all these forms of film derived their appeal from the black between the images. Now HiVision teaches that the video image offered something that is currently being lost: the aesthetics of the scanning line. In cyberspace, it will sink in that the power of all these detached media was that we ourselves were missing from the picture. After that, simstim will show that cyberspace was so pleasant because it took place outside our own nervous system. And so on, and so on.

Chemical media had all the time in the world. If, for the sake of convenience, we add up the five stages of lighting, development, reproduction, projection, and reception, we see that these media allowed the image to fully mature. Even movies intended for immediate consumption at the time turn out to be still in the middle of their period of reception decades later. Decaying nitrate films are hastily preserved to prevent these wet media from spontaneous combustion. Back then, visual light was captured onto an unsteady substance that had to be dragged through a series of baths before it could be made visible by placing it between a strong light source and a white screen in a darkened theater. Reproduction took place through immediate contact between the master negative and blank strips. As for the reception of these fluid media, a special favorite always consisted of the sloshing theories about the flowing unconscious called psychoanalysis. The whole movie business anticipated these wet dreams.

Now that the chemical film process is wearing off under the influence of the home video's user-friendly magnetism, we witness a growing awareness of the divisions between the individual images. More and more, this black edge is being pushed into the foreground and included as an equal element into the semiotics of images. A familiar example of this process is Jim Jarmusch's *Stranger than Paradise*, where black is inserted as an interval between the individual shots. The more the image matures, the more obvious it becomes that it is precisely this dark side of cinema which has attracted

95

movie buffs for a century. The space between the pictures turns out to be the great seducer for these aesthetes of the pure image. The general public has no use for this emancipation of the edit, however, and demands a seamless transition from one fascination to the next.

What the cinephiles fail to see is that the magnetic media offer at least as much visual absence. Precisely in an age that produced such an amazing Technicolor palette and in which the ideal of lifelike representation was so closely approached, the snowy black-and-white tube appeared in the living room. The videotape rearranges molecules in a magnetic field so that they can be instantly read once you have obtained the correct equipment. No fluids or light are involved. Traditional development, montage, projection, and reception disappear in the inordinate accessibility of this medium. This is where liquid theory fails, and to this day, videophilia has not succeeded in becoming an exclusive passion.

After twenty years, the imperfections had been resolved and the large-screen color TV could consolidate itself as a home theater. The daily assembly and fading out of scanning lines had reached such perfection that it was no longer noticed. Besides, interior design had been adapted so as to practically exclude sidelong glances at the screen. The scanning line only returned in the late eighties with VCRs, which could fast-forward, rewind, or pause the picture, and displayed moiré in case of bad copies. An artistic application of the scanning-line principle was shown in Bill Spinhoven's installation *Time Stretcher*, which constructed a video image of the viewer with a lag of three seconds between the bottom and top lines. But these horizontal video stockades were never mentioned for what they are. They were just one of many elements that would provide the videological with its own artificiality. The scanning line has become the logo of an entire era. On the front page, video stills from live broadcasts have a topical surplus value which professional photography can never achieve. Press photographers who refuse to send their digital photos by satellite dish are forced to take a step back and sell their reports as impressionistic documentaries about what took place behind the TV cameras.

Now, with the introduction of HDTV, it turns out that all the characteristics of video can be included in the next medium in a perfected form—except the scanning line. The digitally fostered and designed pixel is left completely alone. The permanent construction work required by the television frame is no longer necessary. A computing center provides the autonomous points with their data, and they couldn't care less what takes place on the rest of the screen. The individual pixel can undergo all kinds of treatments and move through various media via interfaces. Data form images only by accident. The spotless television, which can be enlarged or scaled down at will and produces lifelike images in true colors, produces a view in which twentieth-century material is turned into a historical genre. Only when High Definition is implemented worldwide will the cinephiles realize that even their ancient archenemy knew its moments of absence, and was beaten by the same opponent. Just as the movie screen will be replaced by an HD screen, so the old home tube will be erased by the new standard. Static will enter its golden age and become the material for the AVant-garde in search of raw and elementary images in the age of definition.

Thus, people who currently agitate against the disappearance of 8- and 16- mm film can count on the support of Save the TV, media conservationists and the true video (still) artists who exploit the new visual reality to claim all redundant linear material as art. If at present film allows itself to be subsidized as the seventh art, it will then have to share its synthetic museum with its dialectic partner, television, which will still flaunt its former ratings.

THE DATA DANDY

*"I do not believe in progress, but I believe in the stagna-
tion of human stupidity—I admire Japanese chairs
because they have not been made to sit upon."*

—Oscar Wilde

The data dandy collects information to show off and not to transmit it. He is well-, too-well, or even exaggeratedly well-informed. Pointed questions are met with unwanted answers. He always comes up with something different. The phenotype of the data dandy is as feared as was his historical predecessor, whose playground was the street and the salon. The elegant extravagance with which he displays the most detailed trivia shocks the practical media user. The data dandy makes fun of the gauged consumption and the measured intake of current news and amusement, and doesn't worry about an excess or overload of specialized knowledge. His carefully assembled information portfolio betrays no constructive motive. He goes to the greatest effort to appear as arbitrary as possible. One wonders: why did the data-head want to know all this stuff? He zaps not out of boredom, but out of unwillingness to keep abreast of current events and everybody else's latest worries.

The screen is the mirror at which he performs his toilet. The buttoning and unbuttoning of textile dandyism has found its successor in the channel surfing of on/off decadence. Wrapped in the finest facts and the most senseless gadgets, the new dandy deregulates the time economy of the info = money managers. He spends most of his computing time on the luxurious decoration of his hard disk and the creation of sophisticated circuits among thousands of heterogeneous software trinkets. The PowerBook as an ornament is the pride of many a salon digitalist. He derides actuality, hype, and fashion; wherever he shows up, there briefly appears a self that is its own anchorperson.

In the era of multimedia mass information one can no longer differentiate between uni- and multiformity. Neither broad overview nor clarifying detail can relieve the mental confusion. Against this background the data dandy proves what everybody knows: namely, that information may be omnipresent but is not readily accessible. Certain facts are very flattering and one must develop a fine nose for them. Unlike the data collector, the data dandy is concerned not with the obsession of the complete file, but with the accumulation of as many immaterial ornaments as possible. While the otaku withdraws into himself and will never cross the boundaries of his solitary cultivation, it is precisely the most extroverted newsgroups which the data dandy searches out to launch his unproductive contributions. What the data dandy skims off in order to present elsewhere would be only of secondary importance, if the presentation were not so indiscreet. His freakish wit distracts attention from the run-of-the-mill items. The ingenuity of his bon mots has a duration of 30 seconds, after which they disappear from the screen as suddenly as they came. Our data dandy is a broker in gigawares, with the understanding that your garbage is his makeup, and his substance your fluid.

The data dandy displays a disquieting kinship with the politician, who also forces himself upon us with empty phrases and won't go away. Now that the political classes in their death struggle have discovered the media, they refuse to let go of them, and their fanatical attempts to solicit support are taking on dandyish traits. The data dandy surfaces in the vacuum of politics which was left behind once the oppositional culture neutralized itself in a dialectical synthesis with the system. There he reveals himself as an equally lovable and false opponent, to the great rage of politicians who consider their young pragmatic dandyism a publicity tool and not necessarily a personal goal. They vent their rage on the journalists, experts, and personalities who make up the chance cast on the studio floor, where who controls the direction is the only topic of conversation. Yet they find the data dandy hopelessly difficult, since he refuses to play the sporting opponent and neglects to ask politely critical questions. Our bon vivant enjoys all display of banality and takes absolutely no offense at pointless dedication.

Maliciousness would have been useful, but the flawed subversive shows precisely his engaging side. His charm is deadly. While the no-talent underground goes in search of instruments to cause the establishment trouble, the data dandy lets everything go stylishly haywire. There is no longer any social movement, opposition, or undercurrent, nor can one suddenly appear out of nowhere; they can only sink further into the individual. Once empty the media remain empty forever; no statement can compete with that. Hackers and cyberpunks do not manifest themselves, simply because they do not exist and can only be conjured up as ghosts. Calling upon fictitious social forces is a desperate attempt at one more way to gauge the enemy. The same applies to the data dandy, who is taken for a proto-fascist and briefly appears as an illusory participant in the form of theoretical hooligan during the therapeutic debate about the rise of the extreme Right.

The Net is to the electronic dandy what the metropolitan street was for the historical dandy. Rambling along the data boulevards cannot be prohibited and ultimately jams the entire bandwidth. The all-too-civilized conversation during a rendezvous turns up a few misplaced and objectionable data, but never results in dissidence. The point of willful wrong navigation and elegant joyriding through someone else's electro-environment is admiration, envy, and confusion, and consciously aims at stylized incomprehension. The dandy measures the beauty of his virtual appearance by the moral indignation and laughter of plugged-in civilians. It is a natural character of the parlor aristocrat to enjoy the shock of the artificial. This is why he feels so at home in cyberspace with all its attributes. Cologne and pink stockings have been replaced by precious Intel; delicate data gloves and ruby-encrusted butterfly goggles and sensors are attached to his brows and nostrils. Away with the crude NASA aesthetics of cybernauts! The data dandy has moved well beyond the pioneer stage; the issue now is the grace of the medial gesture.

If the anonymous crowd in the streets was the audience of the Boulevard dandy, the logged-in Net-users are that of the data dandy. He feels forced to employ the other users as the anonymous mass, the amorphous normality to which he is the sharply outlined deviation. The data dandy knows he is never more than one of many crazies in the variability carnival of the information circus. He will thus never present himself as the umpteenth retro-identity or remnant of some twentieth-century fashion, because he can only play with the rules of the Net as a non-identity. What is exclusivity in the age of differentiation? The dandy is not interested in ever-more-secret passwords to gain entry into ever-more-exclusive data salons; he needs virtual plazas to make his tragic appearance. Data dandyism is born of an aversion to being exiled into a subculture of one's own. The dandy's archenemies are camp and cult, which hide themselves instead of openly manifesting. On the contrary, the dandy repeatedly launches meaningless Temporary Common Denominators (TCDs) in which every subculture believes it recognizes itself. He manages thus to attract a remarkably large gray mass with which to stage his own spectacles. He creates a fake publicness and tests conventions. Some arbitrary examples of strong TCDs with a high vagueness coefficient are the anti–Gulf War demos, cyberpunk, illegal knowledge, tactical television, and the Northwest Airlines plane crash. The data dandy surfs along on the waves of these Temporary Common Denominators; it's what makes him tick.

On the Net, the only thing that appears as a mass is information itself. As soon as a new field of knowledge is found, it splits and branches off so that an infinite amount of information flows in and out. Today's new theme is tomorrow's 23 newsgroups. If the data dandy wishes to come across as a real figure, he can only do so in the form of dandy data. These are queer: while the heteroinformative data of straight people are concerned with qualification, connection, and reproduction, fanning out and thus causing further disintegration, the dandies' homoinformative data are eccentric but not peculiar. Homodata associate with others and are lost in themselves. Like TCDs, they attract roughly similar info and achieve a carefree concentration within the information field, where the show can begin. There appears to be an encounter or confrontation with the System, but this contact yields no productive moment, no cause or effect. Dandy data are purely situational, parasites par excellence. What remains is legend, the fuel of all media and the hope of theory.

WETWARE

"Those who want to talk about a New World Order without taking virtual reality into consideration had better keep quiet."

—John Sasher

Contact between the wet and the dry is a risky business, fraught with dangers. In practice these vary from a glass of juice in the toaster, a finger in an electric socket, a burst water main, to the collision of swelling passions with sober incomprehension. With its thin skin, hard bones, and sticky fluids, the human body can be reasonably well defined as a problematic water management system whose boundaries are fluid. This aquanomy is marked again and again by pieces of cloth and scent markers as well as equipped with colorants and an aura of ramshackle social codes. These serve to prevent personal overflows from getting out of hand and to cover up little accidents.

The closer we get to machines, the more wet zones are reclaimed. Depending on how technology approaches the body, boundaries are laid and erotic zones defined. Shifts may be read through clothing fashions, the dress of the poor wet slob who these days goes through life neatly and properly swaddled as a "Euro citizen." At the end of the twentieth century we see this thinking bio-pump being slung back and forth, panting and spluttering, between wet and dry, loose and fixed, fleeting and firm, intoxication and reason, static and signal, suddenly functional in the electronic environment. The watery and steamy human factor has shocking effects on the machinery. The unavoidable contact between the wet finger and the keyboard has sparked a technological civilization offensive. Economy comes down more and more to the tightest possible interweave between social structures and electronic circuits.

Until recently, sexual boundaries marked the danger zones. Because of this there had to be, for example, separate ladies' and gentlemen's fashion. This necessity has disappeared, and power is reaching for other means of stylizing fears and desires, while changing form itself. Fascist power was once a bulwark of sexual metaphors which could be reduced to one's own firm soil and pure, flowing blood. Divisions on grounds of sex and race were intended to destroy hybrids, and had political and military consequences.

The antifascist cold war which followed lasted long enough for racist and sexist thinking to bleed to death. The body politics of this era, now over, were characterized by the conditioning of the body on the new machines, which were no longer driven mechanically but electronically.

Space travel furnished the basic model for electronic clothing, which, like power itself, has its attractive side as well as its frightening one. The first astronauts were animals, plastered with electrodes to register the reactions of the biological water management system. The futuristic spacesuit, in contrast, glittered and shone as the prototype of the electronic New Order. The cosmic costume withstood the new dangerous conditions and came out shining, offered freedom of movement, provided protection, and guaranteed communication besides. This required a retraining of the body, which no longer came under the regime of religion or politics, but under the supervision of science. Extraterrestrial space travel, it turned out, was not an invention which would become available to the consumer after a developmental phase, but an experiment to test the body's reactions in an electronic situation under extreme conditions. Here, too, the clothing was not only outward show but dressage, and made it clear to the world population via the media what it means to be connected to a computer. The extraordinary quality of this superhuman performance in extraterrestrial space convinced humanity, the folks left at home, of the overwhelming success of a sojourn into electronic space.

After the explosion of the *Challenger* and the end of the dream of space, the path was cleared for ordinary mass production of the spacesuit. It has been redubbed the datasuit, with an introductory bonus known as the data glove. This awkward outfit provides the data worker with a fascinating evening dress, in which he can visit any location in all possible disguises. It lets him get acquainted in a pleasant and noncommittal way with the new power type of the New Order. The premises of this are as follows: as commuter traffic dissolves and national borders blur, we enter a clean, dust-proof, sterile, medicinal space, which generates its own conception of dirt. Analagous to the danger zones in the era of sexual power, the thing now is the banishment of threats to the electronic condition. Classics like narcotic drugs, stupefying liquors, and suffocating hazes of smoke appear as hot items of the reclamation politics which are spreading the New Order worldwide. This politics demands a strict anti-intoxication diet, if you want to ascend into hallucinogenic dataspace. Otherwise you will lose the necessary concentration, and produce static.

What is new about the electronic condition is the sitting still and the minimalization of biomechanical labor. This fundamental modification in human water management, which just like the Delta Works could only be realized under cold war relations, causes a potential adjustment static in the introduction phase of digital hegemony which is combated by an aerodynamic exercise program. The motorized Citybike as a fashion is an integral component of data policy, and is not ridden by health devotees in fluorescent spacesuits for nothing. Unlike the profligate yuppies of the eighties, the Euro citizens of the nineties strive for total moderation: of their own nutritional and media diet as well as in government spending. The subsidy tap to them symbolizes waste, in flagrant contradiction to their recycling mania and investment sense.

These cozy cocooners enjoy the freedom to stay at home; their greatest concern is the data roof over their heads. Refugees, who cannot be traced in the files, are supposed to stay in their own area, otherwise the U.N. and E.C. with their developmental armies will lend them a helping hand. "If you people refuse humanitarian aid, we will have to open fire." The underlying motive for this military intervention is making global connections, which span the globe like a metastructure, healthy. To facilitate further expansion and innovation, those who are switched off and dataless must keep quiet and stay in their own places. If necessary their ghettos and their written-off social wastelands are sealed shut by electronic security.

Hardware, software, and wetware are the three forms which the human machine can take in the era of the New World Order. This trinity possesses its own geographical and historical coordinates. The hardware on which we play out all our culture and communication comes from Japan. The programs which make it possible for us to read, see, and hear all this precious data come from the United States. Finally, the role of Europe is to deliver the necessary cultural products for shipment. Wetware's task is to cough up culture, which will be run on the Japanese hardware with the help of American software. In this international division of labor, what is expected of Europe is to properly administer the legacy of Bach and Beethoven, maintain the paintings of Rembrandt and Van Gogh, and extend the theatrical tradition, from Shakespeare to Beckett, into the future. The same goes for the media art of the last few decades. Europeans must figure out what things of beauty can be coaxed out of all this new equipment, for there is little pleasure to be derived from the functional use of technology. Art is only charmed into being when the equipment is connected to the history of art, to philosophy and literature and those typically human character traits which have become European hallmarks. This is the lot which the Europeans, after so many blunders in this twentieth century, have called down upon themselves. Wetware means that we are condemned to making culture which avails itself of technical tools that have been designed by others. This need not be a subordinate position. On the contrary: a great deal is expected of us! What, after all, are laptops and word processors without all the wonderful stories that are written on them? Or a synthesizer without experimental compositions?

Wetware is a body attached to machines. Wetware means that we have long been connected to the machines surrounding us; something which, as in the case of television, affords us a great deal of pleasure as well. If it is up to wetware, submission to machines, as predicted by Orwell in *1984*, need not be so dramatically represented. It need not result in slavish submission, for wetware has a secret weapon up its sleeve: its human, all too human traits. The nickname "wetware" is an homage to the do-it-yourselfer who tries to make the best of things but always forgets the instructions. Flaws are deployed to safeguard dignity. Through ignorance, the urge to sabotage, and unbridled creativity, technology always goes haywire; from these accidents the most beautiful freaks spring forth, and after aesthetic treatment are effortlessly declared art. To wetware the user is not a remnant or something suppressed, but a born hobbyist who can hook together any old or new media into a personal reality, where an error message is at the beginning of a long series of resounding successes.

The term "wetware" was coined by Rudy Rucker. He defines it as a collection of technological innovations: chips which are implanted in the brain, organ transplants and prostheses that replace or extend bodily functions. Unlike Rucker, Adilkno considers the wetware idea not as a following phase to upset the wobbly self-image yet again after the revolutions in hard- and software, but as the human remnant which stays behind as the extensions go on longer and longer trips.

At the end of the twentieth century, the autonomous individual trying to bring his gushing fears and desires into balance has come to stand in the shadow of the technological imperative. Managing or throwing open the channels appears to be dictated to a high degree by the available equipment. Wetware is conscious of this dependence and thus sees itself not as a potentate that rules over the machines, but as a watery auxiliary that must adjust as well as it can to the digital conditions of electronic data traffic.

Acknowledgment of the technological a priori should not be confused with the hype which always arises when a new system comes on the market. The buzz generated by the new equipment creates an amnesia that results in a familiar pattern: the short-term effects of a technology are overestimated, while its long-term effects are given short shrift. It is characteristic of wetware to soak in a Jacuzzi of simulacra, and lose sight of the military prehistory of communication technologies and the nefarious plans being hatched by technocrats and marketing divisions. Wetware lets itself be easily fascinated and is not so quick to criticize when something new presents itself. We have become accustomed to the constant introduction of new products and techniques. A cycle is slowly becoming apparent: after a phase of rumors and spectacular presentations, the first lucky few get to show off the gadgets, and critics have a free-for-all. Only then can there be social acceptance, and a market large enough for capital to be interested.

The new technologies cunningly present themselves in the form of fashion and then fade into obscurity. This has recently happened with Minitel, video phones, and mind machines. At the moment it is virtual reality's turn to make technological dreams material. Until now VR has been no more than one big flood of rumors for wetware. The global village where the techno artists live has been turned upside down for a few years now: something big was supposed to happen . . . a megasystem was on its way that would nullify and engulf all media productions manufactured up to now, and suck on wetware like no other before. In the "out-of-body" experiments conducted in high-tech laboratories, VR has been described as a "doorway to other worlds." The distance between us and the screen becomes nil and we enter a "mental environment." VR is the "ultimate human/computer interface" (Rheingold) which encompasses all bodily movements and requires not even fingers nimble enough to operate a keyboard. VR (potentially) takes possession of the whole body in order to let the mind travel as far as possible. While the senses are in a state of maximum titillation and undertake exhausting expeditions, the physical body stays behind in the "non-virtual world."

Because all VR efforts are focused on the conquest of the sixth continent, the part that stays behind is temporarily overlooked. But then the wetware factor reports and returns to its own "tele-existence" as a "human bug." This is the instant when wetware actually appears as a form. Despite hysterical stories about the instantaneous omnipresence of the zapping body in live broadcasting and the dissolution of locality as a natural environment for the process of ego formation, the media user still stands up at regular intervals to grab a beer or take a piss. These moments of absence from the media do not occur in the cyberspace myth. In it, the body is in fact an abandoned station, and life is tantamount to data travel and digital immortality. Wetware finds this a fascinating thought, but laughs loudly, because something always gets in the way. The soggy human recognizes himself for the first time as an equal counterpartner to the immaterial sphere. The wetware story begins as soon as it is clear that technology cannot live with or without the human.

After the presentation of VR a Babylonian misunderstanding arose over what the consequences of this next techno revolution would be. The first report: the cyberpunk world portrayed by William Gibson would come true. Succeeding reports told us that the Gibsonian matrix, where the most intense hallucinations were to be had, was still fiction: virtual reality in its infancy was nothing but a simple computer animation of a building or landscape in which you could rather jerkily look around. But even this disillusionment, which was reserved for the few who had gotten the chance to wear the VR helmet and the data glove, could not squelch the hype. By publicly distancing himself from the evangelizations of Timothy Leary and other electronic cowboys of the VR business, Gibson narrowly prevented his term "cyberspace" from being tacked onto assorted carnival attractions. By Gibson's definition, cyberspace is more like a neospace where social fiction about human and machine unfolds than the name of a new technology. The first commercial applications were simply far too unvisceral for sopping cyberpunks.

The first VR systems are already in operation on Wall Street, in the arcades of the amusement industry, in medical laboratories, at architectural firms, and at NASA. These are hardly places where techno artists, hackers, and cyberpunks tend to have admittance. Thus, for wetware VR remains no more than a fleeting item about which exciting science fiction and hefty volumes are written and critical documentaries are aired. So far the public market is nowhere to be found.

Wetware

To reassure the folks in the street, John Perry Barlow, head of the consumers' association Electronic Frontier Foundation, has proposed to stretch the definition of VR and bring it closer to the people by defining already existing electronic data traffic as part of cyberspace. He is trying to achieve a legal breakthrough by declaring this new imaginary zone free from copyright. Since, according to him, cyberspace is transnational, an international constitution for information ought to be drawn up.

Now that hackers in the United States are being persecuted by the CIA and the FBI, slapped with hefty fines, and locked up, association with the world of virtual reality looks like an attractive option for hauling the hacking movement out of the repressive corner. Barlow's reasoning blames the problem on a fundamental lack of understanding about the current technological developments on the part of the authorities. Big names from the software world ought to call a halt to criminalization. But the question is how much we can expect from their end. Dreams of a great coalition between the upcoming VR giants and cyberpunks seem a bit naive. Even inside the small world of the VR pioneers, a tacky war is raging over copyrighting of the names given to homemade projects. On the Electronic Frontier big capital and military interests silently recede into the background.

Is it wetware's task to fill VR with European cultural values, as Jeffrey Shaw did in *The Legible City*, in which he connected the Dutch bicycle to the city maps of such European cities as New York and Amsterdam via VR? This classic wetware strategy turns high-tech back into art by splicing the newest medium to a quaint, ecological, and sweaty means of transport. The continental approach to technology always has an eye for the funny sides of the human deficiency. For if the human bug is not treated with respect, the buckets are poised ready to cool off the new medium. The new monsters must not be understood as a threat from outside, but made to dance in the new space. William Gibson articulated this insight in the phrase, "There's weird shit happening in the matrix," and had Voodoo *loa* trot through cyberspace on horseback.

A more realistic approach is the notion of virtual sex, as safe as it is extremely dirty. One must understand a medium's pornographic potential in order to make it a success. In Europe, telephone companies were forced to conclude that the introduction of the teleconference was a flop, until the same switchboard connection on the 900 party lines made the wildest fantasies reality. The question immediately popped up in virtual reality too: Was sex good there, and which body parts get the nicest stimulation? Wetware will not get excited over a slicker design for the personal cognitive cluster. What is important is whether mistakes can be made in virtual reality and what kind of Faustian and/or Dionysian chain reactions they lead to. Culture is always the consequence of decline, decadence, clumsy maneuvers, and misconceptions. Technology must establish itself inside it, and not make out to rise above it in order to magically evoke something of a higher order. Only then can there be a fusion between the wet- and its hard- and software.

ARTIFICIAL LOVE:
AN INTRODUCTION TO
FANCY DESIGN

1.

Contemporary sex designers bear no relation to power. If the traditional question of power has become empty, then we set foot on a new, unexplored terrain—or so it seems in the hype surrounding "VS" at any rate. The reason this promising discovery raises so much enthusiasm is because sex has finally returned to its pre-Fall paradisal condition. If the sixties needed a revolutionary social approach to liberate sex, the nineties lack all legitimation.

"Virtual sex cannot be real," mutters our critical-ethical consciousness. It must, by definition, consist of lies and deceit. Many have claimed that "virtual" sex simply can't and shouldn't be. Prophets of doom warn against the first signs of decay. VS causes addiction, paralyzes the Net, signifies narcissism, cynicism, and autism, and is assumed to encourage the loss of reality. The cyberjunkies' automated surrogate sex is seen as a detestable escapist reaction to AIDS. Safe sex, it is true; but this condomless gratification could well be worse than the ailment. In short, this typically European line of thinking still thinks of sex in terms of danger and ruin.

The traditional critique of VS is a masked appeal for the survival of actually existing sex. What the critics conceal is the ongoing crisis in current intercourse. The United European marital bed is used to talk, watch television, sleep, make phone calls, do sports, or read in, but begetting offspring is limited to a minimum. The European population increase is an imported one. The link between a critique of VS and the explosive increase of immigrants and refugees cannot be made, because it falls under the racist taboo. The waxing middle classes beat around the bush, smiling coyly about the whole affair in an act of willful repression (Freud). In fact, the best thing to do for Europeans would be to return to Victorian sexual intercourse. Don't get immoral with machines, rubber, pets, booklets—get real, in the sense of "legally joined in marriage." Any criticism of VS runs the risk of getting caught in this kind of cramped, law-and-order conjugal ethics; after all, the antithesis of "virtuality" is "reality," and is sexwise in a terminal condition. Jokes about the disabled Other, condemned to mechanized copulation, bear a bitter connotation: What is disapproved of is unproductivity, but what is really meant is one's own (white) impotence.

After the feminist critique of masculine sexism through man's behavior, through advertising, on the job, and between the sheets, we have entered an era of hypersexual awareness. In magazines, art, on the dance floor, in music (Prince/Madonna), we witness a passionate revival of hard, playful, expressionist sexual techniques. The body needs to express itself, while sexually correct body culture requires maximum effort to get what you came for. "Suck it, baby!" Guided by a mass culture of signs and regulations, the postfeminist body, propped up by a variety of academically sound gender constructs, once again becomes a "sex machine." But it is not the same body that James Brown knew. The point is no longer to liberate sexuality or practice perverted urges, but to circulate them. Sex has reached the superstructure, where it is traded as an intangible asset. Whereas Freud still had the illusion that sex resided in the substructure, nowadays we are all superconscious of it. Sex is not to be suppressed or liberated; it must be celebrated, is the present motto. Sex is a sacred activity which is not to be taken lightly because of its image-quality.

What is the secret of Intersex? This is no innocent question by some sympathetic newspaper journalist who wants to have a go at a nice, hip story for a change. The question of VS can only be seen within the context of the classical European tradition of Sex, Knowledge, and Power (as analyzed by Foucault in his three-volume "History of Sexuality"). The "concern with VS" many times surpasses the actual state of affairs. The number of "VS-related" special issues, legislation, scandals, art installations, books, Master's theses, prognoses, movies and TV items, sects, postcards, and sex fiction exceeds the imagination. Fooling around with "real personal" computers has once more been overrun by representation. Neither hardware nor software will ever manage to live up to their promises. The intense interest in VS should not be interpreted in terms of marketing strategy. No matter how exciting the stories may seem, they do not advertise an impending reality, since their effect is ultimately a reactionary (and racist) one. What seems at first glance like the promotion of cybersex and supertechnology in general serves no other function than to make VS more pliable in order to bring it back under control. Thus, the supramechanical expectations turn out to be a cunning strategy to frustrate the excited user.

2.

The virtual-sex discourse, furthermore, is part of a long prosthetic tradition of man and machine. Starting with seventeenth-century automata, there has been the question of humanity's domination by inert machines. The history of this is recorded, for instance, in Sigfried Giedon's *Mechanization Takes Command* (1948). It even features a chapter on "mechanical fertilization," in which he warns against a "point of danger" that is reached when human beings become capable of artificial reproduction. In Karl Marx, too, we see an analysis of human exploitation by machines as a condemnation of inhumanity. It is not until the 1960's with their automation that the emphasis is shifted towards the libidinous, productive relationship between human beings and their "bachelor machines" (from Reich to Deleuze/Guattari). Machines become toys; an unpleasurable machine is a bad machine, something well understood at Nintendo. Donna Haraway–style cyborgs and Net sexologists may claim to be part of a future underground movement all they want, but they have long been incorporated in the dominant discourse. Cybervisionaries, from Howard Rheingold and Michael Heim to Mark Dery, Douglas Rushkoff, and Sandy Stone, look at machine sex as a new productive force that needs to be released. The "body electric" must be electronically dressed up to help it escape from everyday dreariness, with all its sociable rubbish. It accepts the proclaimed abolition of the social and the disappearance of public space, advocating total abandonment to "virtuality"— in the full interest of the emerging "virtual class" described by Kroker and Weinstein in their book *Data Trash*.

The West Coast prophets always describe virtual sex as an ecstatic connection of body to machine. Therefore, the "cyberculture" discourse may be defined as "fancy design." Thus, "Get Wired!" is to be taken literally, as a simple exhortation to connect your body parts, rather than communicate. To the extent that exchange occurs, it takes place on the level of the "interior dialogue"—of fancy. Virtual sex as we have encountered it possesses no haptic or sensual qualities whatsoever—nor does it need any. Plastic accessories strike us as asexual, too clumsy and heavy, too garish and elaborate, lacking the subtleties of seduction. However, as fancy design, situated in a dreamy, hallucinatory environment, they are quite successful, both sexually and financially.

The design of fancy simultaneously speculates on and denies the human surplus. Virtual sex as a concept accompanies a shift in the body's sensitive, erogenous zones. If we stick to Sigmund Freud's lectures, we find that imagination which does not result from a specific temptation no longer requires the "user's" masturbation, the "sex without secretion" mentioned by Arthur and Marilouise Kroker. With the appearance of cybersex, the erogenous zone shifts from the genitals to the hands, fingertips, ears, eyes, even to such metazones as the abstract matrix of one's own mind and personal display screen. Fancy design collects and organizes the methods and techniques of these shifts. It knows how to appeal to, and tap, the weak spots. In this specific design, dreamwork is charted and condensed under electronic circumstances. The point is the power of imagination, not the perfection of machines. Fancy design as a positive science acknowledges the limits of mechanization, and does not give in to paranoia. Virtual sex as a successful phantasm is an explicit continuation of the Gospel according to John the Lennon: "Make Love, Not War."

3.

Virtual sex as fancy design no longer considers the link between man and machine to be problematic, since that classical antithesis has been turned into a natural symbiosis. Machines do not operate well when tampered with by human beings, but man has become next to inconceivable without a mass of machinery. Even mechanical sexual props—from vibrators to love dolls— have become an established social fact. But the step toward electronic sex opens up new perspectives. If the human body sufficed itself, there would be no sex. Every body suspects it contains far more exploratory potential than it can realize with the available partners and accessories. For centuries, the solution has been sought in the exotic, localized in racially other bodies. Because the foreign races are nowadays available on the sexual market, this creates an interest in a new exoticist experience. The foreign is now pro-jected onto the level of chips and sensors. There, something is conjectured, a link which none of the earlier fusions managed to produce. VS, if it is to be successful, must never be realized. Talk about the technological obstacles that remain to be cleared is no concern of ours. As long as fancy meets the G spot, hardware is irrelevant. "Gratification through fascination" is the new device.

TRIPTYCH ON DRUGS

"Inasmuch as there exists a history of art, there exists a time for art. Yet underneath the creative process, art also harbors a different, volcanic element."

—Ernst Jünger

I. Drugs as Media

As soon as mushrooms begin to speak, we enter the domain of true knowledge: "I am old, 50 times older than thought in your species, and I come from the stars." When asked what brings it to earth, the mushroom refuses to answer: "If I showed you the flying saucer for five minutes, you would figure out how it works." Then why be a mushroom at all? "Listen, if you're a mushroom, you live cheap; besides, this was a very nice neighborhood until the monkeys got out of control."

Psychotropic plants are teleports to parallel worlds. Moreover, they help us visualize immaterial data; one can actually see the words drifting from mouth to ear. But are drugs clusters of information in their own right, or merely channels for insights that originate elsewhere? McLuhan's drug use is proved by his thesis that the medium is the message, although we know that he never used hallucinogenic plants. The sixties generation could only come to the conclusion that McLuhan's body produced its own LSD. A peculiar thing about the media guru was that he circulated his trips in the form of aphorisms, whereas the average user, unable to match the learned scholar, received nothing but images whose info value rose to dangerous synaptic levels. In the end, the democratization of total insight may have resulted in a new aesthetics of images, but it hardly produced the kind of world literature to pull the reader into the intoxicated universe.

Nowadays, knowledge about the gods, golden ages, extraterrestrials, little green men, the primal band, and the global conspiracy is generally available, but turns out to be practically useless. At best, it stops us from acting and inspires us to stage effective power strikes. "To stand on the brink of unnamed regions, where no victory is to be won" (Benn). By definition, drug use is a form of entertainment, stuck in the stage of Shangri-la daytrips. Hang loose. The only scope narcotics have to offer is their dosage: Shall we take heroic doses or remain weekend users forever? Just as each medium creates its own mass, so drugs have conquered their own global markets. No creation without recreation. Provided there is enough room on your pocket calendar and bank account, those boring old personal surroundings can suddenly prove full of unsuspected suspense.

Because drugs distort and enhance local experience, they stimulate our acceptance of the world as it is. Everything is all right and the other is OK. The power of cinema and literature to give meaning and coherence to a series of unrelated details can also be attained through botanical means. Thus, a walk around town can turn into a video clip, Carnival in Rio, a Flemish primitive painting, a Robert Frank photo book, a Godard film with independent audio and video tracks, or a visual version of *The Soft Machine,* or it may end in a meeting with the zombie. Again, the happy end is a matter of knowing what dose to take.

II. Media as Drugs

Television boasts a strange creation myth. In the early 1950's, the CIA found itself faced with the question of what would become the postwar mass drug. It hesitated between LSD and television. The possibilities for control originally discovered in psychedelic drugs turned out to have several undesired long-term side effects. Subjects developed a cosmic awareness that transcended social order and professional ambition. It was decided instead to boost television's disappointing results in mind manipulation through the large-scale distribution of television sets and programs. The effectiveness of the new medium's stupefying power relied on the radical colonization of leisure. The televisual image package is much easier to control than the trip's sovereign phantasms. Television's side effects are negligible. Only a handful of civilizationists still warn against TV addiction. The rest of us have long since accepted the electronic drug's actually existing fascination and democratizing effects.

New media only exercise a hallucinogenic effect when they are first introduced; think of the first time you took your Walkman for a bicycle ride, or your first steps in cyberspace. The mild intoxication caused by information-overload disappears once the user learns to divert 95 percent to the subliminal level. The two-minute trailer carries enough info for us to deduce the entire movie. Even video clips, for all their frantic editing, contain the 5 percent needed to give the full story. The latest thrill is when the obsolete 95 percent is presented as essential with omission of the 5 percent that really matters (as in *Twin Peaks*). Television's illuminating influence continues unabated: Year in, year out, it's always nice to bob on an ocean of information that bears no relation whatsoever to your own life. Television must keep up its touristic appeal: 95 percent bullshit and the promise of a real 5 percent to come. The zapping multimedia users are driven by their obsession to be there on time. Meanwhile, they keep on paddling and accept the general stupor.

III. Media and Drugs

The sober perusal of the media message soon results in isolation. In an effort to prevent this, coffee is now being served with the news and cans of lager accompany the feature movie. The ashtrays will be emptied at the end of the evening. Still, the recipient's dazed condition is considered taboo in media criticism. Movie critics get sick at the thought that the audience is usually stoned or drunk. Inebriated interpretation seems to be an insult to art. The pleasures of sex and drugs should be confined to the screen. Western civilization insists that the distance between work and appreciation be respected. It is unacceptable to hand in your social baggage with your ticket and watch the movie within its own context, rather than from some theoretical framework. The impending overdetermination through consumption frustrates cultural transmission. Feel free to give a personal twist to the plot, but do not exploit the images for a journey of your own. Now that we can understand the whole movie at once through expanded consciousness, the social ritual of reevaluating the movie later seems ridiculous. The only entertainment left is to have a snort, drop, or smoke pending the next kick.

Conversely, drugged data preparation has become an established practice. Among musicians, the interval between consumption and appearance has been carefully laid down, something that is gratefully used by the audience to adapt its own dosage to the volume. In the computer industry, the use of smart drinks among software writers has become an accepted fact; so have the trips that make the money market so profitable. American artists take pride in their top dealers, while newcomers have to resort to suspect hustlers. Experienced readers have a flawless sensitivity to their authors' level of intoxication. What is interesting is not writing about drugs or filming the act but Ronell's drugged writing, Lynch's stoned shoots, Benn's coffee-table oeuvre, Blavatsky's hash revelations, Turel's Burgundy thinking, Baudrillard's cigarette hype, Scholte's cocaine paintings, Perry's XTC art, Marley's ganja songs, the speed of punk rock, the grass dialogues of Altman, even the High Politics of a Clinton and Gore.

Drugs and media are equal partners. Until the computer is directly connected to the brain, and thus to the process of creation, accelerating and decelerating substances will be necessary to keep a cool head amid the immense number of data interactions underlying the production of artificial realities. Drugs can be used as the metamedium to manipulate the technological media. Without them, we soon reach the limits of the tolerable. Drugs enable communication with (extra-)terrestrial intelligences. But at the same time they transform our individual nervous systems into technological media operating at the same speed as the noncorporeal equipment. Now that data generation without drugs has become inconceivable, it is time to let the drugs speak for themselves. Install Coke for Windows.

THE DOMINANT EAR

It is often said that we live in the empire of images. While in the beginning was the word, it is believed that in our final hour the flesh has become image. The occident on which night has fallen is lit by flickering signposts that guide our stumbling sight through the labyrinth of speed. It is believed that in this dreamland, reason can no longer write its name and has become a PIN code. Uprooted metamorphoses herald our downfall while we watch, dumbfounded and fascinated by its sheer visual beauty. Involvement has zero force in the mediacracy. So power runs no risk, and is hard for the stupefied senses to locate.

The above specter, as propagated by cultural conservationists, is meant to avert the threatening decline of literacy by restraining visual consumption. Language as a national culture carrier is assumed to guarantee profundity, in contrast to the addictive superficiality of R/TV/VCR/CD/PC/VR, which only stimulate passivity. The bourgeois character, who turned out immune to fascism and communism and is doing so well materially, is feared to collapse under the internal assault of zappable impressions in the third dictatorship of images.

This specter has an audio equivalent. The ear is believed to have been dismembered and surrendered to the senseless but excessive noise of trail bikes, fighter jets, loudspeakers, chainsaws, dogs, factory floors, cloudbursts, carnivals, loading zones, and parties. Parallel to their literacy campaign, the opponents of noise are lobbying for the allocation of sanctuaries where tractors have been replaced by horses and the scythe will sing again. It is the sound of nature, which humanity, with all its rights, must obey under penalty of mutation.

The preachers of pure sound and vision accompany the disappearance of an audiovisual culture that gave us a Goethe, Rembrandt, and Bach. From Altamira to Bikini, the primary task of our legators' civilization was to fell the enchanted forest of the cracking twigs, the indistinct fluttering, the piercing looks and the rustle of leaves and nocturnal animals. The acoustic space of the first human being on earth was a constant flow of quadraphonic input with no locatable sound source. The struggle for civilization was an effort to realize clearings and local silences, to be filled with the mystique of the unreproducible work of art. Through human intervention, a harmonious order could be installed in the primordial chaos in which the subject knew its place among the ranks of higher beings. The singular quality of the great artists was that they knew how to evoke and exorcise the threat of original anarchy, in a gesture which helped the petty bourgeois to overcome their most individual fears.

The highlights and evergreens of Western civilization were part of an audiovisual regime that imposed its coordinates by means of the clock tower, with its 3-D dial and carillons. Power produces not only images but also sounds; it enters the body through the ear and the eye. The image, although it ensured a continuous norm, could still be ignored by the people at large, but the intermittent chiming of the bells had a range that was impossible to escape. Until, when the industrial machinery was started up, the volume of acoustic space was increased so that the masses were subjected to permanent acoustic pressure. This gave the image a suggestion of silence. In this vacuum, impressionist painting, photography, and the silent movie could rise to full glory. They accompanied the transition to a power type whose secret derived from the hidden power of the image. For a while, the proliferation of visual flora was curbed by the retro-futurism of European fascism, which harked back to the auditive media of radio and the public speech. When, after some insistence, the marching music died down, the rodeo was replaced by full-color movies and the flickering screen, which were celebrated as democratic achievements. The civilization fan club at the time immediately ascribed pagan characteristics to rock 'n' roll, which belonged to the haunted forest where cultural beings indulge in their most primary passions.

Through the flexibilization of taste, musical preference has become a condensation in the global and historical network of styles, trends, and genres. To each state of mind its musical genre and vice versa, and that twenty times an hour. The listener who as a fan was once defined by subculture and identity has suddenly become receptive to every sound wave. If in the fifties only parents couldn't handle rock 'n' roll physically, today the physical border experience has lost its age- and group-defined character. The dislike of certain video clips reflects a similar effect on the social body as swing has on the lip-synch show. Everyone is open to anything, but each reserves the right to his or her contemporary favorites. Every audioviewer can read and interpret any musical genre. A socio-genetic approach to music is the only mode of promotion. Rap is a ghetto thing, house comes from an empty warehouse, trashfolk from Ireland, indiepop from London, highlife belongs to chic Ghanaian dance clubs, and speedmetal to suburbia. Once culturally tagged, each new beat contributes to the soundscape.

A precondition for this is that music, which always results from local experience, is freed from its origins, to become a contextless, universally understood global language. The experiential media of the sixties neatly screen a whole era with a kind of freshness and radiance classified as original in the age of the digital drone. The universal musical-sociological retraining of the ear has created an immune system which prevents music from penetrating those primordial cerebral layers that might be aroused by it. As entertainment, even the crudest sound lacks the Dionysian élan of the primal band.

Music, the dominant mechanism of the social organization of personal memories, immediately makes us forget the social misery as sound. Pop music is such a perfect system of auto-reference that there is immediate appreciation for people who copy the guitar play or voice of one or other predecessor who died too soon. Pop musicians who wish to charge acoustic space with dangerous signals engage in a battle against the transparency of their own style, in an effort to render the singularity and qualifiability of their methods more opaque through increased complexity. The existing openness to all continents and eras provides the material for minimal classifiability. But pop music knows its own history, and can endlessly and rhizomatically copy it in a way that is effortlessly shared by the media masses. Is it possible to make timeless, abstract pop music which refers to and derives from nothing?

The limitations of pop music lie in its technological a priori. Not only is music technically easy to date based on the samplers used, but the transition to new information carriers also filters out an entire musical collection from the hole in the historical memory. Who will make the switch to CDs, who stay magnetic forever, who vanish into the hobbyist sphere along with untraceable spare needles and racks of 78-rpm singles? Again, music reacts with a defensive attack. In the first days of the gramophone, vocalists sang directly onto a wax disc. Later, only live performances were cut into vinyl, with no dubbing. During the next phase, studio recordings were produced in which each instrument was independently recorded and mixed in. In the terminal phase of the LP medium, records provided the raw material for the direct scratching process. Now the LP seeks to survive by becoming the content of the CD, which, however, is actively and digitally emancipating itself from its source material. Soon, it too will be forced to become the material for a subsequent round in the inevitable economic transition to a new generation of noise carriers.

Time and again, musical workers blindly submit to the secret power of the medium offered them. Before, there were guitars or pianos; now there are fully integrated audiovisual circuits. Acoustic emptiness screams to be filled as it deserves. Whereas the guitar still depended on the guitar player's fingers and fits, the beat box needs no physical movement to perform. Musicians never controlled their guitars or drums; the keys themselves imposed a kinetics on the hands. The musical instrument sought to rid itself of the soft machine's touch. Punk understood this, and reacted with an unrestrained attack on the predigital equipment—neat material for another compilation CD. The next phase will be synclavier microchips flying about as house DJs smash up their mixing desks. As soon as the audience becomes interactive, the laser projection reveals its destructive side. As digital culture reaches its zenith, noise once again invades acoustic space.

THE THIRD BODY

I. A Private Reality

Music is not sound but ambience, a sensory space, omnipresent and forever open. The neonatural environment generated by audio signals reconciles the unconscious with its vague condition: the intermingling of to be and not to be. Music is a normality-expanding substance that brings on drowsiness. The general human tendency to dissolution is counteracted by rhythmical sound wave interruptions. The definition of a musical piece with a beginning and end leads to punctual interruptions of consciousness that build up tension between the here-and-now of local experience and the wherever-and-whenever of the brotherhood of consumers. In the musical sauna, the human will to unreality is kept awake through periodical cold silence showers. The intermission between songs prompts social reflection regarding the *zoon politicon*: "Eh?" This dialectic of absence between slow musical intoxication and the rapid sobriety of thought intensifies the subcritical attitude required for adjusted behavior. As the arbitrary medium between contained savagery and rampant civilization, music is a touching achievement of the family of man. In music, man the muse finds delight in culture.

Every musical form creates its own space. Although the boundaries of each of these premises are clearly defined, they manage to create an illusion of boundlessness and totality. A straight line runs from cradle rattle through teenage stereo to Walkman and car radio. This musical educational trajectory aims at the highly individual design of personal reality. Music serves as a public means of production for the manufacture of intimacy. "My moment of awakening was when they played the Bee Gees' 'I Started a Joke' at the ice rink" (John Sasher). The discovery of a personal sensory space is an irreversible point in the shaping of identity. Any possible later fusions with favorite tracks refer to that primal scene's intensity, no matter what subsequent shifts in musical taste may occur. The initiation into the universal audio archives results from a sudden and inescapable detachment from the social context: that first musical space-time journey into unknown territories. Once evoked, the promise contained in this possibility never loses its attraction. The recognition of a similar intensity in other musical forms is the driving force behind the metamorphoses of personal taste, a unique secret shared with millions of other teenagers, hippies, mods, punks, Abba fans,

118

Africans, Hindus, ravers, Bach devotees, housewives, and metalheads. The technological reproducibility of sounds is a social prerequisite for individuality.

II. A Shared Reality

Music is the ideal intermediary between individual and common life. Pop music is not just listened to in the privacy of living room and concert hall, but in all the spaces in between, from bank and shopping mall to construction site and public highway. The normalizing function of public music is constantly disrupted by the brief emergence of private reality's personal intensities. In fact, this intermingling of the public and personal senses is what renders your social adjustment bearable. Public space must regulate its volume so as to keep the body in a constant, absentminded movement. Muzak forces the environment into the background in order to limit attention to the offered goods and services. The aroused boredom must be compensated for by an affirmation of your individual willpower in the shape of an impulse buy. Increase the volume, and the public no longer consumes hard wares but states of mind. The Walkman reverses these sound levels, declares public space a silent zone, and gets on its way, taking with it its own sensory space. The walkman or -woman listens to self-programmed Muzak, the only possible unpleasant surprise being the external intensities in case of empty batteries or a broken CD. Whereas the mall's public Muzak is designed to soften the masses' hard personality, the walkman's private Muzak strives for a hard personality of its own within the soft crowd. The Walkman's problem is that it must be part of these masses, whereas the shop music strategy aims to detach the individual from the multitudes.

You only really listen to music if it exercises an alienating effect; that is, when you detach yourself from your entire sensory surroundings and tune in to one sense alone—the ear. Concentrated listening requires effort, an act of willpower; to listen is to defy music. It is an educational process to enter a previously unknown sensory space. To listen is to exclude and to introduce. New music is a generator of complexity in which it's hard to discern anything at all, whereas old music can be amazingly subtle once you turn on your differential accumulator. Whereas the connoisseur can always discover new levels and elements to a composition, the reluctant listener clings to familiar sounds and older rhythms. Listening precedes the concert; you never know if you'll really get into the music or not. Whereas dance clubs invite you to hit the dance floor without further ado and let your body do the listening, the concert hall initially requires you to be all ears, only later to submerge all the senses in a total experience which it is impossible for the purely techno sound to generate. This is the promise of the live concert. Music that forces you to listen can hardly be kosher. The annoying discrepancy between compact disc and live performance has been averted through unplugged versions, on one hand, and the maximedial spectacle of the megashow on the other. Concert halls and dance clubs are temples of the senses whose architectural qualities lend a touristic quality to nightlife: they enable the mass experience you really paid for. In the case of a techno party in some warehouse, the focus is on the sensory qualities of installation and drugs, producing a mass no longer aspired to in glam disco. With music, one is never alone.

III. The Sensory Body

Let's see what Neil Young has to say about his life on stage. "The guitar and the amplifier work together to feed each other. And you have to get the amplifier big enough, so you're far enough away from the guitar that you can still feed, vibrate the area. And you move the guitar around in the area, finding angles and places where the guitar sits and responds to the sound. And then you start building the sound coming out of the amplifier with effects after the guitar signal is entered. It has to have strayed in. And then you take the effects and introduce them again between the guitar and the amplifier, through a different route, and you blend them together and they start feeding back. It's a very natural thing. And to hear it live is really awesome. You feel it in your chest." The musician's grounds are limited. The barrier between stage and audience is strengthened by the light show and speakers. The musician is not looking for audience interaction. He plays for the installation, working for the interference between his body and technology. He plays no tunes, performs no play, it's a physical experience he's after. It is only when his body connects to the equipment, and technology responds, that the mass follows. The switch may also be made between band members, when the individual musicians suddenly meet and things start to roll. The first link between body and music, and between the bodies as such, is created on stage, before it hits the concert space. Drugs enhance musical attention and increase sound concentration, so the musician can let the guitar do all the work. The instrument is allowed to go its own way, so far that the performer has no option but to thrash the runaway guitar at the end of the evening to silence it. Reggae is the prototype of responsible drug use; music, band spirit, and ganja combine to call forth the cool runnings, much like beer and polonaise. Every musical form uses its own narcotic methods. "We're jamming in the name of the Lord."

The public appears after the transition from highway to concert hall, via the overflowing buffer zone of entrance, box office, wardrobe, toilets, and bar. In these interspaces, the individual body prepares itself for the mass, discarding redundant textiles, buying T-shirts, and effecting the desired level of intoxication. Then begins the ordeal of endless waiting, strangers, the racket of the opening bands, and a generally noisy ambience. The audience begins to show signs of subdivision between the fans and groupies up by the stage, the reserved middle section, the talkers in the back, the wall gang, the barflies. Tension rises as the band appears: a first moment of discharge, after which the audience disperses again and tries to listen. The audience's movement has been halted; people stand or sit around. Only the group in front of the stage goes berserk at the first sound of a note. The concert hall's architecture is designed so as to effect a functional segmentation of the audience, which must be entertained to prevent it from turning its charge of explosive tension into action prematurely and undirected. The audience's physical ecstasy must merge in time with the switch on stage and then die out after the band has left in order to prevent trouble. The concert shows us that entertainment has a physical basis. It is the proprietor's duty to contain the risks that accompany such Dionysian aspirations. Mass ecstasy releases fundamental energies of antisocial inclination. The live concert's ceremonial structure is part of the strategy to contain the pursued mass release. Should the stage be besieged and the equipment thrashed, it would be a case of bad management. Those who physically cross the line between the sensory spaces of stage and concert hall disturb the concert's prescribed peace, be it to party or to run riot. If, after three encores, the ecstasy still hasn't quieted down, the band can always follow Mano Negra's example and dive headlong into the audience.

IV. The Third Body

When we cross the sound barrier the entire body begins to respond. It has found the instrument to hook up with: a reggae bass guitar, a raving rhythm box, steel guitars that give you goosebumps, punk's throbbing rhythm guitar, Irish folk's tin whistle, Nigerian talking drums, rap and raggamuffin's pounding human voices, the great vocalists' lyrical fragments and intonations, a solo guitar's emotional explosion. "Take me to the bridge." At the same time, a single physical zone is discovered to be the key to the rest of the body—the belly in country & western, the hips in rock 'n' roll, the skin in house, the knees in juju, the head in metal, the flying torsos in pogo, the feet off the disco floor, the hands in blues, the ass in qawwal and party, clapping in gospel, jumping in mod, the click of the finger in jazz. "You get the message." The switch between the bodies on stage and those in the audience is made as soon as the music takes over. The third body created is a result of the connection between a specific technology and an ecstatic potential in biological bodies. Techno and bio merge through sound amplification. Each musical form or group has its own third body. The physical experience may be that of universal grace or elegance, aggression, purity, fun, anger, rage, peace and kindness, hysteria, mellow aloofness, doom, or an urge to destroy. Once music produces a third body, it represses all other potential third bodies: It keeps to itself. That is why it is possible to like all kinds of musicologically incompatible genres. Schubert, Bowie, and the Sabri Brothers can easily be combined over the weekend. Where the third body appears, classical space-time limitations disappear and one enters a purely Freudian state. The pop concert offers more than just spectacle and a good show; it manipulates bodies beyond political and sexual economics. It injects the wetware's ego with a stiff dose of id.

The third body is a state either reached during the concert, or not. Musicians are judged according to their ability to invoke and contain it. The concert's logistic apparatus is designed to regulate the switch between the spaces of stage and audience, an issue that is becoming increasingly demanding with the expansion of the latter all the way out to playing fields and stadiums. In the sixties, Ken Kesey visits a Beatles concert: "John, George, Paul, dips his long electric guitar handle in one direction and the whole teeny horde ripples precisely along the line of energy he set off—and then in the other direction, precisely along that line. Control—it is perfectly obvious—they have brought this whole mass of human beings to the point where they are one, out of their skulls, one psyche, and they have utter control over them—but they don't know what in the hell to do with it, they haven't the first idea, and they will lose it. Ghhhhhhwooooooooooowwww, thousands of teeny bodies hurtling towards the stage and a fence there and a solid line of cops, fighting to hurl the assault back, while the Beatles keep moving their chops and switching their hips around sunk like a dumb show under the universal scream. And then the girls start fainting, like suffocation, and getting tromped on, and they start handing out their bodies, cockroach chair debris and the bodies of little teeny freaks being shuttled out over the pitched sea like squashed lice picked off the beast. The Beatles are the creature's head. The teeny freaks are the body. But the head has lost control of the body and the body rebels and goes amok and that is what cancer is."

The third body is not an expression of free will, but an acute metamorphosis spreading through a sensory space. The audio installation and concert hall acoustics see to it that the music fills the entire building, rather than merely making itself heard. The same effect is aspired to by teenagers when they turn up the volume all the way. The third body is implanted through the beat, swing, sound, duende, or vibes, and causes motor reactions: stomping, swaying, wavering, bopping, wiggling, shaking, jerking, twisting, stripping, rocking, or waving. The third body dances, it shuns ideological critique. You either get into it or you don't; there's no in-between. Denounce the cha-cha or breakdancing as the repressive choreographies of actual spasms all you want; it would still be an outsider's observation. The concert is a success if it realizes the third body, no matter what the quality of the performance or the individual pop critic's tastes. In the concert, the human condition is indulged in; whether you agree with that condition or not is irrelevant, for it exists. Since criticism can't make head or tail of the third body, it confines itself to listening, concentrating on musical technique, act, and the politico-socio-cultural backgrounds of lyrics and band members. Conservative pop criticism is aware of the existence of the ecstatic body, for it recognizes its risky aspects that require the necessary precautions. In fascism, dancing is equated with sports and the third body goes up in smoke. Although the third body can be said to act independently of critical consciousness, it does not eliminate it. The audience regains its senses at the end of the song, when the clapping of hands reestablishes the boundaries between individual and third corporeality. If the band has lived up to the indefinite expectations before the concert, the audience will call for an encore. In this ritual afterplay, the audience festively returns its third body to the musicians, effectively bringing it to a halt in preparation of its return to private reality. The DJ's Muzak has already begun. The lonely crowd disperses, some stick around, the bar is closed. Life goes on.

Labor, Sex, and Media

The greater the belief in media supremacy, the more compelling the "question" of media becomes, and the louder the demand for a comprehensive theory to cover the media and provide them with the necessary terms and concepts upon which to base policy. The lack of clear analysis is seen as the main cause of technological and commercial proliferation. However, it remains to be seen whether it is possible to formulate a total analysis of media power. In the early twentieth century, attempts were made in several fields to get such a determinant discourse machine off the ground. In the fields of sexuality and labor, the attempt proved successful. Psychoanalysis and Marxism have not remained marginal phenomena, but have left clear marks on history. They have not only interpreted the world, but unmistakably changed it and rendered it debatable.

The mutually incompatible absolute demands made by both theories gave rise to endless debates within metatheory. On the street level, this clash of discourses corresponded to a revolutionary violence that proved fatal for the democratic nations. Still, the misunderstood forces behind the totalitarian movements could afterward be explained from a Freudo-Marxist perspective: Linking sex and labor made it obvious that the two together had constituted prewar psychosocial identity, and that the workers could be roused through sexual appeals. The disastrous consequences of this belated insight currently hover like a dark cloud over the media theory under construction. If we fail to answer the question of media now, then the Gulf War makes a fine example of what is to come (or so our intellectual discomfort tells us). That is why Hussein is worse than Hitler.

Just as Freud did not take notice of Marx, so media theory does not heed Freud or Marx. Communication experts suggest that the old theories are not equipped to describe or analyze media society. If before, sex and labor themselves were the determinants, now they are considered to be derivatives of a theoretical, not (yet) understood "media reality." Both superseded social quantities still make their appearance in the media, where, however, they are of limited validity. They do not contribute to an understanding of the coordinate patterns thought to propel the media. In fact, psychoanalysis and Marxism aim at nothing of the sort. Through the recognition that the factors of sex and labor have been incorporated into media, these theories have long since put their general claims into perspective.

Labor, Sex, and Media

Thinking no longer has totalitarian pretensions. In theory, democratic Taylorism has triumphed, and it is far from clear what product the research underway is going to come up with. Theory's little stories are half-products that appear in the media under the sign of expertise. Since the latter results from a successful marketing strategy and is always looking out for fashionable trends, it is doomed to perish. This sort of virtual condition remains bearable as long as it is compensated for by material security. The surrender of research institutes to the media is one more proof of the unbridgeable gap between media practice and media theory.

Even the marginal experiment, which does still stake a general claim, operates in a field that is carefully defined by the media. Labeled art or underground, subculture or lifestyle, renounced for reasons of business risk—once form and content have been crystallized, it will be condensed as a story to further enhance the media package.

The business economics of the multimedia spectacle thus control the entire field of research and take on an aura of inescapability. Even the scientific ivory tower has been furnished with King Media's loudspeakers, where King Labor and Queen Sex blared before. This shows that we are still used to thinking submissively in terms of absolute monarchy and universal power. We await the coming of the Sigmund Marx or Karl Freud of the media age who will offer us a vision of a postmedial Empire of Freedom. She or he will put an end to intellectual rigidity and parochialism and topple the tables of the postmodern concept-traders so that theory may once more become the guiding principle of nations. Media philosophy, like quantum physics, should formulate a Theory of Everything under which all kinds of disparate questions can be grouped.

The concept of "media" originates in the modern age with Hegel's phenomenology. His principle of the spirit as medium rendered bourgeois society a practicable entity. The spirit medium enables a qualitative leap, as with the childishly innocent body when it becomes the sexual body and yet remains the same. On the other hand, "media" means that from the viewpoint of power, the body becomes controllable, productive. The medium creates unity by mediating between power and the body, so that both poles forever share a relationship of mutual dependence. Power needs the body, and the body needs power. Thus, the question is never: power or not? but rather: what form of power is at work (as Foucauldians put it).

The twentieth century is characterized by a form of power consisting of the coupled media of labor and sex, which ingeniously interwove the organization of public life with private life. Sex and labor are media in the sense that they mediate between the body and the social. Just as sex mediated between the sexes, so labor mediated between classes. The reason sex and labor as an identity-inducive pair were such an unbeatable medium was that both media, within a cooperative bond, gave productive potential to the division between public and private. Socioeconomic questions could thus be translated into psychosexual terms so social contradictions could be experienced on the psychological level as sexual conflicts. Since the masses thus understood themselves to be psychologically dependent on socioeconomic reality, they were open to irrational demands on matters of national interest. This has been one explanation of National Socialist hysteria.

History can be divided into periods of subsequent power types, with the predecessors invariably incorporated by the successors. If the current type is defined by "the media," then it carries with it the psychosocial complex, without being dominated by it. This explains why the media cannot be overthrown by any offensive (combined or otherwise) from a sexual disposition: the media will effortlessly defuse any revolutionary sexual movement. The same can be said of the social. Whereas the unemployment rate of the 1930's immediately created a revolutionary situation, this is unthinkable under the media reign. All (sex-pol) resistance is highlighted, not in order to root it out, but to test its item potential. The old powers can undergo fundamental changes without threatening the new power type.

The psychological bodily complex is no longer directly linked to sex and labor; instead, it mirrors itself on the media's ever-changing images and programs. Inasmuch as the old media had no option but to equip the body with a fixed and definite identity, the new media are dependent on polymorphously perverted identities. That is not to say that the media do not create an entity. Diversion unifies and occupies the millions. The diversity overload is productive, in that the various elements can be instantly connected. This unlimited potential of combinations has abolished the fixed coordinates of time and space that old labor and sex still depended on. Moving through time and space is pretty cumbersome if one has to drag along blood and soil with each step taken.

Many of the accusations against the media result from adherence to a power type that has lost its function. Media are considered far too shallow to properly shed light on the context of reality. Superficiality can only be perceived as a disturbing element if one adheres to firmly fixed identities accorded such importance that it is forbidden to treat them lightly. The idea that the real forces behind or underneath the screen can be revealed is likewise based on the presumption that the media themselves do not have power, but instead are tools in the hands of manipulating third parties. The invisible links render power itself invisible; the quest for hidden power not only underestimates this feature of media power, it also sticks to the rules of old power, which has in fact disappeared within the media.

The same goes for complaints about the overload of information and entertainment and their synthesis, infotainment. The diagnosed overkill is experienced as a waste of energy, time and money that could have been put to much better use. This waste metaphor is a relic of the sexual disposition, according to which energy must be spent either on labor or on sensitivity. Back then, waste was considered a problem because it threatened the logic of (the division of) family labor and factory labor and laid an inordinately high claim on vital reserves.

But what is waste to the media-ecological mind becomes a test pattern on the media level. Whereas waste is based on scarcity—to which it is itself the exception—abundance is an existential prerequisite of media. If waste once was a devastating explosion, in the media it becomes the productive implosion par excellence that raises the switch potential to the power of n. The media ecologists' real desire is to reduce the media to a single prime-time quality channel, betraying their yearning for the subjection of media to a past order offering fixed guidelines for a life of responsibility.

All this discomfort seeks a way out, so media theory is assigned the task of finding therapeutic treatments for all the discontent, which will restore the user's balanced mind and prevent frustrated contact with the media. When therapy presents itself as theory, it will have to eliminate technological fears, to which end it can basically either express or trivialize them. In contrast, any theory that wants to avoid the social demand for media therapy will have to look beyond the boundaries of media reality. Whereas therapy cures the medially insane, theory ought to treat them as borderline cases that enhance our perception of media power. The media heretics and perverts reveal normality in their aberration.

So far, media theory has done little more than to formulate the concepts to guide the introduction of the new technologies. This is usually done by describing the machine's grammar from within, so that we may understand and communicate with the media using their own language. Media are provided with a history and a future. What remains unexplored this way is the reality production of the new power type, here and now.

The paradox any media theory has to face is that it can only define (hyper-) reality according to criteria that are beyond the media. Theory must absorb resistance; rather than eliminating discomfort, it must reinforce it. It must not oppose the media, but move beyond them. In contrast, to presume the omnipotence of media is to try to summon the impending disaster of a Brave New Media World, in order to exorcise it through the exclusion of subversive elements.

The same can be said of the attempt to put the media into the proper perspective to the point where they become insignificant data liquids. Again, to trivialize is to deny (virtual) reality through the emancipation of the virtual as virtuality. This approach, too, does little justice to the present, with all its paradoxes and absurdities. It renders the careful study of media microphysics redundant, as media are only virtual after all. Media theory tends to lean towards one of these poles; it prefers to make grandiose gestures rather than to record the small stories, a lousy job best left to everyday journalism.

It is only when the media twilight falls that media theory begins to blossom. The theory of fascism needed an entire cold war before it could fully mature. The ecologists' call for a media freeze is a forced attempt to contain the excrescences so that research may flourish. However, they forget that this can only succeed if it is preceded by a catastrophe. To cancel ISDN, HDTV, and VR and stop the necessary permanent innovation would be to rob the global economy of its motor. Ecologists advocate an unprecedented crisis that would make the stock market crash look like a day at the beach. In an attempt to impart an air of reasonability to their apocalyptic yearnings, they propose precautionary reforms to curb the media (so that the book may witness its comeback).

The question remains whether media theory can survive without a global crisis. Will the media walls be made to crumble as the iron curtain did—unexpectedly, and without bloodshed? The dyad of annihilation and modernization that served as the driving force behind the twentieth century can remain operational in the media age without resorting to violence. On the contrary, violence is released, itemized, and finally expelled as the primitive means of communication of the unconnected social wastelands. Media neither feed nor feed on violence. But under the media ecologists' command, they do make a prime target. Their vulnerability compels them to plead for a world government that will exclude violence and render it unthinkable within the networks. No matter how justifiable this eerie media premonition, it still testifies to their continued belief in the (political) power of the labor-and-sex age.

Any media theory that wishes also to be a power analysis is doomed to be outdated the moment it appears. If media theory is to analyze the media without resorting to holocausts or conspiracies within the military-electronic complex, it must abandon the idea that media have anything whatsoever to do with power. Accusations of superficiality are the media's greatest compliment.

KING THEWELEIT

*"Let the dead hum a tune if they will. And let the perpe-
trator shut up please."*

—Armando

According to Klaus Theweleit, the word "media" is too weak. He would prefer to label new technologies in their radical, altering, or programming
aspects as "metamorphosers" or "transmutators." To McLuhan's thesis—
"The medium is the massage"—Theweleit adds, "Metamorphosis is the
product of this massage." Unlike McLuhan, Theweleit is not prepared to
think from the medium's point of view, but instead cherishes a subjective
position. He is obsessed with developments in the new media workplace:
How are media workers to connect their bodies to the machines in order to
render their medium productive? Theweleit is less concerned with the question of what reactions media cause in their receivers than with the mystery
of how they are made to transmit. To him, the question of media is the question of their application. For him, the broadcast of life does not start over and
over again, but is a process of growth. Theweleit observes that producers use
the media metamorphosis to go through the same cycle again and again. His
proposition is that we use the media as growth factors to support the extension of human experience.

Theweleit rereads McLuhan in his own way. Each new medium picks
out a single function from the whole of human experience and magnifies it.
This amputation opens up an entire field of new perceptions and possible
metamorphoses, but at the same time anaesthetizes through sheer force. The
media subject becomes so fascinated with the new devices' unlimited potential that it no longer notices the rest of the world. In this "closed system," the
users adopt a narcissistic position, mistaking their new medial possibilities
for their own identities. The high thus invoked is labeled by Theweleit as the
"narc pole," in reference to both narcissism and narcotics. "It seems
irrefutable to me that, in terms of technological media that interfere with and
alter the body, the path of individual growth/metamorphosis or obstruction
always touches on the pole of intoxication/anaesthesia/narcosis."

The fact that those who are engaged in the construction of artificial realities constantly skip over the intoxication/drug pole is not a matter of choice
or whim. Intoxication is an inevitable by-product, with a hazardous as well

129

as a happy side. New media can cause an addiction in which the mediatist strives after an endless repetition of the same cycle of intoxication. This is a risk we have to take, Theweleit says, since it is only through media that humanity can grow. To him, growth is a prerequisite if we are to shape our own history instead of endlessly repeating past horrors. From his medial perspective, he does not see growth as a natural condition: "People with a history of their own must, by definition, be people from artificial/artistic realities."

In 1988, 10 years after his thousand-page *Male Fantasies*, Theweleit published volume one of his magnum opus, *Buch der Könige* (*The Book of Kings*), whose four volumes are expected to consist of a total of 3,200 pages. *Male Fantasies* has become synonymous with a farewell to rigid Marxism, in that it explains fascism in terms of the male's incapacity to deal with his own body. The *Buch der Könige* tetralogy will comprise a farewell to an equally rigid belief in literature as an autonomous art form by explaining it in terms of the inability of writers to deal with their own history.

With its 1,222 pages and 600 illustrations, *Buch der Könige* constitutes a genre of its own. It is a "second attempt to write unawaited biographies—a whodunit—a case study. More to do with the narrative psychoanalysis of the not-quite-born: Narcissus; intoxication; murmurs." The leading character is Orpheus, in "Landsberg, Berlin (West and East), Mantua, Florence, at the polar circle, in America, Prague. In 1945, 1607, 1283, 1901, 1968. With his lyres: text, music, opera, radio, cinema, paintings." Discourse-jockey Theweleit inserts 312 pages on "Historical Complications," a succession of sources of inspiration, incoming mail, encounters, weird books, memories, auto-psychoanalysis, reviews of Kinks albums and television shows, comic books, soccer heroes, and his mother. Visiting Alice Miller in Zürich with his wife and kids, the "good child" is more closely examined. Over lunch, New York psychohistorian Lloyd deMause is questioned on the cycles of the Fantasy Wars. Velikovsky is consulted concerning cosmic catastrophes, and the Zürich writer p.m. regarding the global system of bolo'bolo.

There is no end to it. "The detective-historian's task is not to reduce; on the contrary, he must add. There are never enough versions." Theweleit manages to restore to art its social role, without depriving it of its element of autonomy. He brings to bear the most wildly divergent texts, without ever misappropriating any of them. As a result, his book acts as a labyrinth of sources that stands in its own right and cannot be interpreted as a transient product of the Zeitgeist. Unlike in *Male Fantasies*, Theweleit now refuses to distill a single conclusive theory from his sources, but instead creates a field of tension between what he terms "poles": "I would exclude as little as possible, and poles are the means to this end. Poles may be added up and connected to one another, after which any short-circuits will occur of their own accord, as well as combinations that amount to a network of poles, in which something may be caught of the currents and waves that are actually en route in reality's net, or which—speaking more precisely, more physically accurate—constitute this net."

In short, his is not a dialectical or deductive method: The currents which Theweleit discovered in the male body in his *Male Fantasies* are now retraced in the world, including his own immediate environment, and he consistently applies this experience to his own writing. Stories and concepts emerge, converge, give off sparks, combine, and gain an intensity for the reader which, after the first shock of recognition, amounts to an experience of "real history." Theweleit even took the consequences to a practical level: He typed his book on a writing table designed especially for him which allowed him to run a text dozens of meters in length through his typewriter without interruption (described in detail on page 1125).

Following the men of war in *Male Fantasies,* the focus is now on the men of art. They are the kings referred to in the title. Theweleit decodes in detail the actual conditions which enabled such writers as Gottfried Benn, Brecht, Knut Hamsun, Franz Kafka, and Ezra Pound to begin and maintain their artistic production. What he discovers is that all these writers followed a specific pattern, based on the classical myth of Orpheus and Eurydice.

After the death of his beloved Eurydice, Orpheus the singer descends to the underworld to demand her return. Moved by his singing, the Hadean gods comply, on the condition that he will refrain from looking back on their way out. Just before their return to the world, however, Orpheus turns around, and Eurydice vanishes forever. This experience transforms Orpheus into the poet to whose lament all of creation bowed down. He refuses intercourse with other women in order to fully devote himself to art. Finally, he is torn to pieces by furious Maenads and cast into the sea, his head to sing on forever.

Why did Orpheus look back? Out of overwhelming love, is the traditional answer. But love of what? Theweleit wonders at the beginning of his book, on rereading Gottfried Benn—Orphic poet par excellence. And he starts to recount: In September 1946, Benn completes his poem, *Orpheus' Tod (Death of Orpheus)*, which begins with the line "Wie du mich zurückläßt liebste" ("Do not leave me behind, my beloved"). A year before, Benn's wife, Herta von Wedemeyer, had committed suicide in the small town of Neuhaus, where he had sent her to escape the Red Army. He had remained in Berlin as an army medical officer. On hearing of Herta's death, some months after the fact, he immediately takes to writing the Orpheus poem, which he completes after a second visit to her grave, a year later. During the war, Benn had written his most important works in Landsberg: *Roman der Phänotyp (Phenotypical Novel)*, *Statische Gedichte (Static Poems)*, and *Ausdruckswelt (The World of Expression)*. As he wrote to his friend Oelze, he considered these books to lay the foundation for a new German culture. After Herta's death, he fears he will no longer be able to write; with *Orpheus' Tod*, however, he resumes production. The question, then: What exactly did Benn exorcise through his writings that allowed him to conquer his stagnation?

Orpheus' Tod is a classic example of absolute lyricism, a high point in modernist writing; brilliant and impenetrable, even after several times of rereading. Theweleit, too, confesses he is always enchanted by it. Then he begins to read Benn's letters to Oelze and other biographical material, and discovers a secret code in the poem. It appears that Benn interpreted the entire story of Herta as his own experience of the Orphic myth. Herta was the Eurydice whom he had sent into the underworld, so that after her death (i.e., Germany's liberation) he might be resurrected as the new poet of the people. The poem's Maenads were the prostitutes who consulted with Benn to treat their venereal diseases and offered to compensate him in kind. He rejected them out of loyalty to Herta. Meanwhile, however, he wrote homosexually inclined letters to Oelze in which he suggested that the two of them were to give birth to the new culture. It is only when he completed his poem that Benn conquered his shame regarding his wife's death and could thus undergo a new transformation, leaving the whole Orphic question behind him. He not only soon remarried, but began writing a new kind of leisurely poetry as well.

Benn was aware at the time that he was going through an Orphic cycle. He had experienced the same thing before with two other women. This is why Theweleit uses him as a starting point for his observations regarding the question how the "production of artificial realities" (in short, art) takes place, and what the exact meaning of love is in a writer's life. Theweleit: "The production of artificial reality is not a matter of a single person; there is always a second or third one involved. Likewise, the artistic offspring is produced—or so it seems—by pairs. Men and women are linked together in an Orphic sense by relationships which may well take on the form of love affairs, but are essentially productive relations. The central productive pair seems to be the combination of two men." (Cf. Plato and Socrates, Freud and Fließ, Benn and Oelze, Brecht and Eisler.)

The poet, if he is to continue to make real art, must constantly renew himself. "If he failed to change, he would be at risk of becoming rigid or turning into one of those half-grown monstrosities that invariably border on his production and life: homunculi, Frankensteins, Draculas, and furthermore, journalists, gurus, and assorted spirits whose growth has been stunted, whom he fears to produce or become himself once he loses his grip on the ongoing changes in reality."

As we have seen, artists use the Orphic cycle to effect this renewal. Man uses woman to start off his production, then sacrifices her to enter a new productive cycle. By himself, he cannot produce lovely songs; the beauty of his art he extracts from the female body. It is only through her that he can develop a relationship with "Hades," with death, and with "wildness," with nature. This is where he finds his material. In this cycle, the male is the eternal survivor, the one described by Canetti as a prototype of the "ruler." The male always ends up on the "Ü-Pol," the pole of survival, where, out of shame, he pushes the preceding history into a black hole so he may move on.

But in so doing, he prevents himself from ever learning from it. He thus has no choice but to repeat the same cycle. To "develop" or "grow" becomes impossible; to enter personal history becomes impossible; the "not-quite-born" need to see to their perpetual rebirth, which they accomplish by slaughtering another.

At this point, Theweleit discards his role as detective and turns into mad analyst. He wishes to be neither cop nor judge and to prevent people from saying: "Benn? He's the guy who murdered his wives—Theweleit uncovered it." He is assisted in his attempts by his male partner, Friedrich Kittler, his contemporary student in Freiburg. Women not only work with media—as typists, telephone operators, or secretaries—they are also equated with media (typewriters named Monica). Women may even be used as media themselves. Kittler's surprising discovery was that almost all the writers of the last century fell in love with female typists or dancers.

Theweleit takes the same approach. The artists' urge to stay in touch with changes in reality forces them to connect to new technological media, since it is the latter that initiate and program those changes. "Because media enable new registration techniques, they connect us to reality in other ways than the modes of (dis)connection of previous generations." Since women have a special relationship to the latest media, writers who seek to get in touch with those media invariably do so through a love affair with a woman.

In the six chapters that follow his exposé of historical troubles, Theweleit traces this pattern back through the ages. Dante introduced vernacular literature as a substitute for Latin, by using Beatrice as the medium for the love rush discovered in the Florentine Summer of Love 1296. In 1607, Monteverdi collapsed polyphonous church music with the opera duet, featuring the first female singers instead of castratos. His opera, interestingly enough, was entitled *l'Orfeo*. In a thorough reconstruction, Theweleit demonstrates how Monteverdi was forced by his royal commissioner to alter the romance between man and woman—Orpheus and Eurydice—in favor of the relationship between singer and king. Only art ought to conquer; all human relationships had to fail. The composer's duty extended even to his own life. Theweleit describes this as a general pattern: Every artist who enters into a relationship with power is obliged to see to the failure of his love affairs— which shun power—and to give permanence only to art.

Theweleit discusses episodes from our own age in the lives of Brecht, Hamsun, Rilke, and Kafka. The most bitter chapter is reserved for the relationship between the life and work of Brecht. Theweleit examines a period beginning in Moscow, 1941, and ending in Santa Monica, California. Brecht used Margarete Steffin as his typist and lover and then finally left her to die in Moscow. But that he should write a poem about her death, in which she rises from the dead as a coughing constellation of stars so that Brecht may say to or about her what he likes—this is past Theweleit's limit. Brecht was shameless. And "it is only where shame remains that history is created. Shame allows our access to what actually took place between people."

In his chapter on Kafka, Theweleit follows in the footsteps of Canetti's *Kafka's Other Trial* and Kittler's *Grammophon Film Typewriter*. Kafka's massive correspondence with Felice Bauer connects all the poles charged by Theweleit over the past 1,000 pages. Following a chance encounter, Kafka decided to fall in love with Felice, who was, in fact, employed by Germany's leading manufacturer of dictating machines and had worked as a stenographer for a phonograph record company. Kafka expressed his fascination with the use of media by endlessly proposing to distribute the new recording equipment. At the same time, he used Felice to boost his own art production. He transformed her body into a not yet existing but anticipated or desired device that registers everything. This explains the enormous extent of his "correspondence" as well as his repeated promises of engagement to Felice, all meant to keep his writing going at all costs.

But Kafka transformed his own body, too. In order to compete with modern media, he had to turn himself into a registration device as "objective" as the dictating machine. "Orpheus must tear himself apart if his tape is to register anything." Thus, the reader's expectation that Kafka, too, will go through successive Orphic cycles is disappointed. With Kafka, it is Orpheus himself who descends to the underworld, his Eurydice remaining above. Shortly after the last letter, Felice Bauer married and gave birth to two children. Kafka had come to realize what writing was and could be. Finally, he writes to Milena Jesénkà: "The curious, mysterious, perhaps perilous, perhaps liberating comfort of writing: to stand out in a row of assassins; to observe crime" (the same insight that had occurred to Benn).

Here, Theweleit asks his final question: "Is this the only alternative? To sacrifice the others, or to consume oneself, for the production of artificial realities and, most of all, to write? Or is this sacrificial urge a matter of the extent to which the art medium (language, music, painting, cinema) forms an alliance with political power, or is made to do so, or thinks it must do so—in other words, of the demand in autonomous activity to compete with political power?" These questions he will examine in the next volumes.

Buch der Könige Vol. I ends in 1958, with H.D. (Hilda Doolittle), who, during psychoanalysis, wrote *End to Torment* about the love of her youth, Ezra Pound. She concluded that she had been Eurydice to Pound's Orpheus. Earlier in her life, she had written a poem about Eurydice which began with the lines: "So you have swept me back, I who could have walked with the live souls above the earth." She and Else Lasker-Schüler, an early love of Benn, are the only women mentioned by Theweleit as writer's lovers who realized what their men were doing to them. He claims that these women were able to write without sacrificing anybody because they stood their ground on the "pole of powerlessness." This enabled them to live their "own history" instead of always having to transform themselves in order to begin anew.

Theweleit generalizes the question of guilt regarding the masculine sacrificial urge. Everyone has suffered one or more attempted murders in childhood by the caretakers at whose mercy the child is defenselessly left (he describes how he himself caused a car accident with his pregnant wife sitting in the passenger seat). By accepting this powerlessness, we can avoid always having to end up on the pole of survival again, where we have no choice but to pound others into the ground. From a position of powerlessness, it becomes obvious how impotent everybody else is (what has happened cannot be changed). And that, according to Theweleit, is the beginning of a personal history.

Theweleit is not against "using" others. In keeping with the psychoanalyst Winnicott, he maintains that the other can be used—and thus deranged—as a mature "object," as long as this does not lead to the "consumption" of the person in question, as was the case in the relationships between Benn and Herta von Wedemeyer and between Brecht and Steffin. Even the "object" must be allowed to survive. The same does not apply to Orpheus himself. "With any luck, I'll have written the book at the death of Orpheus," Theweleit concludes his never-ending scroll.

THE LIMITS OF NOISE
ON KLAUS THEWELEIT'S SECOND BOOK OF KINGS

The long-awaited second volume of *Buch der Könige* (*The Book of Kings*) was published in 1994 in two volumes totaling 1,800 pages. Volume 2X, *Orpheus am Machtpol* (*Orpheus at the Pole of Power*), discusses what happens when writers develop the lust for power. In the introduction, Dr. Gottfried Benn along with Ezra Pound, Knut Hamsun, Gertrude Stein, and Céline are cited as examples of modernists who, at the critical point, could not resist defecting and joined the wrong regimes. Theweleit is not interested in the moral aspects of collaboration. He is concerned with the question of exactly what happens when great thinkers make the "mistake" of siding with power of their own free will. Is this the result of a sudden "bedazzlement," a childhood bug, the wrong friends, annoyance with righteous stupidity, outsider status, the moments of weakness of a misunderstood genius? These, after all, are real problems which afflict us all once in a while.

Theweleit devotes most of 2X to the period between 1932 and 1934, during which Gottfried Benn chose to side with the National Socialists. In his case, neither an incomplete birth nor physical armor is the crucial factor in his "turning into a fascist," nor is it a case of his "coming out" as one (assuming he was one all along); rather, we see a combination of resentment at his own impotence and the desire to gain access to the latest medium (in his case, radio). By the end of the 1920's, Benn had exhausted his poetic program, which for 10 years he had managed to keep alive from the poles of the "underdoc" (the subclass's physician), the weak Ego, the need to save mothers, and intoxication. Benn is tired of his insignificant position and yearns for a bit of promotion, recognition, and financial security. Unfortunately, he has few friends among the writing class, nor is he a member of any writer's organization or political party. He finds himself in deep intellectual isolation (not to mention personal, after his girlfriend commits suicide in 1930). Thus, the usual ideological and sociological explanations for why people become fascists apply as little to Benn as the cliché that aestheticism is the breeding ground of fascism. This gives Theweleit the chance to apply his method of power microphysics to Benn's case.

For 600 pages, Theweleit analyzes Benn's day-to-day activities, thoughts, and writings during his transition from apolitical poet to failed party-political agitator, based on a massive amount of sources and documents collected everywhere. Theweleit and Benn make the perfect couple: Theweleit knows all about his partner, none of whose tricks and devices will distract him from his analyses. Theweleit recognizes the taste of Benn's every word, he knows every distinction of that language, he does not have to prove anything; all he wants to do is to put himself into his subject's position, like a private investigator.

The choice faced by the German intellectuals of 1933 was a choice between two mutually exclusive positions. The first one held that "those who fail to speak up now will be silenced forever," the other that "whoever speaks up now will make an eternal fool of himself." The two poles together could not build up the necessary tension to carry out a successful metamorphosis. Thus, as Theweleit makes stunningly clear, Benn missed out again and again in his attempts to become a fascist until finally, to his own good fortune, the Nazis turned their backs on him altogether in 1934. Had the fascists paid any attention to Benn's radio and newspaper speeches, the poet-physician might as easily have ended up one of Nazism's early victims as he might have a Dr. Mengele practicing Aryan population policies. Theweleit distinguishes between Ovidian and non-Ovidian metamorphoses: In the first, the human being changes into a plant, animal, stone, or other natural phenomenon; in the second, the human being attempts to change into anything at all, from fascist to businessman or whatever. "The petty bourgeois is nothing, he is precisely becoming; he used to be, he prospers and perishes, he soars, he falls down."

By 1933, there were two poles of power available to Benn: his radio speeches and his membership in the Prussian Art Academy, Department of Poetry. Through the Academy, he was acquainted with the "Family of Mann." Although Benn would never equal Thomas Mann, his relationship with Heinrich Mann was far more ambivalent. Theweleit successfully demonstrates how a letter from Heinrich, written in the turbulent transitional period around the takeover, played a crucial role. In retrospect, this letter was a potential medium. Heinrich Mann might have publicly supported Benn (thus denouncing attacks in the communist press). Publication of his letter could have offered a middle way out. But Benn had already been publicly accused of fascist sympathies, a charge no one was about to revoke. Klaus Mann knew better; he had thought of Benn as a leftist from the start (being a people's doctor). In 1931, Benn still had two options: He could have swayed to the left or the right. Theweleit shows that, at the time, nobody was unimpeachable. In the end, however, it was a series of small incidents (unfinished manifestoes, unpublished resolutions) that would determine Benn's life for the next 15 years.

Theweleit does not want to apologize for Benn. For a year and a half, Benn consciously adhered to fascism, but he need not have. Benn and his contemporaries were not the subjects of a history of ideas carrying out a nineteenth-century program, starting with German Romanticism and ending in the gas chambers, in an uninterrupted process of decline. In his resistance against the historians of ideas, Theweleit goes so far as to analyze all content (be it loyal or defective) as symptomatic of a psycho-technological disorder in its author. Thus, when Benn himself took to writing a history of ideas (e.g., on the "Spirit and Soul of Future Generations"), Theweleit interprets it as a text that deals only with Benn himself, because, according to Theweleit, no significant artificial reality can be produced on the pole of power. On the contrary, and with reference to Brecht, any text that is written on the pole of power is the result of a desire to kill other people. Whereas the goal of all of Theweleit's writings is to find a way of living/writing that does not victimize and which, firmly entrenched on the pole of powerlessness, will create a history of its own.

But if it is true that ideas only elucidate their inventor's biography, then the thousand pages on Benn, too, must be read as Theweleit's own life story. Perhaps a man who did not find enough recognition himself, who finds himself in an outsider/underdog position, while he had hoped to be a "professional writer"? If this is so, the pole of powerlessness would not be Theweleit's own choice, but one of those microphysical inevitabilities. Fortunately, in September 1995 he received the Adorno prize in Frankfurt's Paulskirche. Moreover, in early 1995 he published a separate collection of essays entitled *Das Land, das Ausland heißt* (*A Foreign Land*), which included analyses of the Berlin Wall as a "German national mass symbol," male childbirth, the Gulf War, memory films like *Shoah* and *Hotel Terminus,* and the outburst of racial hatred circa 1992.

History speaks for itself. What 1933 meant to Benn, 1989 meant to Theweleit. He hooked up to computers, the Wall came down, the Balkans returned, and "I increasingly resented the thought of entering the nineties with a book that dealt exclusively with Benn. It needed more recent items. Especially postwar pop culture, which has forever shifted the paradigms of the art-states, needed to be included in the same book that discussed the art-state which Benn was trying to save for himself in 1933–34." The result was volume 2Y. Again, it is devoted to the "kings" and their male production modes. It begins by elaborating on *Buch der Könige* Vols. 1 and 2X, by analyzing the biographies of Hamsun and Pound. To Theweleit, the present is history, embedded in his own biography. In order to understand the late twentieth century, we must return to Theweleit's primal scene—the sixties, a decade which, for him, started when he read Benn, and culminated in the student movement and, above all, the critical consumption of American pop culture, as personified by Elvis Presley, Andy Warhol, and Jimi Hendrix. It is the same biographical interpretation of history found in Greil Marcus, Camille Paglia, and Germany's leading pop theoretician, Diedrich Diedrichsen—the peers Theweleit tries to match in his 2Y. This illustrates his proposition that texts deal only with their authors.

The Limits of Noise

Volume 2Y, the 834-page *Recording Angels' Mysteries,* may be read as a successful contribution to the society of the debacle, "the courage to fail." Elvis may have been the King, but Theweleit fails to discover convincing proof that he was also an Orpheus. His analysis is no more than a repetition of the corny Oedipus triangle. It is not Elvis's wives, his manager, nor the drugs, but his mother who inspired his songs and performances. But Theweleit lacks a sufficient grasp of the biographic material of his heroes. He suffers from a shortage of evidence. Since Elvis's letters (the critical edition?) remain unpublished, all the detective can do is review the movies. The other major chapter discusses Andy Warhol's monomaniac, planned-productive urges, his sellout to the aboveground, and his emptiness and artificiality as the condition of his continued productivity.

Theweleit and company are not satisfied with analyzing the sixties in terms of mass culture. Rather, it is a matter of having shared a mystical, collective moment at some point. The private and the historical get tragically intertwined. Sadly enough, no fascinating autobiographies (such as Tom Wolfe's *Electric Kool-Aid Acid Test*) are being brought to bear. Theweleit himself is now overcome by the muse and gives in to free association. He no longer analyzes intoxication, but succumbs to it instead. Finally, he borders on the domain of the occult and of numerology with his play on words ("Connect-I-Cut"), his comparison of soup manufacturer Campbell with others who share the same surname, and his notion of Pittsburgh as the secret heartland of American modernity.

At this point, another of Theweleit's weaknesses becomes obvious: his relation to intoxication. In 2Y, his statement that all art results from intoxication and noise turns against him. The material he presents is intended for further analysis, but the reader is not stimulated to take on this task because, by now, arbitrariness prevails. Theweleit's power lies in the fact that he knows how to articulate theoretical allegories. He manages to shed light on cultural patterns whose validity stretches far beyond his own reach or research. But narrative theory is neither literature nor poetry, nor is it an essay, for which it lacks the necessary density. Theweleit is fortunate enough to have a chance to write down his 2,000 pages, abundantly illustrated, at the risk of succumbing to corpulence. The data galaxis produced by popular culture differs significantly from that of literary culture. The detective finds out nothing about musician-actor Presley, or about painter–movie director Warhol. No written evidence of the song's sensuality or the serigraph's emptiness exists. Whenever Gottfried Benn went into ecstasy, it would result in an utterly coherent poem. A large part of Benn's oeuvre consists of an ode to form as the acme of intoxication. Benn uses intoxication to break the conventional, in order to create new forms in uncoded territories. Whenever Theweleit goes into a writer's rapture, his pages fill up with parochial German odds and ends. Even Wim Wenders' embracing of American culture is treated with Oedipal small-mindedness. And all of this despite the fact that Theweleit, provided he does not lose his composure, is capable of the most astonishing insights. Theweleit, like so many of his contemporaries, is at his best when he tries to solve the mystery of fascism—even though that particular twelve-year period was never a part of their "personal experience." The generation of the sixties is brilliant when it comes to the deconstruction of the world before 1945. The manufacture of sixties mythology is left to the media industry, while its analysis is not the strongest point of those who were there. Apparently, to relive one's own past experiences is impossible; it only works with someone else's moments.

VIRTUAL WRITING

"Everybody is a designer."

—John Sasher

1. Designer Media

To make a periodical, you need a format and a design. Then you just let volunteers and free-lancers fill up the columns, people who think they have something to say. A combination of design, marketing, and distribution determines the magazine's success. Content doesn't matter a fuck. But without a content, the conceptual magazine degenerates into designer gloss, interesting only for professionals. The biggest danger for designer reviews is if the buyer takes the product for a professional journal. The empty look tells readers that they are completely free to ignore the content while enjoying the magazine. If they read it anyway, the word-order is pure coincidence and the provocative quotes, sharp observations, and intriguing associations are an added attraction. Design should be both indeterminate and distinct at the same time. If the image is too strong, the whole thing will be perceived as lifestyle, so that design turns into fashion. As a useless product, design must remain in the model stage to keep one step ahead of hype. It must constantly renew itself through software investments. When a program is understood, it can be thrown away.

For centuries, the book was marked for its contents. The creative monks' designer bibles weren't intended for reading, either. Church Latin had a nice typeface, but it was the pictures that made it ("Were the evangelists moonlighters?"). The male couple of Gutenberg and Luther put an end to this pleasure of text. Only in the era of designer media, in which words have been revalued as random ASCII, has author-related content become superfluous again. The status of books and the prestige of their authors vanish as soon as we realize that they have to make it within six weeks and will disappear from the shelves if they haven't in three months. In the book trade, a vertically stored book is a dead book. The ground material called "book" has fallen into the hands of the window dresser. As soon as the book object stops presenting itself as commodity and avoids the *Gesamtkunstwerk* of the bookstores, it loses its setting and embarks on an unpredictable odyssey. The search for a given title acquires a sporting aspect, while to read the work itself requires an uncontemporary dedication which can only be produced

141

from behind a battery of answering machines, faxes, and disconnected door-bells. Once the designer book discards style, subject, author, and the market, it acquires the brilliance of the prodigious. Design speculates on the exis-tence of the unknown, which it discovers at the moment of design; it seeks not to exploit but to escape.

2. Accuracy Through Obscurity

The computer network liberates writers from their publishers. Unencumbered by reputation or oeuvre, the eager author can hurl one book after another directly onto the Net. Should your masterpiece be wiped off the newsgroups in 10 days, you can park it on your personal homepage, FTP site, or BBS for the benefit of the virtual community. Writers can save their books from certain destruction on the paper market. The only thing that matters to the collection of connected files are the tags. "*Weltfremdheit*" or "discipline research" activate different search functions than "safe writing" or "Ferdinand Kriwet." Electronic writers receive a daily, comprehensive liter-ary update, and this has its consequences. Deconstruction software reveals what grammatical, rhetorical, and educational tricks make a text bearable, in spite of its pol/cul/sex content. The quality of world literature is on the rise. If you can follow the writing activities of renowned authors, the question of how they do it is quickly answered. It's a dizzying thought that earlier gen-erations wrote their books with ineradicable ink. This is why programs are being developed on demand to produce textual-critical editions even while writing, and send these dozens of versions hourly to the fleet of hard discs that record culture in atomic shelters. To give their texts that little extra that separates literature from the rest, authors throw their personality into the struggle: the unique combination of gene package, cultural cross-overs, salient biographical data, and education as used by a Camille Paglia, Donna Tart, Elisabeth Bronfen, or Jung Chang.

The text that chooses to appear in the network instead of on the table strives for the greatest possible economy of the word. Reading pleasure used to be based on piling stylistic ornaments on top of story lines. The literary cal-culator now recognizes this as noise and an obstacle to communication. The electronic readers have all their texts pre-scanned, filtering out added value. For example, there exists a kill-file which destroys all sources and examples from 1989 (or 2012 for that matter), a quotation-eraser that gets rid of every-thing in quotation marks, the command "skip interdisciplines," which erases everything expect the reader's specialization, "create summary," which sum-marizes a text according to the reader's wishes, and "show method," which shows self-referential excerpts and takes out all the exercises. "Textual cleansing shareware" provides access to such mega-oeuvres as that of Goethe, Simenon, Dilthey, Marx, Konsalik, Vestdijk, Balzac, Heidegger, Voltaire, D'Annunzio, and Agatha Christie: The final technological solution to Althusser's shame at not having read the complete Hegel and Kant.

Virtual Writing

Human beings feel a biological urge to string words together before striking the first hard sentence. At the end of the day, writing that makes use of the selection programs preserves the three sentences that withstood the test. Text production the following day starts with those three sentences. Less radical are the help files that remove mistakes, prevent platitudes, and point out bad journalistic habits. The selection program removes all sentences with constructions like "The eminent authority . . . " or " . . . justly remarked . . . ," or the use of italics to prop up weak sentences. The compact text naturally has the density of a summary, the quality of poetry; it conceals a poor understanding of foreign languages, suppresses every tendency toward explanation formalities and replaces the snail's pace of reason with the brilliance of the keyword. The point is to formulate knowledge so precisely and with such complexity that it cannot be hacked by someone else's software. Writing on computers must never reach a conclusion; if it did, the train of thought that produced it would have to be left out. Sentences no longer seek a relationship with their predecessors or offspring. Conjunctions like *because, thus, since, however,* and *but* have been scrapped. In principle, any sentence can follow any other. The mystery of text is that an order of sentences does indeed exist. Text wants to be one step ahead of imagination and accelerates to the point of absurdity. It does not need the logic of machine language. One in a thousand texts contains something new, so that there emerge unlikely correspondences ("between a camera and a fish eye, what are Hindi-telephones?") which stimulate the fantasy. Compressed text is precise and obscure. It evokes a hidden world of thought which apparently no longer needs to be reported. The Nettext is becoming concrete, while readers arrive at a level of abstraction not usually accessible. With all the exit signs that have been placed throughout the text, tourism in abstraction is easy to endure.

3. Writing Without a Carrier

Traditionally, writing involved storage on clay tablets, parchment, paper, or hard disk. Virtual writing means producing a language that only exists in the main memory. On-line text turns the written word into an unstable medium. There is no Nobel prize for the best telephone conversation. All of your genius or love for humanity is lost forever once you hang up. What the Hittites, Aztecs, Mayans, and other vanished cultures talked about will always remain a mystery to us. The written word causes single events. When text becomes as ephemeral as the spoken word, it ceases to be evidence. It does not need to preserve or transmit any culture. Contextless writing does not aim to retell or transmit stories and does not seek to degenerate into some mythological stage. It practices a now-and-nevermore kind of communication and sharpens punctual consciousness. Language turns out capable of correctly transmitting our intentions when undistracted by body language or its setting. "When you narrow the bandwidth, you focus the message."

Actually existing cyberspace is a text-based environment, not because of a cultural decision, but because of a technological limitation that people have to live with at the end of the 1900's. The transient computext represents the ironic reemergence of the written word, after the word had already been declared dead by the new visual culture. Writing has succeeded in renewing itself by finding a new mass medium. All books can be resold anew on CD-ROM. The bookstore can survive, just like the library-cum–data bank. The melancholy warriors for the preservation of the written word should demand that all of humanity goes on-line as soon as possible. Literacy is learning to type on a keyboard.

In the global democratic conspiracy to prevent the convergence and synergy of mass- and written culture, Sega and Nintendo have moved toward non-literary visual interfaces which require no command of language. "Text for some, images for all." The speed whereby the Internetionale spread through the early nineties reveals the strength of textual culture. Virtual writing is the written word's answer to designer media because it is not in search of material form, which is by definition too contemporary. The primitive nature of on-line text exceeds design. The ephemerality of real-time media ignores all good intentions of stylists and conservationists. If writing has been cornered by design in the paper world, it has created a new, free space in the electronic universe.

THE SOCIETY OF
THE DEBACLE
CRITIQUE OF ADULTERATED REASON

Now that the historical figure of the bastard has emancipated into an esteemed member of the single-parent family, he can grow up in all innocence and turn into a fairly grand aesthetic category. Cruelty gives way to beauty (the united bastards of Benneton). By definition seduction incarnate, the bastard is the visible result of an irresponsible high. The modern bastard self-confidently radiates the harmony of a novel genetic, cultural, and technological disposition.

The illegitimate kid as prototype of the Artificial Child (AC) is a figure from the age of the bourgeois family. The nineteenth century was populated by cast-off serving-girls and governesses. Sanctimony made sure that a slip in marriage was covered up in the cloak of love.

Evoking the tender memory of the possibility of innocent love, the bastard is, in the official version, a victim of rape, racism, double moral standards, or world history. Nonetheless, it has been a long time since there has been a slot for him in official statistics. Instead, he returns as a therapeutic case. Child of circumstances, product of shredded families, this miscarriage of a failed marriage is searching for his own father and mother, his own land and language. Is all this really so lamentable?

Christianity provides us with the basic model of the organized bastard. Jesus of Nazareth had a mother, to be sure, but who's the father? Trying to answer this tricky question evolved into a world religion. The savior, as provided for by tradition, has blond locks and blue eyes. To complete this picture, it should be noted that he was born in a barn and brought to Egypt on a saddle, mere pedantic details. The illegitimate status of the Christ Child functions as a bridge to the sacred, the metalegal. Normally we can only expect a few saints per time-space package. As soon as the crisis breaks out, they are allowed to utter their prophecies.

The crooked-legged bastard Aryan, Adolf Hitler, is an expert in this field: "The stronger must rule and must not merge with the weaker which fritters his own magnitude away." Elsewhere he postulates the "valid thesis that all racial mixing will sooner or later cause the bastard's fall so long as the superior element of this crossing remains clean in a context halfway resembling a race." Hence he judges the political situation in the following manner: "the race is 'negrotized' at such a rapid rate that one can really speak about the origination of an African state in Europe. A mighty undivided European-African mulatto state is growing up from the Rhine to the Congo."

Hitler gave expression to an anxiety that has changed today into a desire for miscegenation. Hitler was right about his mulatto kingdom, and so much the better. His passionate warnings are completely out of date. They show that he was still struggling with his own dubious origins. This is true of all interest in the corrupted. Higher or lower, fatter or thinner, darker or lighter, shorter or longer, stronger or weaker: have fun and good luck with the assembly of your "own" identity!

When biological science carried out more exact investigations, it turned out that even today 10 percent of children do not owe their genes to their legal fathers; a healthy situation, one might say. At present the race needs fresh, wild genes from the outside to stay in shape. The blood bastard is fully emancipated and has advanced from genealogical impurity to the enrichment of a genetic landscape that would otherwise be stunted and dissipated (and degenerated, or so the dominant ecological discourse would have it). If you can't sit in the sun any more owing to the ozone hole, you simply adopt a few darker genes into the bloodline. As a professed anti-racist remarked on TV: "In the coming years, all Europeans will simply become a little browner."

The bastard comes from the concept of racial purity and functions as a counterpoint to the cultic family performing rites at the front door. The bastard stands for the realistic recognition that there is no way to hold back nature and that we must consciously live with the consequences of the raceless species. Taking up the testator from the second line into our midst insures that private pragmatism can unfold. From this point on the bastard is not disadvantaged from the outset but has to prove himself like everybody else. Now that the family as the highest form of nepotism is also faced with its decline and fall, one can devote oneself to purifying one's own actions. "I'm PC, you're PC": the dawn of psychocracy. From today on one cannot push the blame on the forefathers with their nature and nurture. This is the time of submission to the dictatorship of the future. Fate no longer chases you but you have to chase it yourself. If you wait passively, you will be passed right and left and nothing will happen at all: the condition of millions of parked lives.

Now the cultural bastard gets to work realizing himself, and has problems with the question of authentic ethnicities. He must always represent his mixture. Cultural criticism remains fixed on the analysis of individual influences in order to raise them to an ethnic, humanistic, and religious plateau. After the explanation follows the promotion to higher culture.

But there is the obvious question of actually existing miscegenation and defilement. This explains why the concept of the bastard will never disrupt the existing order. Impure thought does not observe the limits imposed on cross-fertilization. It parasitizes the beauty of its own impurity. Mixed intelligence lives off of the grace of forgetfulness, morbid fascination, false arguments, and impure motives. It does not promote change but realizes it without being particularly aware of the fact; codes are never decoded but perverted. The bastardized intellect is shaking the bars caging the strong concept. Negativity, as long as it cannot be implemented or arrive at consensus, can carry it a long way and leave existent conditions behind. Clear ideas are of no particular interest to the bastard. Rather he fiddles around in order to cause a short-circuit, always on the lookout for those flashes of thought which are necessarily followed by thunder, on occasion effecting a direct hit or refreshing creativity.

The bastard feeds on decaying fashions, not with the intention of recycling them but with the conviction that the whole is always the untrue. Contaminated knowledge recognizes that truth has its weaknesses, handicaps, superfluities, lack of motivation, and poor PR techniques. Catastrophe no longer hits us but simply passes by. The bastard interrupts the great lines and muddies the clarity of future dreams. He is at the edge of failure, tilting the perspective of good—not from joy in the certainty of failure but from devotion to the transit of the Occident as it smears the pristine purity of boundary-lines.

After the fascination with evil of the 1980's, we now face the failure-hype. We no longer read about seduction, simulation, perfection, glamour, and passion as pure self-expression. Evil had to delete all of the good of the 1960's and was magnificently successful (cf. the breakthroughs of 1989). But later something else came after all. The triumph of the dialectic, the historical synthesis of market and democracy, never occurred, nor could a new antithesis be found. Good socialism rightly gave way to the capitalism of failure. The system and its serfs underwent a revaluation of all values, and in the meantime nothing has changed—an indefinite situation in which nobody was concerned any longer to express the world and one's own ego (and everything related to them) in words. Chaos rules, and this does not stimulate illegal visualizations. Timeless struggle in the guise of destructive private initiative takes place in the midst of rotting cement and bankrupt governmental structures. Here the heroic appearance of the proclaimed end of history is lacking. Spectacular society plunges us unexpectedly into the society of the debacle. "We learn from Guy Debord."

The heathen faith in new media, project management, production control, flexible planning, retraining, improvisation, image, and identity is the tried and true method for introducing new techniques. At first, the functioning of all those curious machines and concepts causes amazement. But once they are generally accepted and actually do their jobs, attention shifts to the moments in which methods and techniques fail, and then they are immediately written off. Once normality is achieved, every cyber technology loses its nimbus and can be routinely employed. Once hard- and software fail to fulfill their promise, consumer rage turns against the machines and their producers. It is magnificent to give way to rage and to throw all the miscarried machinery out of the window, heaps of them piled on the street!

Grunge and Generation X have mobilized the authenticity of elementary failure against the spandex-shine of revoked success. The breakthrough of stagnation is the surprising turn that history has completed since 1989. As long as the end of progress was still being announced, nothing happened. But the philosopher of liberation, Fukuyama, could not foresee that bungling would win out. To be sure, self-organizing principles like chaos, artificial life, fractality, Internet, complexity, Biosphere II, and turbulence are optimistically engaged, but are stuck in their advertising phase. Consequential cancerous metastasis is not achieved and they remain models. Failure on the contrary is in principle not a model, much less a strategy. In this respect, it distinguishes itself from everything that the eighties provided by way of ideas. Downfall is not fate: fate approaches from the outside while the fiasco comes from within without having been able to be programmed ahead of time. The inherent disappointment that unfolds is not a bug that can be removed from the program. In the age of overorganization and a social experiential surplus, avoiding a flop has turned out to be a swamp in which thoughts of success have bogged down. Attempts are still made to redefine failure as an educative moment, but Omo Power, Intel's Pentium Chip, Microsoft's Windows 95, Philips's CD-I, atomic power, the reunification of Germany . . . they all turned out strong concepts which, though not unpromising, led to nothing.

One is mistaken on two fronts: one can accept the wrong position to the correct object or grab the wrong theme by the scruff of the neck and stretch the correct theory over it. After pop culture's loser pose we now have insight into the failure of theory. Derrida confesses that "my Grammatology missed the point." Just like Lacan, who admits that the unconscious is not structured like language after all. Too bad for an entire generation of doctoral students. Now all we are waiting for is a study about Nietzsche's complete wash-out— the eternal return is not possible at all! The Superman is merely a bastard. Sometimes it is said of Marx *ex cathedra* that he was mistaken . . . But what is to remain of Ryle's concept of mind if John Garang decides to use it as the basis for his Southern Sudanese government? The age of random thinking is at hand.

Total falsification does not diminish the possible value of disavowed theory. At close examination, thinking is not concerned with the question how the world is put together but how it organizes itself when observed in a particular manner. The present intellectual climate is dominated by a skeptical consumption of discourse: can anything be done with it, does it represent anything, is it about anything, can something practical be done with it, are there any pictures, is it easy to read, isn't it too complicated, does it lead anywhere, is it marketable, is it convincing at all, is it all really true, can one score with it? The problem with Foucault's notion of "discourse" is that it is unbeatable (or so the cover tells us). Discourses may weaken, digress, take a radical turn, spread out over the entire field of reality, penetrate the most intimate places, be suppressed, seize power, or become a counterforce, but they cannot be exposed by lie detectors. They always exude more of the same truth. In general, discourse is not dealt with publicly, but slyly operates backstage. Will the media discourse ever fail or founder completely, so that everybody will suddenly decide that they have better things to do? You can bet it will.

Provocative Watching

"We're in the Boredom-Killing Business"

Television has left the wall unit to go all the way down. It's been equipped with little wheels to maximize domestic mobility. The late-medial receiver sprawls across the couch, bed, chaise longue, or floor, cuddled up with a pillow and stuffed animal. Video ergonomics leaves the chair (where once the modern monarchs took stock of their media-glacis) untouched and researches horizontal reception. The royal scepter has become a remote control used to admit or dismiss channels. The inner experience of half-sleep in front of the screen is periodically interrupted by visits to the refrigerator, lavatory, or telephone. "Where's the ashtray?" Is this the post-human condition so often discussed, or is that something reserved exclusively for the "other"? The slumped video condition never directly admits the images to perception. Once, TV watching was mediated by radio and television guides and domestic affairs. Slouching in front of the tube, viewing critically, the pace of the serials, the couch potato's total addiction, staring in fascination at the fluctuations of light intensity: all are legends of a distant television era. Today, we speak of filtered watching: a psycho-chemical magnifying glass has been inserted between the naked eye and the radiant tube. Viewers are no longer vulnerable, naked, and innocent, but themselves manipulate the images, including them in personal leisure activities at will. The image regime of yore, ruling over the docile, homogeneous masses, has itself become an inert jumble of icons, ready for unrestrained revision. The trajectory of internalization has been reversed; the images are now assigned the theoretical grid of the relaxed subject. Video artists who wish to breach this order are going to need a lot of violence-and-panic aesthetics.

Audiovisual media have not resulted in the anticipated "inundation by stimulation," but in a supreme state of mind. A space has been created between the classical transmitter and receiver, in which awareness can temporarily expand toward total control over every input. The best quality indicator for video clips and related genres is hashish and its designer variants. Herbal tea, café au lait, a microbrew, a Coke, a glass of wine, LSD, or XTC may as well produce unsuspected dimensions and one-shot viewing pleasure links. Everyone can be a fifteen-minute brilliant media theoretician. The unbearable state of current affairs has been reduced to archetypal proportions. There is comfort in the poetic experience of historical constants (for want of something better to do). Watching someone else's mental images is a form of temporary entertainment which can be extracted from the wealth of historical ideologies. But this is more than mere noncommitment; it is to glance at the final fateful hour. Drugs in hand, we descend into the very blueprint of the collective unconscious. Once beyond interpretation, we are surrounded by the thousand plateaus, here, on this simple weeknight, and all thanks to video. We should not underestimate the dialectics of quite ancient and new media. The technological images mentioned by Flusser draw on an immense, but limited universe: there is nothing new to be found. The attraction of media art is that it allows us to observe the entry systems themselves: Drugged perception consists of exercises in the perception of metastructures. Just as Hillary's account of the first climb of Mount Everest will always make for fascinating reading, even though nowadays we can simply rent a Sherpa helicopter to take us to the top from Base Camp I, so too are video art and computer animation of lasting value. Sooner or later, every experiment is fit into an all-night epic that mustn't necessarily be zapped to bits.

The habit of replacing the old test patterns with all-night aquarium broadcasts (with viewers making furious phone calls about silverfish floating upside down on the surface)—or a video loop of a ride on the back of a garbage truck, a boat through the waters of Berlin or Amsterdam, or a one-way German express train—is an appeal to the normality-inducive characteristics of the zero medium. The attraction of home viewing through security cameras that would otherwise register only audiences appears to be self-sufficient. The question of why this should not be interesting can no longer be answered. In criticism, normality appears under two headings: one pacifying (stupefying television), the other incendiary (mass killers copying TV patterns). The influence of television is thought to have two mutually exclusive extremes, resignation and blind rage, which at the same time represent two aspects of one and the same popular awareness. But normality is always outside of the subject, who gains access to it through intoxication. To the user, the world is everything as it happens to be—all else is superfluous. The material at hand is taken for granted, and enhanced judgment (-through-joy) is not concerned with the critical note that starts off the debate, but with a medial-input analysis that will culminate in a maximum matter-of-factness and outshine all controversies. Ecstatic resignation has a biological basis, and does not result from any cognitive-rational understanding of commonplace affairs: Watching is not a mathematical formula, but a chemical process. Whether it's brutal violence or a corny game show that's being served up, the home front, with its superior outlook, is chiefly interested in its own perceptive reactions, not in the battle of signs that takes place on screen. All images are abstract; they become actual through the suspense created between the content of ideas that remains absolutely clear within the viewer's hypertransparent frame of mind, and the production of bodily juices which occurs now and then, despite everything. Only within the glands can normality be produced; all else is artificial exaggeration.

Today, virtual reality presents itself as the media junkie's methadone. After kicking the habit, the clean synapses need to be offered an attractive alternative. Here, the advantage of video becomes obvious, in that it offered a distance to the image through which viewers could let their creativity flow. VR tries to beat the narcotic three-dimensional interpretation of the two-dimensional screen with the promise of a multifaceted, expanding, iconographic empire to keep you high. Yet VR, with its pseudo-menus, offers hardly a choice. It presents not a trip to the heart of the machine, but a program treasure hunt, an interactive holiday for the eco-minded citizen who prefers this artificial trek to disturbing the remnants of nature. Off the road through cyberspace is not included in the package; you cannot impose your own programs on the entertainment presented. In VR, no matter how far you travel, you never leave the library. The transcendence of the pictorial mountain achieved by the videonomous end-user has been taken out of the cybernaut's datagloves. Now smart drugs are being developed that will allow the production of the most astonishing syntheses, even in VR.

Since it is becoming clear that VR will never surpass the game-room level, the attempt is now to hasten the promised absorption by images through existing telecom accessories. In order to renew connected humanity's interest in the television screen's constitution, the industry is now developing interactive TV, the main motor of which is home shopping. The solitary human being's natural tendency to talk to objects is addressed by those firms who manage to buy access to one network or another. Hair conditioners may be sampled on-screen, ordered by phone, and delivered at your doorstep by messenger services. The object's answer is to deliver truckloads full of flashy gowns, electronic gadgets, and porn movies to the interactivist's home. Teleshopping's educational objective is to make the viewers realize that to switch on the television is to leave the home. Telephonic consciousness must be transported to the TV medium. An impulse-buy in a shop is still an act of relative individuality. The home shopping industry hopes to transform the pre-pay-TV era's receptive rapture into the consumerist ecstasy of "buying-power watching" on two-way channels. We do not yet know exactly what is ruining interactivist thinking; the danger that the expanded viewers will never get down to the decision-making process, will skip the stages of multimedia initiation and elaboration altogether, or will leave the choice of channels to knowbots programmed to their personal preferences, or watch standard channels only, or do something completely different . . . Flick-it-yourself TV is a test of the old premise that the subject in front of the screen is willing to want, think, judge, act. It's comforting to dwell among the temporary autonomous flocks every now and again: a moment of relaxation from the everyday demand for unique creativity.

Provocative Watching

Narcotics enhance our understanding of the nature of media power. They do not produce new inner images, but offer control over the complete old external image package. Drugs do not reduce, distort, or prevent reception; rather, they give the viewer the power of direction, a fact that is hard to accept for the media persons who thought of themselves as situated at the heart of the power disposition centered around technological images, but which considerably increases the silent majorities' joy of living. What remains for the intellectuals, having only just conquered their own alcoholism, is deconstruction sports. This mental fitness training is the current approach to the video medium: to scan all channels for possible fasc/rac/sexism and the according level of political correctness. The media designers are well aware of this, laying their traps for every conceivable cultural-critical viewpoint. Many representatives of the theoretical classes have already defected to the other side of images, taking great satisfaction in the maelstrom of interpretations they evoke and manipulate. Contemporary illustrated stories already offer so much deconstruction by themselves as to dismantle the critical view by its own methods. Reichean movements, Eco-style mass culture, classical Freudianism, new-age healing through blending in with the natural picture, fundamentalist selection methods: All these outlooks appear to add to the synergism of the entire media package as edu- and infotainment. Video is no longer watched as a means to get carried away, but is an interpretable and temporary cultural product from beginning to end. What has Hollywood come up with this summer? What lasting values does European cinema have in store for us this time? What's interesting in video is its production process and financial boards, not the final visual experience. All that counts is the aesthetics of production conditions. The awareness that everything is an expression of the zeitgeist is the most rewarding form of historicism. "A responsible video from the Clinton era; a fine example of nineties engagement."

So far, reality TV defines itself in relation to classical media-user numbness: the rough image is expected to kick the spoiled viewers where they had it coming, a strategy aimed at charging the weakened image package with raw energy. The inevitable consumer's answer is: "Bring me another Coors!" Reality is just another marketing stunt. What's more exciting is the cold turkey of drug-free watching. To sit through the edit, shaking and in a cold sweat—to look the medium straight in the eyes, without the dope, in defiance of any productive relations. Those who place their bets on the return of traditional boredom will note that the image has already adjusted to the masses' level of intoxication to the point where it is impossible to follow without physical intensification. Detox is an attempt to witness the second demise of the Occident—by watching without either being manipulated or manipulating the images yourself. The existential moment of video arises when the viewers and their videos are linked up beyond all power structures. All iconographic metaphysics, every superstructure or supreme violence disappears; all that the viewer without qualities observes is the picture lines passing by. In the material manifestation of the image, we are welcomed by pixels. Techné is a friend for life.

ELECTRONIC LONELINESS

"Change the world; stay at home." Such is the adage of the social ergono-mists who distill a political constitution out of the user-friendliness of con-sumer electronics. The pliability of society having been examined from every angle, the private is now assumed to contain a reservoir of diligent self-reg-ulation just waiting to be tapped. Post-sociologists disguised as trend-tasters project all their reborn enthusiasm onto the homestead. Concerned for the army of stranded white- and blue-collar workers, they seek methods to lift them from their state of anomie and unproductivity through home terminals. Individual enthusiasm for technogadgets is transformed into hope for an eco-nomic revival. Home installation of new media appears to have provoked a working condition. The combination of data highway and enhanced televi-sion leads to an irreversible return of the cottage industry in the form of vir-tual looms. The idea is that the countryside will flourish again, traffic jams disappear, the environment be saved and the family be restored. And who in his or her right mind wouldn't support just that?

In the age of the shop floor, open-plan office, canteen, and conference room, there was still a political work climate. It was still a matter of spatial proximity and visible hierarchical relationships within a broad technological circuit that encouraged the integration of specializations. The commitment to material production induced compulsory solidarity. This lay at the basis of twentieth-century corporate dreams, from Fordism and Taylorism to Japanese management techniques and New Age. The labor unions saw to the pacification of ever-latent labor unrest. Thus, in the postwar West there arose a configuration which guaranteed the manageability of social dynam-ics, a permanent reorganization which ultimately resulted in industrial underutilization. When, in an analogous development, socialist/communist passion slipped out of the picture, the social question shifted from the factory gates to the individual doorstep. The home thus became the object of fantasy for political economists and other social visionaries.

Today, those who take early retirement are simply unmotivatible and are in fact written off. These gray masses belong to the industrial past; they make inroads on the last resources of the welfare state and are otherwise ignored. Yet it is they who consciously dedicated their active lives to interior design. The postwar generation discovered the home as a leisure object and mirror image of the self. Renovation and redecoration became their life fulfillment and relational therapy: an open kitchen for an open marriage. What mattered was the order of purchase and correct arrangement of refrigerator, hi-fi set, bedroom suite, floor lamp, motorbike, lawnmower, awning, and washing machine. A special place was reserved for the means of communication: the car outside and the TV set indoors. The home was a sanitorium where you got the right treatment, a shelter for the practice of family ideals. The fatal turn came with the belated insight that we had all been working toward a realized Utopia where no one could survive for long. The whole collection of luxuries turned into dead capital. The social function of the family reception room gave way to the active temporary arrangement of support functions geared toward the individual. The excess of stuffy knickknacks has been replaced by a carefully selected mix of sanitary objects. This combination of stylized and functional ambiance prepared the home for its current transformation into workplace.

Visions of home telework are on a par with wishful thinking about robots, artificial intelligence, and organ transplants. They appeal to a future stage of development, as yet unknown but imaginable. Working at home terminals creates a work situation that lacks all the traditional attributes (physical exertion, collegiality, competition, movement, noise, dirt). Everything which used to make work such a nuisance seems to have disappeared. Machine operation by the few guarantees the prosperity of the many at home. But the internalized urge to work cannot bear this seeming idleness which is scarcely recognized as such by unemployment statistics. A sense of urgency must be created, a feeling that we've all got to work together to prevent a social regression to decadence, crime, and entropy. The delightful promise is that the masses will have something to do again and can thus be kept at bay. At home, we are invaded by science fiction: Spaceships lodge in the living room and the impression is that everybody is on a virtual journey into space. From "We're here to go" to "We're here to stay": Don't call us, we'll call you.

Video games, 800 numbers, interactive media, and home shopping have created the right mood and acquainted us with the necessary tactile skills to work at a distance for cash. Now, all we have to do is stimulate the decision makers to equip the telesector with the required technological and ideological infrastructure. We can support them by articulating our commitment to create a perspective on economic activities within a positive climate of collective individuals. The axiom of self-realization is casually slapped onto telework: You cannot become a full person unless you make yourself useful. No identity without activity. Pep talks, training, and performance evaluations have to prepare the individualized masses for digital piecework.

Telework is not an institution but a constitution, a frame of mind to nourish the new work effort. It is a matter of psychology before anything else: What used to be called apathy, being glued to the TV set, has become a first requirement for job performance. Isolation must be conditioned to this end: Individuals are locked up in niches where they are at one with the network.

Electronic Loneliness

We are urged to keep our minds on the screen, for it is all we have. No flourishing family life or professional adultery awaits us; even the promised outlet of virtual sex is a dead end. All we are left with is the bill. Since chance meetings have been ruled out, dating services bring us video presentations and careful matching and screening techniques to line up desire with the matching package. No sooner have visiting rights been settled than our all-too-human imperfections rear their heads to pose an acute obstacle before the affair has even begun. By and large, the other is unbearable. The other's ever-absent radiance and perfection form a social basis for boredom and apathy. Intercourse is stifled, and the tele-existences remain otherwise invisible and meaningless to one another. Martin Buber, where are you?

Traditionally, the home has always been the abode of children and their grandparents, but there is no room for that anymore. It's just that people have other things on their minds. By all practical standards, the telehovel has become intolerant of children. In this empty, coated environment, there is no room left to create a world of your own. Visits have been canceled and are generally frowned upon; they can only disrupt the programmed order of the day. Little people are firmly caught in a monitored development scheme. Ever since their moment of conception, they have been clones of a cultural ideal. They are made for perfection. And woe to them who fail to live up to this investment in their opportunities. Play has become education, as exemplified by computers. For example, Nintendo education lays the medial foundation for future generation gaps. Those who have already grasped computers at age four will never experience the Net as the domain of rebellion. So they hang around on the streets, the ultimate forbidden territory (weapons, drugs, sex, fashion, joyriding). Outside is still the domain of the informal, of indefinite chance: fighting over nothing, making out, long waits, breakaways, accidents.

The parents, meanwhile, remain chained to their home terminals, forever unable to break free. They find their peers in miscellaneous media and use them to share their despair. Locked inside a perfect world, they simply cannot imagine that anyone would have it any other way. The primary socialization of people into ill-behaved adolescents, with all the accompanying biological deviations, makes the media into meaningless institutions that neither exercise authority nor manage to inspire. It is the same as with other toys: After the initial thrill they are simply tossed aside. Modern parents lose their last anchor, now that even computers no longer offer a solution. There is no way back, now that the family as a network has been disrupted. The family was never functional to begin with. If anything, it resembled a hedonistic pack, unable to think of better pastimes than harassment, gossip, fooling around, blood and mayhem, ambitious plans, bad eating habits, excessive drinking, and disenchantment.

Actually existing electronic loneliness cannot be expressed in metaphysical or psychiatric terms. It is not a matter of profound melancholy but of shallow artificiality. Desolation is a fatal production factor, a trap one stumbles into by reckless thinking and believing in daydreams. Only organized tourism is still considered a way out: the assembly of a collection of psycho-physical experiences, from meditation, repentance, exhaustion, ecstacy, fasting, and pilgrimage to heroic relief campaigns. But none of these sensations can help one brace oneself for that highly personal confrontation with the machine. Pulling the plug on the Net means suicide. There is no future without the Net, and there are no alternative scenarios left. Nothing seems to prevent the advance of enclosures. We have finally left the age of despair. Get serious. Emotions have settled within the archeological layers of consciousness, in an age in which the history of attitudes is being recorded. The Net as the ideal merry-go-round for self-styled identities will neither create revolutionary situations nor bring the world to an end. Cybernetic emptiness need not be filled, nor will it ever be (with desire, disgust, nor unrest). Finally, telematic energy will disappear into the flatland of silence. Commands may still flicker on the screen, but it is you who have disappeared.

THE REVOLT OF THE
MEDIA ECOLOGISTS

The innocence of the media is no more. A period of stagnation will follow the rampant growth of the 1980's. This is foreshadowed by the propagation of a mentality of moderation. It is made clear to us from all sides that we must stop handling information and images carelessly. Henceforth, the media and data traffic, like other sectors of Western society, must submit their presentation to the diktat of ecology. The environment is more than endangered plants and animals. It is a mentality which, with abstract concepts like "conservation" and "recycling," sees the constructed media sphere as a third or fourth nature. Watchfulness prevails against all possible needless pollution and senseless waste.

Aware media users find a natural equilibrium between receiving and transmitting information. After the euphoria of getting acquainted with the new technologies, they seek a balance between the immaterial environment which evokes imaginary worlds and the biographical one where their own flesh lives. This balance is considered necessary to protect the pioneers in data land (who are working at the "electronic frontier") from cold turkey. After the ecstacy of the emancipation phase we see a dissatisfaction in technoculture, and it may be seeking a destructive way out. High expectations all too easily end in great disappointment, which inspires hate for the machinery. Deleuze and Guattari would simply call it "antiproduction"; the sudden disgust that arises in those who have allowed themselves to be swept away in the flows of signs. Could this be the "drama of communication" (freely adapted from Alice Miller)—that at the moment we only receive and are sending no signals back? Or vice versa: that we are putting too much data into the world, without getting anything back for it?

Among data workers a feeling of emptiness and senselessness is arising, which can only temporarily be compensated for by the introduction of yet more hard- and software. Perhaps an ecological therapy can help; in any case that is what the media ecologists G. Steiner and H. J. Syberberg suggest in their publications.

The body seems likely to evaporate from a long stay in the medial milieu. Along with the boundaries of the personal environment, the definition of one's own body is growing vague as well. But before the critical limit

159

of virtual reality is transgressed, the ecosophers want to protect us. They look wistfully back to the long-ago era when authenticity and real presence so flourished, in an attempt to salvage what they can.

The establishment of permanent media has produced a new longing for direct contact without all those mediating bodies and elaborate prostheses. The unbridled colonization of personal life must be temporarily halted. At the end of the eighties people suddenly expressed annoyance at the tapestry of media we all had to eat through in order to keep up on things. Not more magazines, TV series, and computer software! Not more world-shocking media events! The media diet people automatically imposed on themselves lest they get swamped was becoming the done thing. Boredom and indifference mingled with active forms of refusal to keep consciously consuming. Best-sellers could be left unread, TV could be watched zapping, sleeping, or not at all. Unconscious registration of the headlines proved enough for keeping up in conversation.

The French theories from the 1970's, which turned against concepts like unity, truth, and meaning and practiced unrestrained deconstruction and difference, were no match for the supersonic world of simulation. Endless text production turned out to offer no solution, but rather to cause the problem. Moaning and groaning about the excess of interpretations turned into a public lament that appealed to many.

According to the media dietitians' diagnosis, we are currently in a media vacuum caused by the drivel of journalists and the endless academic discourse of the specialists. We live, they say, in a corrupt world where the parasites of the secondary call the shots. These second-rate writers and filmmakers who populate editorial centers make sure every original experience is nipped in the bud. According to this media criticism, a real present no longer exists, just imaginary zones, indirect discourses, and staged events. Above all, access to the work of art is being closed off to us by a garbage heap of exegesis, commentaries, and criticisms. If anything can recapture meaning, it is real art, which strikes you dumb and requires no further explanation.

George Steiner's *Real Presences* (1989) articulates the antipathy for emptiness which accompanies the flood. In his essay he seeks alliance with the modern struggle with media overkill and arouses the reader's interest in a "society of the primary," in which "all talk about the arts, music, and literature is prohibited." In this society all discourse is held to be illicit verbiage. Criticism can be put on the shelf, since "all serious art, music, and literature is a critical act" anyway. We don't have to worry about "a blank and passive silence" prevailing in this counterpart of Plato's republic. After all, all presentations of the great works are to be considered as interpretations and are "understanding in action."

Steiner is without doubt playing with a full deck. He is well aware of how difficult it is to draw a dividing line between primary and secondary texts. We must see his call for the dismantling of the culture industry as, above all, a sign of despair at the fleeting character of modern products. "The great bulk is totally ephemeral"; it will be "soon out of print" and "sepulchered in the decent dust of deposit libraries." These works come and go "like querulous shadows," at best providing some "transient pleasure" and the necessary job opportunities for the "secondary souls."

Indeed, today's works do not dedicate themselves to an imaginary eternity as once existed. They are manufactured to be recorded and reproduced—more precisely, copied. Their manufacture is entirely dominated by possible media connections. The fleetingness Steiner so deplores is nothing more than the speed of modern registration techniques. The media alliance into which the "eternal" works of art have been incorporated is a dynamic multimedia archive where technological connections between word, image, and sound are created. Without calling this development by name, Steiner sees a loss of authenticity here. The modern media alliance, in which culture moves forward as information, in no way resembles Steiner's model of secondary layers with an authentic, primary core at the center. In information science there is no difference between first- and second-rate data; at best there are processed and raw data. In principle, they are all subject to static and erosion and at the mercy of the state of technology.

For Steiner, media are synonymous with the immanent fall of the subject, which would express itself in its own way, but cannot because it is bowled over by an avalanche of information. "Literate humanity is solicited daily by millions of words, printed, broadcast, screened, about books which it will never open, music it will not hear, works of art it will never set eyes on." Not even the computer and electronic databanks can process this mass. Steiner is mainly looking to arouse self-pity. It's all simply become too much for the scholars. Even worse: the media are impairing their intellectual capability and are becoming superior. "A mandarin madness of secondary discourse infects thought and sensibility." He tacitly hopes that history will pass devastating judgment on our "imperialism of the second- and third-hand." "Perhaps our age will come to be known as that of the marginalists, of the clerics of the market."

Media ruin the mind, and pointing out the culprits is sufficient. They are the press hounds: "Journalistic presentation generates a temporality of equivalent instantaneity. All things are more or less of equal import: all are only daily." (All data are equal, but some are more equal than others.) Poets, composers, and painters, according to Steiner, should not be satisfied with their five-minute fame. They are, after all, "wagers on lastingness." That the media are concerned these days with the incorporation of art into the mythological universe (think of Van Gogh, Mozart, or the Doors) has not yet occurred to Steiner. Meanwhile, the media have produced their own immortal heroes and myths, which can compete with the traditional ones and moreover happily embroider on them.

"Journalism bids us invest in the bourse of momentary sensation." Whole masses of people who practice "serious art" are caving in to this seductive offer. Actually they should display a radical disinterest in topicality, since according to Steiner "meaningful art" is by definition not new, and just as timely 30 years later. "Originality is antithetical to novelty." But creativity has become fatally entangled in the academic-journalistic discourse which twines around it. In placing such emphasis on the compulsion to present oneself as shocking, new, or modern, and succumbing to the patterns of fashion, Steiner cannot get involved with the current use of media in art. In his view, the media still maintain themselves outside the creative process. They attach themselves like parasites onto the work of art and nibble on it from the outside. When this gnawing reaches the threshold of pain, we can indeed expect artists to become frustrated with the "paper Leviathan of secondary talk" of which they unwillingly comprise a part. At that moment, the ecological appeal can strike a chord and give restraint a moral fundament.

If, on the other hand, we see the media as platforms, and start with the assumption that the arts must seek contact with other data currents if they are to survive, finding an interpretation-free work space outside the media does become quite difficult. The longing for this kind of extramediality is nostalgic and timeless. Leaving things as they are and applying yourself to new work in your media-free surroundings has a touristic quality. If we see the media as more raw material, they and all their secondary replays are freely at the artist's disposal. Then the wastefulness is back on track and we can calmly let babble ("the busy vacancy") continue to grow rampant over media excess and mental moderation. Criticism is applause in the form of static.

The same unholy alliance between media and art bemoaned by Steiner is also the bone of contention in the controversial book written by the West German film director Hans Jürgen Syberberg in the turbulent transitional period of '89/'90. *Vom Unglück und Glück der Kunst in Deutschland nach dem Kriege* (*On the Misfortunes and Fortunes of Art in Postwar Germany*) immediately drew attention to itself when published because of the author's unrestrained use of Nazi terminology. The scandal prevented people from looking more closely at his line of reasoning. The "secondary talk" indeed had the effect here that primary theory remained out of range. What is remarkable about *Kunst in Deutschland* is that it articulates popular prejudices about postwar art and then connects them to a theory of art. Syberberg sees an era coming to an end with the fall of the Berlin wall, and is there in no time to fill the need for new paradigms. Finally he can say aloud what everyone was already thinking, namely that contemporary art is second-rate garbage. Like Steiner he thinks back nostalgically to an art that radiates purity, durability, and beauty: authentic monuments for eternity.

In order to be included in the media, art has had to defer to them. That is the reason for postwar superficiality and pollution. This "art without a people," according to Syberberg, results in "disposable commodities like punk, pop, and junk." "Everything mutates boundlessly, everything degenerates into unhealthy decay, with wholehearted approval." In the boom period an anti-art triumphed which was pounced on by the media: "All doors opened for this anti-world of beauty, grinning, dominating the market, shameless." Syberberg sees the preference with "the small, the inferior, the deformed, the sick, and the filthy" over brilliance as the hallmark of this art form. "The command of ugliness dominates life and art and the rat becomes the symbol of what is interesting, as does the swine."

Hans Jürgen is livid with annoyance at Hamlet in undershorts, Don Giovanni in the whorehouse of the fast-food chain, the poet Kleist with a steel helmet, William Tell in a Jeep, and Richard Wagner's *Twilight of the Gods* cut up into "a fast food porno videoclip." The reader has to laugh involuntarily at the bombastic drunken language in which Syberberg spews out his frustrations about poor Germany. He rants about all those filthy artists and their hollow products that culminate in self-destruction ("the rocker who smashes his violin"). A neurotic mannerism typifies the contemporary art sector. "A subsidized and organized apocalyptic mood abounds; culture without identity, crippled by inauthenticity." Although Syberberg achieved success with his monster films after WW II, he nevertheless considers this period a kind of hell "which unfestively celebrated its triumph and was nauseated by its own vomit."

His hallucinations betray a tremendous fear of the chaos of hybridization, in which everything is connected to everything, everyone sleeps with everyone: "nations, races, food, plants, animals, populations." The media in particular have become too much for him. He cannot distinguish between the many images, and sees only the masses of media that engulf him. To him, the "international arbitrariness" of "multicultural media charisma" is a mess emptied over the "bloodless soil" from above. This he frankly admits: "So here we are, in the land of plenty of realities, on five to 40 channels from all over the world, our lives lonely, sated, and incapable of art."

The media officials who call themselves the mouthpieces of protest speak with a forked tongue: "life-lies arise from the media markets as a result of the dialectic of minorities." The "wars from behind the desk of the opinion industry," according to Syberberg's masochistic cultural philosophy, result in a gigantic "environmental pollution of the soul." Art has degenerated into the "show business of the leisure industry." It has been reduced to "charismatic electronic art." Even his own medium turns out guilty of "dissolution into the international electronic multimedia marketing show," when he writes that film has reduced art to pure industry. The aesthetic situation seems so hopeless that he himself is no longer embarrassed to come out with such rubbish.

Steiner and Syberberg fill a temporary need. For the time being, experiments with electronic art are unresolved and offer no certainty in the unstable art world. As long as the electronic media are still in their phase of introduction, the call for a return of authentic art can count on public approval. Fascination and boredom constantly alternate. The importance people attach to the media is just as great as the disbelief they are overcome with moments later. This zigzag motion causes confusion which cannot be resolved except by switching off all the media. The media-ecological laments are a waste of time because they appeal to a sense of responsibility that is not of this age. The media dietitians demand responsible behavior from tele-civilians. If all of us would collectively persist in doing the same, our impending destruction by digital multiplicity might be averted by ecological simplicity.

But the assumed will to consistent behavior has long been replaced by a range of more or less interesting options that are constantly changing (or not). The user is no longer overcome with apathy, indecision, or indifference, but examines miscellaneous paradoxes quite apart from the complex of responsibility. Superabundance is a natural background factor, as a set of possibilities that are open to all. The conscious on/off choice has been replaced by a vagueness-coefficient: today, one works in several menus at once. The option of a media diet may be one such temporary menu—until information regains its old fascination.

CONTEMPORARY NIHILISM
ON INNOCENCE ORGANIZED

"When reflection has traversed the infinite, innocence is regained."

—Heinrich von Kleist

With the emergence of a privileged mediocrity, the innocent life became accessible to the masses. No longer was John Doe part of a class striving toward historical ends, e.g., revolution or fascism: Enter a cold era, now devoid of passion. While outside, storms raged and change rapidly followed change, one's own life was left to grind to a halt. Time, regardless of history, fashion, politics, sex, and the media, was to take its due course. The innocent made no fuss; they despised it—"Come what may." Average folks considered themselves cogs in some giant machine, and were proud to admit it. They saw to it that the trains ran on schedule, and returned home at night in time for supper. Instead of the old barriers, such as caste, sex, and religion, innocence introduced such bromides as tolerance, openness, and harmony. Positivism become lifestyle. Positivist critique served the reconstruction of politics and culture. Good times were had, one was busily and dynamically engaged and abundantly employed. There reigned a clear and simple view of reality. The innocent did not incorporate the Good, they just hadn't a clue, though not lacking in standards. Crime was not for them. Thus, they involuntarily became the objects of strategies of Good and Evil.

We are speaking of a life without drama, immediacy, "decision." Things will never get hot. Nothing will ever have to be decided on. You don't need to break out in order to be just you. Rock ye no boats. The innocent thrive on everyday ritual; it's what makes them happy. A failing washing machine suffices to drive one up the wall: The bloody thing simply must function. The plight of materiality is that it's always breaking down, failing, malfunctioning, and generally behaving in odd ways, and that it cannot be quietly replaced. Untrammeled consumption holds a promise that from now on, nothing will ever happen. In this undisturbed existence, luxury becomes so natural it goes unnoticed. The innocent consciousness is distinguished by its air of cramped grass-rootsiness, evoking a universe where personal irritations may explode without warning: Time and again, streetlights, traffic jams and delays, bureaucratic hassles, bad weather, construction noises, diseases, accidents, unexpected guests and incidents comprise an assault on innocent existence. Nonetheless, one is caught up in uncalled-for events. This attitude of disturbance-deterrence, devoted to job and professional affairs, excludes all risk and has bestowed the status of sole criterion upon the attainable. The summum of happiness now consists of soft porn, moped, the new medium-priced car, one's own house and mortgage, interesting hobbies, club life, kids, elaborate birthdays of family members and friends, book clubs, Christmas cards, cross-stitched embroideries, ikebana, tending the garden, clean clothes, the biosphere of pets and indoor plants, guinea pigs, the rabbit in the yard, the pigeons in the attic, holiday destinations, dinners out, a bit of catching up or a general chat, Greenpeace membership, or tele-adoption through the foster parents plan. This ideal of an unrippled and spotless life is characterized by its endearing pretense of being literally everybody's goal. Innocence is under constant treatment from doctors, therapists, beauticians, acupuncturists, and garage keepers. Innocence likes to be tinkered with. It considers it its duty to develop and, if necessary, reeducate. Courses are taken, Adilkno sessions participated in, the theater, concert halls, expos visited, books read, directions to forest walks followed, and martial arts actively engaged in. Innocence as a universal human right encompasses animals, plant life, architecture, landscapes, and cultural expression. This is the condition under which the world may be ultimately salvaged: neither utopian nor fatalistic, but smoothly functioning.

The advertisement campaigns accompanying this way of life appeal to the childlike joy of having one's accomplishments rewarded. Scenes of smiling dads and mums who can afford anything. A reference to the authoritarian circumstances in which the child is raised to maturity and learns to talk. Innocence presupposes the enclosed security of family, school, company, and sports club. Under "infantile capitalism" (Asada), desire is tempted by the offer of a secure existence. By displaying good behavior, one is assured that the ongoing changes in the vast world outside will not cause any catastrophes. Rebellion is punished and virtually pointless. The household comprises a fortified oasis. The others are just like you, and moving from one cell to another you get the impression that life is swell. Surprises are solely permissible within well-acquainted constellations. The crush alone makes for a composed exception to the rule. In sex, there may yet be room for assaults, with all that may imply. This is why the personal ad is such an innocent medium, having nothing to do with prostitution or moral decline whatsoever. The highlight of innocent existence consists of the wedding day, the happiest day of your life. Marriage is the one occasion in their existence on which John and Jane Doe may dress up in all their decorum and show themselves to the world at large. The ordering of the wedding gown, the white or red worn for all to see, the bouquet, the bridegroom's shoes, the orchestra outside, the cabriolet or carriage, the cheering onlookers, the historical wedding room, the clergyman's moving little speech, the standing ovation and gifts, the dinner at some fashionable restaurant, the subsequent feast till the small hours: No trouble or expenses are spared to create surroundings in which everybody ends up getting terribly pissed, yet never severely disgraces themselves. A day to remember in horror for the rest of your life, but forever impossible to forget; a wound in your life, a mental tattoo ruthlessly inflicted by family members. Millions of couples shack up forever just so they won't have to cope with it. The pressure lies in the fact that there is no option but for the whole thing to proceed smoothly, so that even if it does, any fun that there might have been is definitely out. The greater misery the night before, the bigger joy come the wedding night. Afterwards, it's safe havens forever.

As innocence, to a substantial degree, consists of defense, it cannot remain neutral under the continuous outside threat facing it (thieves, rapists, hackers, counterfeiters, the incestuous, psychopaths, renegades, bacteria, missiles, toxic clouds, aliens, etc.). Neither can it summon any childlike curiosity concerning events in the outside world. Innocence's protective coating mirrors any threat posed by its environment, thus causing it to take on an aura of organization. The Mafia, youth gangs, criminal conspirators, sects, drug cartels, banditry, pirates are all thought to be after mediocrity's naiveté. They're omnipresent spooks. Before you know it, you may be involved, guilty of or victimized by fraud. Innocence, desperate to turn its head, to pretend that nothing's the matter, threatens to succumb. Ignorance may prove fatal; a more practical strategy consists of localizing and channeling attacks. Hand out to each individual an electronic guarantee of innocence and sooner or later any felon will end up in some specialist jail. In fact, innocence shouldn't need any legitimation; all this registration and surveillance merely causes it to lose its aura. Everyone is a potential illegal immigrant; even if the contrary is proven, one remains a risk factor. In the present phase, escape into anonymity becomes daily more dangerous and undesirable. Neutrality thus appears a chosen isolation, the final outcome of which is grotesque exclusion. Those who aren't thoroughly on line can make no appeals to organized innocence's compassion.

Organized innocence is obsessed with Evil, gazing at and dissecting it, categorizing and exposing it, in order to finally bypass it altogether. Innocence owes its existence to its seeming opposite. One cannot confess innocence, for every confession must needs be one of guilt, any gesture a false pose pertaining to goodness itself. Everybody is informed to start with, everyone knows all about the next person and there's a silent agreement that some things are best left unsaid. The innocent are discreet and do not interfere with certain hidden domains (of power, lust, death). No boundary violations here. Holidays may offer some compensation, but everything has its season. Next of kin are those who cause maximum annoyance. They are parsimonious neighbors, noisy kids, funny couples. First annoyances are quickly made emblems, forever there to fall back on. The others are scrutinized distrustfully, in a form of surveillance which it is impossible to sanction since there no longer exists any common exchange to define a norm. Normality can no longer define any aberration. Only drug-related nuisance, street-walkers' districts, travelers' sites, and refugees' centers may now temporarily unite citizens in mobs, for fear of declining property values. This neighborhood resistance is not ideologically motivated; one simply never gets down to the point of formulation of transferable ideas. The neighbors are doing model airplanes, oneself preferring Pierre Boulez; what room is left for any exchange? There is more to separate us than mere garden fences. Therefore, too, accusations of racism or discrimination are off the mark here. There isn't any moral order to deteriorate into bigotry.

Stereotypes get blurred. No one knows what a Jew might look like, or what distinguishes Turks from Moroccans ("All Turks are called Ali"). The other's features don't stick, since one has no sense of identity oneself. So much for PC advertising, public information campaigns, even cookbook recipes. Multiculturalist society is a clash of featureless citizens and the heirs to identities. There is a severe misunderstanding with the Innocent concerning the Other come from afar. There is a great readiness to accept the concept of differing cultures. They're assumed to function in the same type of isolation as ours. Who would wish to visit upon another a dull life like our own, culminating in likewise padded solitude? Tolerance means envy of the other's simplicity. Friday rounds are not considered backward (as the strict Reformed once were), but as proof of a devotion and consistency no longer available to oneself. The suburbs are polytheistic; everything is believed in. There is more than what's been taught you at school—but what? Seeking, one has found, but anxiety remains as to what more is going to show up. Gurus, healing stones, skyward apparitions, voodoo, and encounters all slip past without one having ever a chance to share these experiences. For a moment, one gets the impression that there's quite a bit going on, that the surrounding world is full of deep acquaintances, of promises and optimistic prospects. Before long, one finds oneself alone with all the acquired cross-country experiential attributes, the textbooks, perfumed oils, the neat windbreaker the two of us bought together, remember?, the empty personal organizer and holiday photo albums. What macrosocial guiding principle will dissolve all this weeny human suffering, will resolve our confusion? Where are they, the builders of this new state of affairs, amid and around us? The refugee, as a cultural carrier, may prove prophetic. Ultimately, it is they who reintroduce to us our exiled spirituality, so sought after in the West.

Innocence may be lost through committing murder, participating in a little S-M, joining a bike club, opting for art, going undercover; yet the underworld of entertainment offers no consolation. One final option much in vogue consists of defecting to war or genocide. There can, however, be no refuge from the conglomerate and its diktata. The mountain bike, T-shirt, Oilily clothing, computer games, graffiti, bumper sticker, spoiler, cap, sloppy casual wear, hair gel are all the nomadic objects of Jacques Attali's Europe on its way to a stylized uniformity. Innocence cannot be negated, or compensated for, by its opposite. The one thing it can't stand is party poopers.

This process of decomposition within normality offers no alternative and puts up no fight, nor even does it make a point. Through it, innocence is exhausted. One cannot be bright and happy all day, forever dissolving the grime through constructive thinking. Innocence is not in danger of being wiped out by either revolution or reaction. It can only wither, go under in poverty, slowly vanish out of sight, as though meant to waste away. Grounded love affairs are resolved by ordering a dumpster in which one's accumulated innocence is disposed of, in order to make a cleaner, wilder start after interior redecoration procedures. A generation ago, the politicization of the private managed to get some innocence out the door, but it has regrouped with a vengeance and now has grunge rockers, generation X'ers, trance freaks, and other youth categories all searching in vain for some firm footing they can react against, in some format other than that of fashion or the media, innocence's latest organizational modi. Government itself is now the most outspoken antiracist, antisexist, antifascist, antihomelessness, and generally anti anything the well-intentioned insurrectionists are liable to oppose. The only things left for innocent young generations to vent their anger on are all forms of organized innocence itself. Abundant material for grounding an enormous social movement, to start working at innumerable separate issues, in order to discover a common ground in all those disparate little divisions. Boycott insurance companies, raid those self-assured infant clothing shops, torch those redundant gift stores—we've a consumer paradise to destroy! But let's not get excited. We'll have innocence fade away, see it quiet down; tell you what: We'll not even mention it.

THE HOMEOPATHY OF EVIL
THE COMING MAN REVISITED

"The superman appears where man becomes meaning-less. He is man capable of life in a world without meaning. The shattering of the old moral and hierarchical order does not shatter him. He finds his own rank and morality. All things become fluid again."

—F. G. Jünger

Disaster no longer threatens from outside. There no longer exists a tempting external world, inhabited by some evil genius who stains the virgin soul with propaganda. Society is no longer to blame. Nor does evil come from within anymore, out of some cesspool of banal urges and repressed desires that return with a vengeance. Nowadays, evil resides between the self and the world's double glazing. Beyond the id and its environment, there presently appear unforeseen thermopane spaces, the "interhuman sphere" where evil flourishes. Evil is not an absolute value, but a transient, indefinable vacuum created at ever-different points. You can neither submit to it nor support it. To resist it or to profess it is impossible. Flirtations with evil are idle. The slogan of the ecstatic nineties—"Dare to be wrong"—is imploding.

Lombroso is a legendary figure from the age of determinant science, when moral standards still existed and Good and Evil were still interrelatable. Today, images of the hairy-face, the hook-nose, the pockmarked cross-eyes, the hunchbacked witch, the driveling lecher, the Neapolitan starter, and the Caucasian type mainly betray ethnic innocence and folkloric naiveté. Something similar is happening in psychology. The categories of both inner and outer have become popularized and implausible. Today, people suffer from troubled childhoods as they used to from complexion problems. There was a time when causes still had effects and both were stable, but nowadays people just don't know what they're doing anymore. A chain of missing links: "I'd never suspected it of him, not even in retrospect." Life's stages: Those who don't side with the wrong camp before they turn thirty have no conscience; those who fail to see what's right after that have no common sense. The cultural-despair model teaches that good automatically culminates in bad: Every good intention already bears the trace of a miserable outcome. Every personal initiative ends up as fierce commerce. Good takes root in Evil, where it flourishes till its inevitable return as Evil—"Ashes to ashes, dust to dust."

The only way out is to do nothing—that is, the safe Nothing, not the horror vacua of men like Cioran and Camus. Conversely, malicious intentions need not necessarily exclude a positive outcome. The U.N. peace mission's adage: "Withhold all aid until a country is completely in ruins." The Internet, formerly a decentralized World War III command structure, is now leading to an unforeseen friendship among nations, a pen-pal club without borders, in the best UNESCO tradition. Nowadays, one progresses from evil to good; but those who still stick to the "golden age of the cold war"'s supercooled model, which saw advancement and progressive conformation as signs of personal development, inevitably end up members of the melancholy platoon of demagogues like Buchanan, Haider, Zyuganov, and Helms. At the same time, there remains the possibility of a pole reversal at all times: the Internet's cowardly child pornographers turn out more cunning than the benign intentions of vigilant Netwatchers. Porn for kids is the key that will lock up the Net, though it remains unclear whether the evil resides in the Web regulators' puritanical attitude or in the software of smutty sex search engines. The craving for the Positive is the abstract vector. The sanitary organization of life prompts unlimited optimism and an obligation to look hopefully at the future, despite everything. Assume the American smile, and you will be beyond blame. Once liability has expired, there is no one to stop you from going on your way. Behavior and furniture indicate a susceptibility to anything that might pop up. As long as the sanitary attitude's contributions are duly paid, you may rest assured of the promise of a containable existence. But as soon as this personal economy of Good Hope collapses by painful coincidence, there is nothing to prevent a free fall into the dark.

As soon as we leave the bad-to-worse model in favor of the phantasmatical from-bad-to-good—or the more realistic "not-very-good-is-it"—or possibly even from-bad-to-indifferent—then life loses its unequivocal orderliness. There is no longer a point in defining or pinning down Evil: to understand it has become impossible for simple laypersons, now that the list of evildoers and baneful causes has grown so long and vague that even negative thinking cannot grasp it. Try, yourself, grappling with the question of whether capitalism is the problem or the solution some consciousness-raising weekend; it's enough to break anybody's back. No one even considers presenting the computer with this kind of mega-question anymore. Now that causes have ceased to matter, attention shifts to the design of the golden mean. "Why have airplanes at all, now that we have the Internet?" "Africa shouldn't need to be poor now that we have low-orbit satellites." Having a blast for one night prevents long-term flipping out. Wrongdoing in order to prevent worse: Steady decline can be averted by surgical operations on the level of politics (the Gulf War), the social (business junkets, inspiring informal conferences on new media), and sports; but also on the scale of individual psychology: a personal acceleration, alternated with extended low-intensity lifestyle periods. We know the outcome of World Revolution and the Long March: The former changes nothing, the latter gets bogged down. What remains is the spasmodic initiative to save the whole mess. As in those T-shirts: "No Time to Waste." Where engagement and no-nonsense may intermingle in either direction according to the time of day, ethics have no role to play. Polarization or reconciliation? Sure, nice idea. Midlife crises lead to nothing, now that people grow old too fast and are forever young. The converted fifty-year-old who crosses over from problems to solutions; the catechism as an unread best-seller; the absent fantasies on reading De Sade; the former dissident who thinks of the Communists as the great democrats; the suicide guide for bon vivants; the Liberal who warns against the consequences of global deregulation; the 95-year-old who died "completely unexpectedly"; the American neo-Nazi extradited to Germany; thieving police; battering in lesbian couples: "All of that, and much more." The revaluation of all values has begun, and there is no way of stopping it. Nietzsche served his turn; none of the good man's anxious and excited writings can impress us anymore. When the masses and their elite pass beyond Good and Evil in a single move, the whole theology of ethics becomes a mixture of private notions. Everyone has their own day about it; "I'd just as soon say nothing."

When Evil becomes a fleeting hobby—a process of growth we all have to go through, a chance experience, a good idea taking a wrong turn, a vain bid for worldwide renown—then even conversion and reflection won't help. Dallying with texts or brooding on personal experience is just another pastime, not serious study, let alone harsh criticism. The distinction between the interpretive clergy and the mucking about of perfidious commoners has been lost. Sinister "hate speech" is at odds with the academic (in)difference industry that dumps every conflict on the theme market. The delinquent rhymester makes a fine confessant who can count on the judgmental classes' recognition without the need to provide insights. The relation between action and words has been disturbed; we now enter the stage of failing judges and impotent politicians, at prey to the hegemony of ambivalence or, rather, multivalence, like everybody else. The old specter of Evil keeps on haunting massive European Liberation Festivals, restored concentration camps, the Anne Frank House's new visitors' center, and American Holocaust museums. These exorcist rites no longer find a foothold in everyday order; they take provisional refuge in their monumental antithesis. Italian neo-Fascists present themselves as outspoken anti-Fascists. There is nothing left to say about historical Fascism, but plenty about its ill-considered presentation back then and the present logistical inability to cope with historical tourism's traffic flows. The urgent appeal of "no more Auschwitz" has lost all meaning after Bosnia. It's become a truth well understood by the perpetrators. What moral power could there ever be in the slogan "no more Bosnia"?

The Homeopathy of Evil

"We are agreed, then?" Beef-fed cattle, Japanese car industries taken over by Americans, South Korea as Great Britain's main investor, Walkmen used for insulation, the gathering of knowledge supplanted by that of information. Pragmatism turns against itself on pragmatic grounds. The incongruous has become the reasonable. Now, all we have to deal with in the line of orientation is the last of the negationists, the buffoonish and dismal who deny the Holocaust, adore Stalin, still defend the Molotov–Von Ribbentrop Pact, and approve of Hiroshima. They are not the eternal have-beens, but the scapegoats who channel our fears as a conversation-starter—drifting Sputniks used for orientation by opinionating bodies running amok. Every consistent disturbance factor risks ending up part of this role play.

Medially speaking, the talk show's evil of the day—mass murder, civil war, blind terror, kiddie porn, earthquakes, epidemics, airplane disasters, etc.—is as neutralized as the old evils. "How could this ever have happened?" The idea that there's more to it than meets the eye is accepted from the start. This is where the mentally disturbed among us step in, joining the weirdest sects because at least they offer a coherent story. "Gaia's upset, what can you do?" TV and the media's non-dimensional data can't cope with the human story's bouncy dialectics, and are too soft for the complexity addicts at any rate. At the expanding core of major events and obscure modi operandi appears a domain of a new species of political intervention with well-defined objects (i.e., victims) and identifiable suspects, but whose motive remains shrouded in mystery. Plans are never unfolded, nor can they be reconstructed in hindsight. The whole sad state of affairs should have been solved long ago through level-headed interventions by SWB (Soldiers Without Borders). So far, all we hear is more of the same; we're still waiting for the qualitative leap whereby disasters may radically exceed their regional limitations. Chernobyl gave a foretaste of the way in which humanity might be aroused from its slumber. It established a yearning for what might have been—something like a real stock market crash. The idea that the other is temporarily or permanently up shit creek no longer mobilizes; it inspires. It's still unsatisfying to see evil reduced to a local, temporary, and elusive affair all the time. Evil deserves better, what with the bad state of the world.

OUT OF CONTEXT

"Sometimes, a child's laughter frightens me."
—F. Hölderlin

1.

Life's course has come to an end. Before you've even had a chance to manifest yourself, a resumé, full of impressive positions, is required. Love-engagement-marriage has been replaced by a patchwork of afflictions, such as coming out, crisis, relapse, and a second or third childhood. One no longer gets down to promoting one's career: It simply takes too long, and who knows what things will be like five years from now? With linearity broken, the accumulated past no longer offers a foothold. The best thing to do is to take courage and make a new start. Feel free to forget or deny your personal biography. The betrayal of friends, party, creed, family, and business is a litmus test to prove your ability to keep up with the rest. Professed loyalties have turned out to be nothing but a décor in which to watch time go by. The past is merely today's overture; it does not interfere with the current future. Looking back now, past commitments turn out empty and meaningless. Been there, done that, time to move on. What on earth have I got left to say to those people?

All change is no more than a dietary variation in an unchangeable existence. There isn't any experience left waiting to be articulated. On close examination, people experience nothing whatsoever anymore. Biographies constitute a tactical standstill, a drama without movement. Life, above all, is a matter of inner experience. We bathe in a profusion of interpretations, whether to do with suppressed lives, automobile makes and holiday destinations, or domestic problems. The last anchors to cling to are the collective childhood experiences, enlarged to mythic proportions: the pop concerts, parties, summer camps, military service, a strike or a riot, a soccer championship, campsites, and favorite pubs back then. These scant experiences of life make up the ground material for one's debut presentation. The 25-year-old bestseller author already looks back on a libertine life, feeling free to deny our fettered existence like another Proust. A loop is created, from the past which meant nothing to a future that will have nothing to offer. Existence without context is condemned to the present, the available, and the possible. No breakout, no despair, not a dream.

Success is not a triumph but a necessity; otherwise, what story would one have to tell? There's no mistaking it: You are only rewarded for the risks you are prepared to take. Once out of context, actions become indefinable. Any will-power or ambition that is brought to bear is arbitrary. There are no external, urgent necessities to justify choices of profession, hobbies, or partners; no force or coercion to render life evident. Thus, everything must come from within. There, all is barren, empty, and cold. Thus, actions take on the character of a flight forward: a submission to fate, sought anywhere one can, without ever finding a thing. The result is the diversified extremism of workaholics, Doctors Without Borders, the Guinness Book of World Records, raves, mountaineering, and bungee jumping. Backlash effects consist of disablement, senior workouts, walker shopping, insomnia, chronic fatigue, agoraphobia, and incontinence—including the accompanying therapy package.

2.

Now that the neo-Liberal ministers of the 1980's (the Thatchers, Reagans, Friedmans, and Hayeks) have stepped down, the congregation has dispersed, left to its own devices. Before, a primary motivation consisted of resentment of the megalomaniac welfare state, the proliferation of social legislation and the communists disguised as civil servants. Encouraged by the revival of cold war thinking, one imagined oneself to be engaged in a liberation struggle against line after line of bureaucratic fortifications. The leveling of these overgrown moats around the institutionalized working classes induced a state of euphoria in the higher-educated middle classes, aided by the whining media, the nagging "new social movements," and perestroika in distant Russia. Neo-Liberalism found so much response because socialism had lost its vitality, while the ruling Social Democrats were already thinking along similar lines.

The collapse of the structure of social achievements, justified demands, seasoned executives, political parties, and their yuppies was not brought about through effective power coalitions among the opposition. The bottom dropped out from under the ideologically righteous because the executives of the welfare state had lost their religious confidence. There was more talk about neo-Liberalism than there were actual gestures toward the new Liberals. The message was eagerly heard out because, essentially, Liberal thought appealed to a guilty conscience which had reached maturity. The officials were fed up with the promises and effects of their interventions in the social sands. Policies collapsed under the weight of their own measurability. A whole new sphere was discovered, incomprehensible and uncontrollable, beyond regulation, forms, and policy documents. A no-man's-land was sensed to exist. Entire populations got projected into an involuntary parking gear, encapsulated by regulations and arrangements. Who could have defended their predicament? This had nothing to do anymore with the intended emancipation of the working class, which had itself long ago turned into something else. It had lost not only its recognizable contours, but its expression as well, including its spokespersons.

Neo-Liberalism encountered an easy opponent in drifting socialism. Now that everyone has become allied, the political classes share a similar uncertainty. No one knows why they act as Christian Democrats, leftist Liberals, Republicans, Social Democrats, or Conservatives within this constellation anymore. What's left as residue is the scandals, files, disturbed relations, agendas, and procedural mistakes. After solving the social question, it is now time to face the political one—something our highly dynamic neo-Liberalism has no answer to. Further deregulation would mean the elimination of the very political class to which one belongs. Parliamentary democracy cannot be contracted out to freelance/part-time temporary flex-workers sure to get the job done within the agreed period and budget. Management offers no refuge, because the managers themselves have become the objects of drastic restructuring. Even the concept of media democracy—with its ad campaigns, image control, and PR officials—is doomed, because these bunglers have to compete with MTV heroes, Hollywood stars, royal families, and weatherpeople. Here, the impending constitutional crisis is no more than another fleeting item.

Many have suddenly pinned their hopes on the free-market economy. A vitalistic ideal is projected onto business. One imagines energetic yet reassuringly uniformed employees who will get down to business without wasting words. People move through a flexible infrastructure, smilingly exchanging last-minute services. They part as satisfied customers and partners. Here, male and female, black and white are equals, putting maximum effort into correct task-performance—all for the common good, naturally. Here, there is no more whining or arguing about irrelevancies, only concentration on the essential. After executing production performance, there is room for spiritual growth, network development, physical exercise, and recreation within the private circle (from golf club to mosque). Here, the aura of advertising is still fully intact. One wallows in service, quality, reliability and trust, guarantees, positive test results, and consequent share prices. Thus, we return to the stage which Akira Asada called "infantile capitalism." People are more than prepared to assume that all good springs from the economy. Far beyond the horizon lurk bribery, corruption, fraud, and deceit, as characteristics of regions so poor that even tourism scarcely finds a foothold. One idolizes pleasant efficiency and stylized perfection, a form of worship that is not interrupted by asking tricky questions.

3.

On embracing paradigm, science became aware of its own context. Reflection on one's own premises was itself a product of massification. Lecture halls grew too big to nip all critical questions in the bud any longer. The academy as a disciplining institution, once designed to mold the elite, lost its consistency and became an amorphous, uncontrollable body. This process produced doctrinal opposition in the shape of neo-Marxists, feminists, postmodernists, and ecologists, who started to pen down their own diktats. As a result, the university lost its educative character and became a copy of social programs carried out outside the institution. Yet these social movements were not autonomous; they were grafted onto a decaying and expanding university and consisted by and large of students themselves. In the long run, these movements too found legitimacy in the faded educational factories. After a delay of some five or ten years, the presence of media and university had grown so great that people imagined themselves to be a political force, whereas, in fact, on the "outside" nothing happened at all anymore.

The university ceased to be a hazing institution, something to be endured in order to acquire status. Afterward, you'd do your job, not glancing at another book until retirement. In your college days, you ground away at courses, made friends for life, met your partner, had a ball, and still managed to graduate. Today, those student years are no longer to be seen as a closed period. One is forced to return to the classroom periodically. At work, one must constantly compete with younger generations who effortlessly acquire the right specialist knowledge, under great pressure and ever so flexibly. Knowledge is no longer inflation-proof. It is no longer something that is transmitted in college, to be enhanced and expanded upon over the years through actual practice. Those professional qualities can suddenly and unpredictably become utterly worthless, no matter how differentiated and well grounded they might otherwise be.

By inventing the concept of "paradigm," an entire generation of committed intellectuals had dug its own grave. So high were the expectations regarding the paradigmatic change one found oneself in, that it was forgotten that this particular changing of the guard was by no means to be the last. From a rare reversal within the scientific ground model, the paradigmatic change turned out to be a permanent fluctuation from one standard to another. This instability structurally undermines the social position of all those who are directly related to the manufacture of knowledge. The labor relations of this industry are characterized by the deployment of temporary workers, freelance specialists, traveling visionaries, and wonder children uprooted before their prime. People grow old too fast, because no one stays young forever. All of this is not without reaction. Everything that offers reliability, security, certainty and coherence is clung onto and advertised as the latest discovery: Ortega y Gasset, the catechism, Saabs, marriage, Heidegger, a strict upbringing, buying a house, neckties and women's suits, zinc buckets, reading a good book. The return to tradition should by no means be interpreted as a collective experience; rather, it is an expression of the personal and its attempt to withdraw from politics. Similarly, the shift to the right is not a movement or struggle, but an expression of an individual form of protectionism. This artificial reliability is neutral and pale. It strives to keep all novelties, with their colorful aspect, at bay, out of resentment of all radical expression. It smothers all commitment to be oneself in a lacquer of antique finish.

4.

Once the structuralists had carried out their demolition work, comfort was taken in Foucault's good old history of institutions. With Baudrillard, moreover, things lost their scene altogether and started to drift. In an environment of polished simulacra, one could be sympathetically enthusiastic about every new idea that managed to put the old behind it. All breakthrough thinking and farewell philosophies still referred to a shared heritage: the Marxism one used to advocate, Freud in paperback, Darwin as a compulsory high school subject, World War II and its manuals and TV serials, Camus and De Beauvoir, the second Vatican council, jazz and the Beatles, Martin Luther King and Godard. Thus, they acknowledged a continuity people thought they were doing away with. The notion of the death of God can only appeal to the faithful. That is why postmodernism is a kind of aftercare; Lyotard comforts those who know they must go on alone.

Semiology, dynamics of science, systematology, mediology, and poststructuralism each pretend to be a new science of fundamentals. They are lectured disciplines that offer psychological security, a jargon that sounds reliable, and an alley into the future. They absorb the unrest which accompanies the state of permanent change. But that which presents itself as metatheory is, in fact, the theory of orientation; that is, the successor to the theology of ethics. It presents regulations of action, directives for task forces. Heavy theory has thus been devalued to the level of marketing and management. Stunned by daily practice, it has reduced itself to its own passionate promotion. Its use lies chiefly in the fact that it's never at a loss for words to guide the disoriented. The urge to give useful advice culminates in the manufacture of progress reports, final conclusions, brainstorm weekends, and study conferences which are never unwarranted, too demanding, or controversial. The aim, after all, is the vortex of ideas that give a new direction to the available forces. A world without painful memories, incongruities, or unanswerable questions.

The dismantled social sciences concentrate on the massage and magnetization of humors. They keep a tail on despair. There is no longer a question of interaction. Theory no longer turns itself against phenomena; nor does it declare solidarity with its object. There is not even the slightest trace left of sarcastic irony or heartfelt cynicism. Theory swims with every tide and exceeds its demonstrated craving for profundity by suggesting themes, finding temporary connections, pointing at analogies, referring to historic precedents, and briefly digressing to customs and traditions. Indefinable unrest is temporarily filled with fleeting moments of charisma. From the involution of problems to the flawless orchestration of good ambiance. Since the great party poopers—Stirner, Nietzsche, Cioran—wrote their programs within the limits of the ego, these have currently become isolated within the aesthetics

of attitude and identity. The present challenge is to trace and eliminate contextless "lite" theory.

THE ALIEN AND ITS MEDIA

"The soul feels like a stranger on earth."

—Georg Trakl

Media are the sum of alien and human being, an unholy hybrid which never distills into pure form because both elements forever compete for meaning. In an attempt to neutralize this eternal battle for significance, three strategies have surfaced, each of which seeks to silence one of either interferents or else force them into harmonious partnership.

The first strategy aims to civilize the media, a democratic movement which puts its faith in the interference-free communication of a wide-open society. With its belief in the existence of pure information, it naively presumes that the others will voluntarily restrict themselves to the human, all too human. It believes that mutual understanding will naturally arise on the level of pure communication. This form of censorship exiles the alien to the same camp that has long been used by humanity to incarcerate the mentally disturbed, diseased, perverted, racially impure, animals, and criminals. It is claimed that the free distribution of information will result in an increased awareness and thus contribute to the dialogue between the free citizens of a free society. The alien, who has accepted this challenge, turns this strategy against itself by becoming the leading item in its guise of catastrophe.

The second strategy defects to the alien, the absolutely foreign. The price it pays is the reduction of media to art and of alien to evil. This typical nineteenth-century charge against the hypocritical bourgeoisie is a demand on modern media to become appallingly strange. Its program is not recognition, but confusion. This way, it believes it can evoke the "ardor of a foreign seduction"; profound awe; fascination. But by surrendering all pretense of communication on the premise of artistic freedom, it hopes to avert evil by creating it itself. The sublimation of evil into the sublime intends to confine the alien's dangerous unpredictability to the aesthetic experience of the uncodable, to be consumed within an institutional framework.

The third strategy flaunts the friendly relationship between medium and alien on the level of everyday life. The incredible is banalized by imagining a benign creature behind the terrifying masks of alien and human being. The alien high, such as the experience of speed or the void, is interpreted as a spiritual initiation into an environment that is a part of the cosmic universe.

The Alien and Its Media

In this view, man has a natural gift to translate incomprehensible alien messages into words like "Auntie Hedl is with me" or "My name is Ashtar— greetings to my friends." The divine laser beams use state-of-the-art media to mediatize the elect who, in turn, use the same media to achieve a global output of their contacts. The hybrid character of mass media is not considered a threat, but is peacefully shared as a harmonious get-together.

The media are not out for communication, but for alienation. "Inasmuch as media communicate or enable communication, they do so as, and through, alienation" (Hegel). Natural contact with the media occurs only as long as their hybrid character is not emphasized and our attention remains focused on the human factor. Once the media makers and users become aware that it is the alien who drives their production of signs, the alien will opt for a new approach to the world. When a medium has exhausted its potential for the casual, it will become pure art, to be consigned to history as an example of degeneration. Artists who evoke the principle of evil can only accelerate the demise of their own genre. The new media launched by the alien will absorb so much enthusiasm that the bizarre alienating effects of the previous media's terminal phase are promptly forgotten.

The media genealogy is to be interpreted as the chronicle of the coming-out of the alien. Before the twilight of the gods, one still prepared for the material arrival of extraterrestrial brothers and sisters. Runways and signposts were constructed in the shape of earthworks and pyramids. It will always remain an archeological mystery whether the aliens landed just in time, left again after implanting the subconscious in primates, were here all along ("Are atoms spaceships?"), or arrive every day at the touch of a button.

They certainly must have felt at home in the Gutenberg galaxy for centuries. It has also been established that they have currently switched to immaterial modes of manifestation, through the intermediary stages of photography, film, and radio. From the nineteenth century onward, the soul (subsequently to be remodeled as the unconscious) in literature is increasingly experienced as a foreign body within the human body. Writers become "increasingly" receptive to the fact that their poetic mechanism is a vehicle for "outside powers": "I no longer think; I am being thought" (Marx). At moments like these, the alien feels obliged to steer humanity toward new media techniques. Through poltergeists, it introduces the Morse code, and through spiritist manifestations it creates the principle of photography. Soon, this in turn is used to record spirits, after which movies and television show nothing but ghosts.

Contemporary media are hybridized by the alien through images tapped from the human unconscious: an inexhaustible reservoir of werewolves, holy virgins, superstars, teddy bears, oil barons, press hounds .. . everybody on screen can be the alien. As soon as viewers come to realize this, television will be updated with equipment to eliminate the distance between image and experience by jacking in to the cerebral sensory center.

From then on, the human factor will return as a personal hallucination within the unconscious, which will literally coincide with virtual space. As long as the alien is free to mix up images, it will not need to make any qualitative leaps to completely different kinds of media, although the possibility must never be excluded. It is only when we leave our own space-time and the alien drags us through the wormhole into the hinterlands that the end of the media as the hybrid principle is achieved.

The alien follows its own trajectory. It will not be confined, sublimated, or reconciliated. Its goals will remain hidden until the final message. But what is clear is that it is fond of intermingling with humans and feels no urge to disassociate itself from us. Its code of behavior is that it simultaneously clings to us and observes a suitable distance. But the same rule applies to theory, which strives to coincide with its subject without being completely absorbed by it. Theory, too, defies dogmatic excommunication, considers delirium to be its limit, and requires a critical distance to retain its hybrid character. Just as the media are the alien's gift to humanity, so theory is humanity's gift to the alien.

COMMUNICATION
CATASTROPHE

"That which can be said must not be said."
—Antagonist

The virus scare logged into the PC proletariat by the world government is inspired by its apprehension that it is not the free data-flow between civilians but the absence of exchange which threatens its omnipotence. Through delete and overload, the virus creates a temporary sanctuary, previously occupied by data communication. The virus is a full member of the democratic community and participates in every debate. It is not a disease, but an experimental mode of argument. The virus is the consistent extension of the long institutional march, which intended to change society from within. It has discarded the masquerade of meaning and good intentions and treats the data world at hand as material to be used against itself. No new creations are being dished up; techno-revisionism remains forever empty.

The data nihilist heeds the words of the political anarchist Bakunin: "Even destructiveness is a creative impulse." The deposition of spirit into information was never in itself subversive. Information itself is a virus, infinitely multiplying. The effort to contain hacked data requires more information, which requires more information, etc. The ecstatic virus brings this festering growth of information to a climax by causing the network to head straight for total overload. The hungry virus, on the other hand, drains off information and aims at total delete. It creates emptiness by burning up data. It prevents the computerization of consciousness, which is always a process of pacification.

Every nomadic thought must account for itself as historical information in the full light of political codification. A lack of consciousness is the biggest crime; antisocial, immoral, unrealistic, irrational, mental. The virus has turned its back on common sense, to defect to the paranoid pole which is after antiproduction, after absolute, data-free communication. The virus is the computer's prayer.

The virus is a data string which sets out on a journey of its own, leaving its author behind within the social to be labeled a "criminal." Since the virus builders can never reveal themselves, they have no choice but to participate in the dialogue concerning the democratic significance of information. Here, they are up against the classical hackers, who think of their network rambles as a struggle against secrets. The hackers claim that all information must be made public to give meaning to the concept of democratic citizenhood. To them, info is not a toy but serious business. Because from a technological standpoint the distinction between 0 and 1 is immaterial, they find themselves forced to fall back on old social techniques to regulate information communications.

Hacker ethics attempt to revive the classical discourse of police-thinking by taking metaphors from the "regular world" and introducing them into the network. Traffic rules, responsible driving, clearing the bicycle path, cleaning up behind you . . . The fleeting contacts engaged in by network users are sexually charged and burdened with the demand for safe hacks. But the data world is nothing like that which used to be forced upon us as social reality until quite recently. Nothing exists by itself; there are only character sets and their compulsory reading codes ("common sense"). Whoever masters the code is fit to rule, control, and exploit the world. Still, even within the global system, ethics have been abandoned ever since chronological time was swallowed up out of the historical order and into catastrophic chain reactions.

For instance, environmental pollution cannot be controlled through a change of attitude, because it has left the human standard behind. It appears that cyberspace's virtual reality still resides within the human condition. Hard- and software have been cooked up by businessmen looking for patents, and are every bit retracable. This is why the ethics hackers still think they can appeal to the possibility of sensible keyboard use. But the virus is already one step ahead. It has abandoned the human, all too human and places its bets on the inconceivable that lurks beyond the world of ideas. It sends out a message to the network aliens, the other-circuit warriors, the pink panthers who have escaped the cyberzoologists' bestiary. It feels at home within the biological complexity of infinite relationships, mutations, and crossovers. Free of objectives, it is only alert to the chain-reactionary liberation of the astonishing. The virus may appear catastrophic to the order of rule and control, but in fact it is the messenger of a different, metarealistic order.

During the first stage of the computer medium, the hacker's movement supplied the military instruments with a democratic ideology. Thus, the merging of military and civil space through the massive PC armament of the population could take place under the historical heading of liberty, equality, and fraternity. Once the electronic cottage industry had been fully accepted, the traditional military apparatus could be dismantled and we entered the stage of the disarmament race between Gorbachev (1985–1991) and the NATOs. Its stake was no longer to hold the global population as hostages, but to enforce a global consciousness among the legions of utterly isolated PC civilians. Thus, the awareness (still doubted during the cold war) has now become generally accepted that we are all on the same disk together, which may be erased at the flick of a wrist.

During this second stage, the professional hacker community is unpleasantly surprised by the sudden emergence of cybergoofs, software traitors, and wise guys who are frustrated with hacker hierarchy and carry out their own radical data actions on the principle that "we are the hunter/gatherers of the world of CommTech." Its answer consists of "one network or none" thinking. Since absolute security is impossible within the data industry, the hackers need to secure their morality through "information responsibility," quite aware that this is a one-way ticket to rejection and rebellion. After all, they themselves, too, once started out as whiz kids who stood up to info screening by data Securitates in a techno-revolutionary spirit.

What lies ahead of us is not data traveling along secured roads but absorption into cyberecstasy. It may as well be governed by the hacktic riot of a total sensory clash, as by the New Age's spiraling bliss. Even in this respect, there will be nothing new. Still, in its imperturbable urge to multiply, the virus already transmits a message that metareality is prepared to enter any zone suffering from deranged codes. The alien is not yet among us—but she is ready. She knows. She waits. She awaits us. It is up to the cyberpunks to make a pact with her. The future is outside.

THE FATAL ATTRACTION
OF REALITY

"Don't want, don't want, don't want to be part of your world."

—David Bowie

"Move those cameras! Out of the way! Sit down! Get out of the way!" On the balcony of the "Stadsschouwburg," Amsterdam's city theater, a lively Suriname band was staging a colorful show in anticipation of the arrival of Nelson Mandela, who was going to deliver a speech to the 15,000 Amsterdam citizens who had gathered there. But the musicians remained invisible behind the row of (white) press cameras in front of them, much to the crowd's annoyance. When word spread around that the "King of Africa" had entered the building, the media gathered around the microphone at the center of the balcony. The crowd, realizing that they were about to miss out on this sight as well, started to chant. Catchphrases like "Move your cameras!" spontaneously turned into the angry slogan of "TV get lost!"—a variation of the traditional slogan "Riot police get lost!" suddenly equating the image hunters with state troopers. In a crowd that had been dismissed as meaningless décor or consumers for a decade, the years of vague antimedial discomfort now turned into an awareness that the media agents have taken over the role of the peacekeepers in robbing the mass of its event.

Increasingly, the media have declared themselves the real event, forcing themselves ever further into the picture with all their technological prostheses. To the press, the actual mass gathered on the square in front of the theater had become just as imaginary as the viewers at home, and equally uninteresting. The "masses of the people" feared that all they would get to see were the backs of some media guys, although they knew that Mandela had come to meet them, and that the happening was not intended as some open-air press conference. The journalists, sensing that the first brick was about to hit their portable hi-tech, swiftly retracted from this 1.5-meter demediatized zone.

Then his exiled royalty appeared in the press-free zone, patiently observing those who had gathered to see him. Noticing that there stood more thousands of cheering people down the sides of the balcony, he pushed his

186

way through the cameras to greet them as well. In contrast with all the pop musicians, soccer teams, queens, and politicians who use the crowd as just another PR tool, Mandela, instead of making a dash for the mike, took his time to meet the mass. Even he himself brushed the media aside to make room for the event. There was a sudden hush as Mandela, contrary to expectations, did not deliver a speech but had the simple nerve to give a full explanation of current ANC activities, without succumbing to sloganeering. The curious experience shared by those present was that of a mass being brought to discharge without any incendiary ranting and raving. The crowd turned out to be capable of more than just ecstasy or boredom; it could simply and quietly contemplate what was being said. After half an hour, Mandela concluded his address by saying: "We respect you, we thank you, and above all, we love you"—something the media have yet to come up with.

The media anticipate a battle of life and death in the coming age of digital interfaces. The bit's 0/1 principle turns out to have a yes/no analogy. Two breathtaking scenarios impose themselves on us: If we say yes to the media, we emigrate to cyberspace, abandoning our physical hardware and inscribing our consciousness into software. If the answer is no, then we take the "exit to reality," with media ending up either as household goods or as museum art, along with vacuum cleaners and country wickerwork.

Although the extent and frequency of antimedial incidents daily increases, they are carefully kept out of or not recognized as such by the press. Not one Dutch paper reported the abovementioned assault on consumer-hostile media behavior. Still, there are already signs of an international "anti-media movement." Its motto is that in order to meet someone you must first disrupt a few connections. Today, the habit of wrecking a telephone booth, short-circuiting a cable TV socket, pouring concrete over an ATM, removing video cameras from intersections, or cutting up street cables at random before tucking in no longer raises anyone's eyebrows. So far, this shared *savoir-vivre*, inspired by do-it-yourself-help and out for simple pleasures, has not yet exceeded the stage of local disturbances. But when the uplinks to the global village are cut short en masse, we may safely assume that many more earthlings will put their media-free time to other uses.

For years on end, viewers used to enjoy their TV sedation, but in the end even that became a bore. The argument in favor of responsibly programmed educational television only deters them even further. Recent research has shown that viewing rates are "dropping dramatically." Even the remaining TV-set owners deny ever using them. "The hesitation to admit to the habit produces an answer similar to that given by alcoholics: 'Drinking, me?!'; 'Those few shows, that's not watching.'"

The mediatist caste moves about exclusively within permanent topicality, because it considers it its social duty to avert the danger of a sudden return of history. To accomplish this, it strips every event of its causes and effects in a production of unrelated and inconsequential items. It realizes that if the masses regain their capability to act, the media will be the first to suffer the consequences. Once, the media were an exceptional case. The impressiveness of live images of the moon-landing lay in the fact that no one had ever seen anything like it before: The whole world was switched on to the fascination of leaving earth at home. It seemed a fulfillment of the promise that we can leave the unbearable weight of being behind and finally enter the technological universe, where we can whiz from one spot to another in a condition of zero gravity.

Two decades later, viewers began to realize what all this really means. By turning everything into information, the media can level all incidents to the same images (all of the Dutch media compared Mandela's address to public celebrations of the national soccer team). Because media are omnipresent, space has lost its substance, to be filled up with images from an inpeculiar elsewhere. The place viewed has no other context than that of the item that follows it. The medial outlook has become coincidental with the touristic experience of "here today, somewhere else tomorrow." There is no need for confrontations with the others, when all you have to do is check out their accompanying info. "Why talk to one another when we're communicating so well?" The others have become obstacles or objects which possibly reveal interesting characteristics. If not, all you have to do is to walk on.

At present, reality is the exception. The fact that it should thus exercise a dangerous attraction is not altogether unfamiliar to the media workers. They identify it in psychological terms as the romantic feelings they themselves have had on occasion, or dismiss the call for reality as nostalgia or fear of technology. No doubt, the assault on media will be misrepresented as vandalistic and undemocratic actions, and indifference as an alarming development that needs to be reversed through information services. Still, the aversion to TV is no more than an expression of the general human need for an outside in which to experience something personal. Reality is seen as the realm of the unpredictable, which no longer coincides with the technological miracle. The antimedial movement's moral values (respect, gratitude, love?) may prevent it from taking its resentment to the point of a final destruction of media. The media just have to cool down a bit. The movement might give the information channels their own place within the machinery of everyday life, then stop arguing about the whole affair.

Now that the media find themselves cornered, they come up with the answer to suck up their users into the screen once and for all: Cyberspace, the "medium to end all media." Rumors about the "new space" that roams through the actually existing global village have charged current investigations with huge expectations and unlimited possibilities. The cyberspace saga has already been written down by Gibson and Sterling; video kids nervously guard the gates of their arcades; the military are diligently experimenting with the total interface between body and machine. Old hippies don data suits and gloves to realize their Oriental dream of unrestricted journeys through the universal consciousness without the traditional withdrawal symptoms. Finally, there are the media artists who try to use their aesthetic morality to keep cyberspace empty, to prevent it from being filled up with nothing but banalities. So far, the early works of these pioneers do not tell us whether cyberspace will remain a private experience, or rather become the virtual vehicle for hypercommunication between global citizens in the near future. The synonym of this public space under construction is "Cybermedia."

In cybermedia, the distance between subject and object which caused the old media so much trouble is all but eliminated. It was about time we put an end to all those reflections and criticisms regarding the ego's place in the world, all that bitching about a presumed reality that doesn't fit in with the general picture. The puritanical small-mindedness which strives for a sharp distinction between human and virtual reality is banned to the prehistory of political metaphysics by the cyberspace scouts. They replace this old-fashioned need to draw a line by a democratic view of reality: If you don't like what you see, why not simply reset your cybergoggles?

The twentieth-century media have not lived up to their promise of the global village as a resort of maximum mobility. The predicted uprooting of the entire world population by an advancing mediatization was seen as a part of the inevitable process of human progress. Finally, the construction of a worldwide infrastructure for all would place every region on history's conveyor belt toward an affluent and convenient life. To this day, technological progress consists of the construction of a set of ideologically neutral networks and facilities: from cable television, freeways, and (air)ports to sanitation and the mobilization of labor, resources, commodities, and information. These transregional structures are thought to hover like a cloud above traditional customs and nationalities. The idea of media was that the transcendence of local identities would automatically lead to their disappearance or (if not) at least render them uninteresting from a global perspective, compared to infrastructural developments. In this scheme, the region functions as a supplier of cultural resources for a variegated media package. Regions that cannot or will not play the game end up on a list of no-go zones doomed to cry in vain in an information wilderness.

But the media have never internationalized; on the contrary, they turned out to be a means of consolidating local relations. With universal communication, everybody can stay put. Not everyone has mastered the touristic experience of the personal lifestyle and environment. Ever more parts of the world (Mesopotamia, the Balkans, Central Asia) are starting to act as a nuisance to the project of transnationalization. Old media such as religions stubbornly stick to their own absolute values and try to cause a stir among the Family of Man. The religious still refuse to believe that we inhabit one world (perhaps they've missed the moonlanding coverage?). But they will learn in time, the day they discover that the rest of the world couldn't care less about their local nuclear wars. We don't need your fucking catastrophes.

Cybermedia are the terminus of the idea of global networks. They aim at completion of the infrastructural, on the urgent principle that there will be "one system or none at all." Their dream is to accommodate all medial spaces in the House of Cyberspace. The idea is that until now, humanity has wasted its time lobbying in little rooms, but now there's a chance to get the general picture and connect the lot. From now on, we will be able to hop effortlessly from every radio program, movie, data bank, archive, and library to every conceivable private conversation, tele-conference, and teleshop, no matter where.

The nagging on of past realities which have frustrated the project of modernity for a century is cut short by replacing them once and for all by a new principle of reality. In cybermedia, all formats of language, time, territory, identity (sex, race, lifestyle), environment, health, and age have been converted into the universal 0/1 code. To log in means to be a little bit of something everywhere. The ancient desire to leave the mortal body behind is combined with the equally ancient pursuit of a masterless, communicative society of pure human beings. World peace is realized on a level of abstraction where to play war games only causes one to lag behind. Historically, cyberspace may still be retraced to war as the father of all things, but in actual practice the fatal transmission of genetic material has ruined our Father even in terms of technological genealogy. Similarly, SDI, scheduled to be a cold war highlight, caused its sudden end instead, much to the dismay of the military-industrial complex.

The threats encroaching upon the cybermedia's Empire of Freedom are legion. On the one hand, there are the pigheaded dissidents and their collective attempt to impose their own format on all the data-flows within the global infrastructural empire. They see the disappearance of space-time differences as a chance to impose their will directly on the users. On the other hand, there emerge sinister figures who break the common consensus and break out of their own loneliness by running amok in cyberspace. With their electronic creeses, they blindly slash away at passersby. But there exist internal threats as well. As Gibson pointed out, corporations are creating new barriers to guard their data buildings, and might well take over all of cyberspace—a form of exclusivism that undermines democratic intentions and invites to acts of resistance in the name of total accessibility. Moreover, the electrosphere can quickly silt up with self-duplicating data trash, defunct environments, drifting noise, virtual billboards along data flows, and spontaneous crashes through overload or insufficient computing capacity. Cyberspace allows for repressive or therapeutic applications as well, which infringe upon the faith in the non-normativeness of communication.

People ask us: "Is there any perspective in cybermedia?" Artistic and non-specialist journals put up a smoke screen to make the introduction of cyberware as attractive as possible. Those laypersons who don't give up beforehand never get much further than the question of technology, while the more advanced get caught up in the question of ethics. They anticipate a broad public debate on the safety of the new media and the redundancy schemes of the old. Consciousness must not be allowed to be harmed by the latest psychedelics. Meanwhile, NGOs such as "Save the TV" demand guarantees regarding the preservation of detached media. Skeptics claim that, like Star Wars, cyberspace may be technically possible, but in practice it will never get beyond the stage of simulation. Its introduction on a global scale like TV or telephone would require such enormous investments in hard-, soft-, and wetware that it would withdraw all productive power from the area of civil consumption. They predict that cyberspace will never exceed the level of private consciousness and will end up as a hyperindividual, out-of-body fairground attraction, similar to the orgone box, dreamachine, or megabrain. The neo-materialists point to the limits of communication. They claim that we have nothing left to say to, nor any wish to meet one another—not even in cyberspace. The Other can easily be consumed without necessarily getting in touch with it. Media may convey something, but they radiate nothing. Real contact is made with a nice chunk of steel or concrete, without the need for input or exchange that is inherent to cybermedia. Finally, the visionaries issue ukases predicting that the whole cyberproject will end up as one of the ruins of postindustrial presumption. They do not mean this in a derogatory sense. To them, the failure of the quantum chip is a challenge to the artist to use defunct electronics to bring the aesthetics of ruin up to date.

In an attempt to hush this interpretative onslaught, the cyberphilosophers fall back on a figure of thinking which has been quite a hit for centuries now: the Hegelian construct of "reconciliation." The contradiction between the virtual (formerly Spirit or the Imaginary) and reality (as the Absolute Principle) is reconciled by the ringing advertising slogan of "virtual reality." But the promotion capacity of this logo may not be all it seems to be. Among the antimedial in particular, there is great resentment of the whole marketing idea. They see cyberspace simply as an actual increase of the available media, and reject its critics as noise that naturally accompanies the introduction of a new product. Their confidence that cyberspace simply consists of all the former media together renders them indifferent to the promise of a new, mythical space. They might have settled for a fully animated image package, as this would at least remove the cameras from the public highway. But cybermedia must be more than just a 3-D video game; their lust for images will continue to drive them out of the studios to feed on extramural street-scene material.

The charm of cybermedia lies in their naive approach to the world. They presume that artificial fascination suffices to extinguish reality. The world is removed ever further from the personal terminal. Reality is not in the least bothered by this. It knows the all-too-human craving for the illusory, and that all it must do is wait for this, too, to blow over. The question, however, is whether the antimedial movement will prove capable of the same kind of patience.

THE EXTRAMEDIAL

"The real Other is different shit."
—John Sasher

Everything is medial. There exists no original, unmediatized situation in which "authentic" human existence can be experienced. That which is not directly audible, visible, or tangible may be stored somewhere, but is still inaccessible to knowbots. The idea that an extramedial remnant still exists is the engine of exclusive tourism ("See Yemen the Different Way"). The extramedial experience is what makes scanning a unique event—"I took the first picture of the Yeti." From this angle, the extramedial is seen as a zone to be conquered, or as a neglected area that can be rediscovered at any time. The idea that an extramedial reality exists is itself an effect of the media, and the first amendment of the media empire. Media do not merely transmit information. They do more than just charge data with symbolic values and meanings. They add up to more than a collection of technological connections. Besides their productive and repressive powers, the media also have a moment of negation. If an extramedial realm exists, it is to be found within the media themselves, not outside them. It can be located at the intersection of two media, between the no-longer of the one medium and the not-yet of the other. In this black hole, they reach the limit of the senses. Conditioning is temporarily lost, the power of the media falters and faulty connections are made which fall outside the domain of information. The content of a medium is the preceding medium, wrote Marshall McLuhan. An inevitable consequence of this rule is that those who strive for a deeper content always land up at a previous medium. For writing this is the voice; for photography, painting and graphics; for film, photography and the theatre; for radio, the narrative and the concert; for the media package as a whole, it is the opera in its nineteenth-century form of the *Gesamtkunstwerk*. All possible combinations achieve profundity in the same way. In terms of the present medium, the writer focuses on the enigma of style, the photographer concentrates on the technique of framing light and its relation to dark surfaces, and the filmmaker experiments with the combination of stationary images and the darknesses in between. Expressive content is always the result of a retro movement. One must immerse oneself in the medium used in order to hold on to one's creative moment, to prevent oneself from being misled or misused by one's own instruments. Only complete control of one's medium leads to authenticity; in other words, to the totally controlled downloading of its data flows. Authenticity is the obstinate use of a medium's resistances for the sake of ensuring the longevity of an expressive work. "And words obey my call" (Yeats).

According to McLuhan's rule, at the boundary between one medium and the next there is an instant when medium *A* loses its original content and becomes the content of medium *B*. At that moment, *A* loses its immaterial function and becomes a mere empty channel, transporting nothing. For a moment medium *A* is free of information, devoid of content, autonomous, concrete, and thus becomes conveyable material itself. In the transition to film, unique photographs are sequentially prepared and linked on a strip of celluloid. The photograph loses its individual content and meaning: the isolation of a singular instant. Medium *B* manipulates the emptiness of *A* to create new contents. Those who negate their own medium do so in order to make it so empty that a new medium must appear and provide a new and satisfactory context for the meaninglessness of the old. Negators do not seek profundity, they seek a way out: that which the authenticists glorify, they have rejected. Their medium is no longer able to function and the new medium has not arrived yet. They gamble on the unpredictable which lies beyond the borders of the old media program. They dare media to prove that they do more than just process information.

To track the specific characteristics of a medium, you must find the moment at which it lets go of its content. This happens when the medium has exhausted its program. At this. moment of completion, content and medium converge and can be seized as raw material for the next round. What is a climax on the medial level is a moment of panic and inspiration on the user's side. It is the arrival of the unimaginable; the media answer.

The experiments of what is called, after the fact, the avant-garde, are never carried out with a specific goal in mind. You are always either too late or too early; only fashion is always on time. Negation fanatically persists in a particular use of a medium, in order to evoke something which is understood as unhappiness with the possibilities of the usual medium. "You can paint like crazy, but so what?" Until the experiments are finished, the medium keeps pumping, churning, shooting, until "it" either comes out or not. "It" is not an experience which results from the mediaworker's subjectivity; it is a techno-effect, an object strategy, a gift from the other side—technological happiness. Happiness is a definitive perception, the experience of that emotion, tuning in to a frequency only you can pick up, here and now. In 1922, Gottfried Benn looked back on the ecstatic time he had spent in occupied Brussels of 1916: "An extraordinary spring, three months completely without comparison. What was the cannonade on the Yser, without a day going by, life trembling in an atmosphere of silence and lostness; I was living on the edge where being fails and the self begins. I often look back on those weeks: They were life, and will never return; all else was rupture." Those weeks will never return because they remain stored in the stories of the Rönne and the poem "Caryatid," which Benn wrote during those months. His medium, writing, had him completely under control, and he, it. The result was absolute prose, sovereign poetry. As he makes the connection between his body and his medium, between *A* and *B*, between self and being, across all rifts, Benn locates this experience on the brink between life and death. In this atmosphere of silence and lostness, Benn has nothing to contribute and no defense; he is in the position of the photograph, a single image on a strip of celluloid: a part of the larger whole that effaces individual existence and renders it productive. The establishment of media connections, the moment of absence of any media message, comes through in the sphere of experience as the link between being and self. The media link gives him his own moment. For a time he balances on the brink between humanity and media.

Media start out by taking over previous media as content. On television in the 1950's you could see plays lasting all evening (including intermission); in virtual reality the first things built were stark office interiors. But then someone discovers, or makes a medium discover, that something different may be done with the old material; this is the only possible way to hint at a mystery that was missing from all previous media. It adds a zone to the province of experience or renders one newly accessible. But as soon as the medium reveals its mystery, it leaves the transition from the previous medium behind it and becomes sovereign. When a medium is no longer anything but a medium and brings its unique moment into play, it no longer forces the data it is supposed to transport and exerts no pressure on those who are tuned in.

Benn wrote poems "without faith, hope, or love." In Benn's Brussels experience his medium brought something to life which did not exist as long as his medium was sovereign; in anthropological terms, something that was dead as long as the ritual was not performed in which the dead and the living are interchanged, the silence and the words on paper. The ritual of wandering and writing in Benn's "three months completely without comparison" kept his life livable and ensured that he was more than a survivor. It offered a way out and a way back; it kept his world alive.

In 1949, Benn wrote in the introduction to his first work: "In general I do not know what I am writing, what I plan to do, or how something arises in me, in the past or now; I only know when a work is finished. But the whole is not finished. 'The crown of creation, the swine, the human,' writes my friend Oelze, dissuasive and doubtful; it is a decisive verse in this book. Not only diabolical, but un-Goethian, it tastes of sulphur and absinthe, but I return to it throughout my life in my work." To precisely what was he returning? After cutting up 2,000 cadavers in medical school, young Benn lost every bearable image of humanity. Everything became quite still; six poems were entrusted to paper—his first. Art appeared out of the emptiness after the body-as-a-corpse, after the total negation of the body as a medium for life, and the emptiness answered and became the voice of his poetry. The medium of poetry chose him. The connection between the disappeared body and the written text was the media link which Benn had put into writing. Whether he wanted to or not, in order to write each new poem, Benn had to return to the gate of the morgue in which he had emptied the body forever in order to turn it into poetry. To be able to write a handful of consoling lines, Benn always had first to see the total deterioration and corruption of life behind that one dissecting-room door which was meant for him—which had chosen him. Everyone has such a door. It is one's point of view. Benn cut the medium of the body to ribbons and landed up in the medium of poetry. Thus the body (his own as well as others') became the basis of his language.

The "media" in their current form are also searching for the door to the next medium, to an outside, though they seem far removed from that point. Contemporary media still derive their content from exteriorities; they want to be filled, to try out their whole program. The mass media are still at the stage in which they must destroy all the material they have sucked in to be able to function. Those who allow themselves to be placed in the picture or recorded "die" in the process, lose their corporeality, their presence in one place and become a collection of bits that can be transmitted everywhere at once. These vampire media have not yet found their special mystery outside material reality. Only when they have passed through the full dematerialization can they enter into the immaterial. The media already make up a system in which humans are no longer necessary, except as fodder for the scanner. In the media network humanity is more of an irritating obstacle, a jamming station, a noise generator, than a condition of its existence. If the media really want to feel the rush of their own functioning free of static they will have to get rid of the human being. The power of the digital media is that they produce images, sound and text solely through mathematical formulas. They do not need an outside world to live off at all.

The extramedial is that which, however complete the media are in their techniques of representation and however the users control their medium, can never be expressed, never understood within the performance of the media package in question. The media exclude the extramedial from the domain of knowledge but at once make it possible to experience it—as that which is missing. And that is the special moment of a specific medium. You can only hear silence when the voice does not speak, but speech is only possible with silence. The extramedial is like a model of the atom: if a three-dimensional representation can be made of it then it has not been understood, and still it is the basis of all that exists. The extramedial appears as the negation of the information in a medium. It is not the bit of data that has appeared in a certain situation in front of and behind the camera, not the thing depicted in the photograph, but its photogenic quality. Without photography, no one would have known that some faces, postures, and elements of the landscape, in a certain light and from a certain angle perhaps, possess something which is invisible without the photograph: they are photogenetic. But this says nothing about what is depicted in the photo. Photogenius is technological happiness. When the photographer glances over the contact sheet, it is this power which determines the final picture. What was a representation (the photograph) metamorphoses into something which was never present in the thing represented (photogenius). In movies, the photogenic effect is known as the third meaning: that which is left over after you have analyzed a movie sequence's importance within the story and its symbolic interpretation. An alarm clock, the bun in someone's hair, a pair of slippers, sheets on a clothesline. The added value, the presence of death, that silence—evoked in the text of photography, language, film, or video, in narrative forms or symbolic contents, but remaining outside either range, no matter how far it is stretched. And it is precisely because of this that it is stretched. The extramedial is the most uncritical category imaginable, and the most rigid. Only from within another medium can the special moment of one medium be discovered, but what that special quality is can be expressed in neither of those. It exists only as a connection between two media, and what the photograph sees in the film is different from what the film sees in the photograph. But there exists another special moment, when a photograph is viewed from within painting, writing, sound, or the tangibility of things. The content of a medium is the user of that medium. Communication does not exist. Two media touch, each registers what is perceptible from its own perspective, and they experience this as communality in the recognition of the other's medium-specific moment. That is understanding: A sees in B what only A can see in B and B says nothing back, seeing in A what only B is capable of seeing in A. If there exists any communality on this planet then it is that which is fundamentally incommunicable, extra-informative, nonmedial, recognizable only as the shift from one medium to another. This misunderstanding generates creativity as no other factor can. In transactions, we find each other, we build things. Just as a director can be called a nostalgic nationalist at home and a prominent artist who takes cinema to a new level abroad, misunderstanding is the vehicle for cultural transmissions.

The extramedial is not a subjective, psychological reaction, but a physical experience generated by the media. Take the third meaning in movies. In black and white movies, the third meaning appears as an erotic effect. The hyperproportional enlargement of a face on the screen creates the effect of the face getting so close to you that you are tempted to kiss it. A combination of acting and lighting divests the face of all recognizable expression and gives it its physical power. Garbo and Dietrich did not need lascivious glances to inspire physical reactions in the audience. Color close-ups have no such effect, but achieve the same by showing the full body. Madonna manipulates viewers' bodies, not with her face, but with full-length shots. With her it is breast and thigh movements that do the job. Considered from within the media themselves, the extramedial is not the third meaning or the photogenic effect; it is the bodies of the users. Hence the camera's obsession with endlessly circling the body. Everything and everyone must be forced into the picture, completely, live if possible. In movies, bodies are extra-informative: The images, the informative, may touch the bodies but never penetrate further, which is why the audience never tires of seeing more movies and keeps an industry in business. Media actively seek ways to realize their extramedial, which is the only possible form of corporeality for them. But the click does not simply happen once enough bodies are in the picture. It happens only when Meaning III comes into play. It is more than quantity or quality, it is a hook you get stuck on.

Media cannot create material bodies; at best they boost physical awareness. Media produce only subsequent media and carry the secret of their approach around with them. The secret of still photography is movement; the secret of movies is the omnipresence of television; the secret of television is its autonomously generated digital images and the autarchic standstill of biological and chemical drugs. Seen from the body, all images are external. The body got by just fine without celluloid and the silver screen, but the visual media could not do without the bodies. This changes only with the arrival of computer graphics and psychedelics. The old media did not reveal the existence of some universal mystery; quite the contrary: They showed that every empty space contains its own mystery, its own extramedial, the secret which can only be detected through that specific medium, just like language discovered silence. In every use of media, the connection is what's important. "Make it new" (Ezra Pound) means making an old medium contemporary by linking it to a new one, as Pound did in his Cantos. "We must be absolutely modern" (Rimbaud) means exactly the opposite: Leave behind the old media and be absorbed into the new. All media that have existed up till now could be put into language. Even cyberspace made its debut in book form (William Gibson's *Neuromancer*). Language absorbed as many older media as television had and flourished, while photography and film had a tougher time. For the time being, the language program remains universal, or at least as wide-ranging as that of digital data.

In media theory there is no death; it is a vitalist theory. Media merely have a line to dying and the spectacle of it. Death is not medial. Nor are there really any near-death experiences here. The extramedial is not the same thing as this unmedial, for the extramedial is unthinkable, impossible to experience without a media interior. The extramedial is the negation of the information content of media; death is the negation of the media themselves. The extramedial is the experience of that which is not information, but death is the realm of that which cannot be experienced. Perhaps death is not even the limit of experience, but more like an offshore island. It is as easy to communicate with the dead as with the living; each discovers his own. Snapshots of ghosts, zombie movies, knocking on tables, closed rooms for angels, muffled voices on tape: No medium is afraid of making the dead speak up in a format we can understand. But just as the living have given up the search for a definition of life—the impossible question—the dead remain silent about what death is. They have nothing to say to each other about it.

On August 10, 1941, Klaus Mann sits in New York. It is a hot summer, and everybody has left the city. But he has to stay and work on the fifth issue of *Decision*, the magazine he's started for American and exile literature. Heat. Not a sea breeze that blows. He opens his journal. The last entry dates from the twenty-ninth of July. Hitler's army has just invaded the Soviet Union: "How quaint, this Hitler. He has made a mistake, a decisive one. This is the beginning of the end." The friends and family members he usually hangs around with, the interesting contacts and encounters, have all departed for cooler places. August tenth. "Never lonelier than in August. . . ." In the space beneath the lines about the invasion in Russia, Mann notes down a vague memory, an almost clichéd quote. Just a sentence. Then he begins to remember the name of its source and, then and there, he writes down two couplets by Benn that have stayed with him:

Einsamer nie als im August
Erfüllungsstunde, im Gelände
die roten und die goldenen Brände,
Doch wo ist deiner Gärten Lust?
Wo alles sich durch Glück beweist
und tauscht den Blick und tauscht die Ringe
im Weingeruch, im Rausch der Dinge,
dienst du dem Gegenglück, dem Geist.

Counterhappiness. Something in Klaus Mann has changed.

Me and that fascinating life of mine. Nothing but success. And nothing achieved. One columnist among many. Everything came too easily. Always listening to others in order to learn something. Always intoxicated by things and exchanging glances and what comes after. Yet this doctor of ours . . . Is *Decision* counterhappiness? Is it enough that I can no longer stand to go on for the sake of happiness? Why am I not in the service, like Tomski [his friend]? Calls every weekend from training camp: marching, shooting, angry sergeants! And me so lazy. He envies me that. Is this freedom?

Klaus Mann thereupon encodes the metamorphosis he is undergoing as follows: *Decision* is not enough, writing articles is not enough, I want to write something bigger, something magnificent: a book! He has always lived in a literary milieu, and now it produces a literary encoding of that which is beginning to flow in him. And the atmosphere of friendship he has always lived in inspires him to write: " . . . so that I will have some news for Tomski when the person-to-person call comes from Savannah. 'Imagine! The first chapter is practically finished. . . .'" After writing this sentence, Mann suddenly gets up and walks outside. Gottfried Benn had written his verse on September 4, 1936, in Hannover, almost as an affirmation of what Klaus Mann wrote to him in 1934 about his partiality to the Nazis: "If some high-ranking minds do not know where they belong, those fellows know precisely what does not belong with them—the human spirit." Benn sent the poem that same September 4 on a postcard to his friend Oelze. It was first published in his *Ausgewählte Gedichte* (*Selected Poems,* 1936), which Klaus Mann reviewed in 1937. On that occasion he had remarked: "Is it not obvious that he [Benn] is lately disappointing himself, isolating himself, finding himself disillusioned, that he has manoeuvred himself into an impossible and awkward, even grotesque position? Because the Nazis do not want him, and have an unmistakable instinct against all his qualities? Because he can no longer find an audience in Germany, since the few readers he had have been deported or silenced? Now he is a surly army medical officer in Hannover; hardly an enviable situation." But, he added, it no longer matters; Benn is a bypassed station.

Until the poem resurfaces in him years later, an articulation of the hardly enviable situation of an army doctor who knows that his few readers have been silenced. And a shift occurs in Klaus Mann. An assurance. This poet, and all my interesting acquaintances here, forget them—only the work itself counts. The great work. Mind your own business and let others do theirs.

When Mann returns to his quarters he continues to write in his journal, whiskey and soda at his side: "But what sort of book? This is a serious moment. I know it is. Seriousness is something I feel deeply. I want to write a serious book, a sincere book. Can a novel be totally serious, totally sincere? Perhaps. But I do not want to write one, not now, not at this moment. I am weary of all the literary clichés and tricks. I am weary of all the masks, all the tricks of simulation. Is it art itself that I am weary of? I do not wish to play anymore. I wish to confess. The serious moment—that is the moment of confession."

And he decides to write a book in English: *The Turning Point,* later translated by Mann himself as *Der Wendepunkt,* supplemented by his wartime journal entries. Mann is undergoing a period of metamorphosis, the completion of an oeuvre: a completion that consists of the negative version of his own existence, including his books, not considered as something he has lived and written, but as material meant for treatment on a higher level, the level of autobiography. And in this new space, finally he no longer needs to be brilliant. The strictest criterion. But what does the absolute poem do to Mann, what does an old medium do when it becomes the content of the next? Rilke explained this in one of his absolute poems, forty years before Mann experienced it. In this poem Rilke described a sovereign medium: a perfect statue from antiquity, completed by the disappearance of the head, arms, legs, and sex. There was only a torso: closed in on itself, without so much as a glance outside. Hermetic. Rilke's description of this medium was itself closed, everything fit in with everything else; his total control of language led to a total authenticity of expression. But having finished his perfect description, he bluntly followed it with the sentence, "Change your life." All at once, an exit is offered. The "change your life" experience of seeing/reading/listening to sovereign media—that was what Klaus Mann had experienced. He realized it, and took the consequences. Of course, Rilke's sentence is an ambiguous one. There are infinite ways to interpret its meaning. Does it mean: "Change your life so you can create sovereign art yourself (as Rilke did); leave your wife and child, go wandering"? Or is it: "Change your life so that you and your life may become sovereign?" Or maybe it means: "O statue, change and become flesh." But for those who are touched by this absolutist magic, such hermeneutics are only a part of the game. "I do not wish to play anymore" (Mann). Change your life: In this moment of completion there exists an opening, here and now, which beams the sovereign medium through. The change has already begun. You are already an other. Later, the astonished discovery follows: I can no longer imagine life without that poem, without that day, without that shape which appeared in the doorway and suddenly made me realize what a fool I had been. The fact that the absolute takes no notice of what goes on outside reaffirms the person who observes this about his own life; that is the change. From this eternal and universal longing to be elsewhere, to be delivered of oneself, one moves to the security of being here, at this single point in space and time, in this ego, in this being. Only those who are completely at one with themselves are capable of the metamorphosis which leads them to ecstasy and changes them. This is completion. Hermeticism is the production of discontinuity. A space appears beyond self and being; metamorphosis begins. Something from elsewhere, from outside, appears in the present. It. The unspeakable. An atmosphere of silence and lostness. Technological happiness. Sovereign media. A line read. A beam of light. But it was an insanely clear day. A silhouette before a window. I thought: Is it you? Human consciousness shifts from one medium to another and becomes aware of its mediality at moments of transition. Where one medium ends and the other begins, for an instant there exists no medium. The unencodable presents itself; the unchanneled, the silence of the godhead, the inhuman. Space. Spaces of possibility. Unearthly silences. This extramedial is negativity. Negation is the unencodable that flows through a medium and causes its collapse. Only those who destroy their medium can express that which needs to be expressed; that which has no expression exists outside the media. Therefore, sovereign media combine the medial with the media's destructive urges and demand perfection from every medium, for perfection is the best destruction. Then the next medium reveals itself.

Remember Baudrillard

"Beyond fascination and the word, there lie enough dark-nesses and existential abysses to satisfy the most serious of minds."

—Gottfried Benn

In 1972, Jean Baudrillard opens his "Requiem for the Media" with the observation, "There is no media theory." He continues: If we are to understand media, we must abandon the idea that media establish communication. There is no question of an exchange between transmitter and receiver; there are only messages. If the media are to be understood, they will have to be destroyed first.

A few years later, in a jocular mood, Baudrillard replaces the verb *produire* (to produce) by *séduire* (to seduce). From then on, the combination of transmission and seduction will provide him with the materials to construct a media theory which has freed itself from Freudo-Marxism. Media do not aim at satisfying the needs and desires of receivers, nor do they produce such subjective needs and desires according to a rational scheme. They owe their impact to their sublime gift of one-way communication. The stranger the transmitted signs are, the more intense their seductive power becomes, and the more fatal their effects on public consciousness. Realizing this, Baudrillard takes a radical step. He leaves the subject behind with all its alienation and insecurity, to defect to the side of the "appallingly strange" object and its fatal attraction. "The subject can only yearn; the object alone is able to seduce."

In *Fatal Strategies* (1983), his definitive essay, Baudrillard explains the mysterious intelligence of this object. Referring to Freudo-Marxism, he portrays woman and the masses as classical examples of the object. "The masses are not at all the objects of repression and manipulation. The masses do not want to be liberated; nor can they. All their (transpolitical) power lies in the fact that they are a pure object, that is to say: They confront any political coercion to make them speak with their silence and their absent desires. Some cardinal problem inevitably arises when we analyze the media and the sphere of information using the traditional concepts of the subject: willpower, representation, choice, liberty, knowledge, and desire. For it is quite obvious that they are at perfect odds with the latter, and that the sub-

201

ject, in its sovereignty, is completely alienated from them. There is a fundamental disparity between this sphere of information and the moral law which governs our every action and tells us that we must know what we want and desire. It suffices to reverse the idea of a mass alienated by media and to inquire how the entire media universe—perhaps even the entire technological universe—results from a secret strategy by the so-called alienated masses, a secret form of rejection of will, a different, sovereign philosophy of unwillingness, a sort of antimetaphysics, the secret of which is that the masses (or humanity as such) are really quite aware of the fact that they mustn't have an opinion about themselves or the world, that they do not need to want, know, or desire a thing."

Because of this radical inertia of the media masses, the "content of the media" need to be reconsidered. "The phenomena of mass and information are proportional quantities: The masses have no opinion and information does not inform them; they continue to feed each other in a monstrous way— the orbital velocity of information by no means increases the awareness of the masses, only their weight. All the information, the restless media activity, the scores of messages are only meant to contain the lethal contamination by the masses. Today, the energy of information, media, and communication is only used to extract some sense, some life from this cold, indifferent body, these silent masses who become ever more attractive."

With these insights, Baudrillard had realized the conditions for his media theory. In order to pose the problem of media, we must abandon the classical view of their social function as that of informing the masses. We must prevent our media theory from becoming a lower form of energy of the media themselves. That is why it does not try to ascribe all sorts of (subjective) intentions to the media, but rather allows them their own moment, seduction, or fatal strategy. Media theory considers the media an object and starts reasoning from there. It challenges the media to render their fatal strategies operative within the development of the theoretical expositions themselves. "This is how we must look at things: in terms of humor."

Media do not answer when approached in a critical manner; they demand the same frivolity and irony from their theorists as they have been reared on. Before it can defect to the side of the media object, media theory must become even more virtual than the media themselves, even more unsteady and implausible. To Baudrillard, this implies "something obscure and impenetrable," but in fact it amounts to "simply adopting a different logic, developing other strategies, giving free play to objective irony. This, too, is a challenge that may be absurd and which runs the same risk as that which it describes—but the risk must be taken: a fatal strategy's hypothesis must itself be fatal."

"Just as the world drives to a delirious state of things, we must drive to a delirious point of view." Baudrillard's thinking was originally concerned with leaving behind the academic context of his education. This he accomplished by declaring the revolt of signs. He claimed that reality had disappeared, since everything had come to signify else. Everything had become political, a social process with a psychosomatic explanation. Signs derived value only through circulation in information networks. He described this condition with the word "simulation," a word that, for him, would prove a fatal object. The concept allowed him to account for everything. He discovered three historical stages: imitation (until the nineteenth century), production (until 1950), and simulation, the present stage. In this last stage, the truth-falsehood opposition has become obsolete. Simulation has more truth than truth itself, because it is not a mirror image of reality but a model for it. Regardless of the truth value of this observation, his audience kept harping on the question of the dialectics of simulation and reality. One book after another, Baudrillard found himself obliged to explain to his thick-headed readers that simulation means the end of dialectics as well. His strategy was to use the word *simulation* so often that people would get completely fed up with it—which they did. But the moment they did, the author had become one with his concept, and must exit. The same went for keywords like *sign, simulacrum, fascination, seduction, obscenity, ecstasy,* and *implosion.* The inevitable result of liberation from Freudo-Marxism was the slogan "Forget Baudrillard." By then, he himself had long given up on his evangelistic activities as missionary of the silent majorities. His masses of readers were free to be as inert as they liked; he didn't need them. There could be no question of a new balance between simulation and reality, as suggested by the well-intentioned phrase "media reality." "The universe is not dialectic—it is devoted to extremes, not balance; to radical antagonism, not synthesis or reconciliation." The publication of *Fatal Strategies* signaled the end of Baudrillard's long good-bye to outdated patterns of thought, and his discovery of a new theoretical space. This is where artists and scientific journalists lost him. From now on, to write about Baudrillard's writings meant to construct a new theory of your own. Summaries and criticisms are always beside the point. Baudrillard comes close to Paul Virilio's approach when he starts philosophizing in an anticipatory, evasive fashion. "To survive, groups or individuals must never pursue their own properties, interests, or ideals. They must always pursue something else, something aside, beyond, opposite— like the warrior in Japanese martial arts." The same rule applies to writing.

"Theory can be no other than this: a trap laid with the hope that reality will be naive enough to fall into it." In *The Transparency of Evil* (1990), Baudrillard no longer considers the media worthy of analysis. The media belonged to the "orgy of liberation" raging since the 1960's, which has now come to an end, thank goodness. If, before, he discerned a "trilogy of values"—utility value, exchange value, and structural value, analogous to the historical stages of imitation, production, and simulation—he now adds a fourth level. Value has entered its fractal stage, in which a sort of epidemic of values, a general metastasis has broken out. Every single thing has become valuable; value steers toward its maximum circumference and may indeed be expected to leave the earth soon. This outbidding of all previous affairs takes place within what Baudrillard calls the "extreme phenomena," which he denotes by adding the prefix "trans-": transaesthetics, transsexuality, transpolitics, transeconomy, transtrans. Because all resistance has vanished, we are suddenly faced with superconductive events. A medical discovery like AIDS can become a global phenomenon in no time.

Baudrillard's strategy is to stop pointing at the simulative character of the media age. He no longer practices radical negativism, but starts looking for radical difference. His theories can no longer be translated back into sociological jargon—the only language still recognized by journalists. "Eclectic Paranoiac, Pharaonic Hypochondriac, Typical Troglodyte, Hepatic Brute, Pathetic Libidinous, Glossolaliac Ambidexter, Soft Exophtalmiac, Inverted Cerebrospinal, Recycled Tetracyclic" (*Cool Memories II*). In his aversion to media culture, Baudrillard places his bets on the secret power of the Foreign, which he had previously localized within the object. He opposes the principle of the clone, of the asexual and monomatic multiplication of the same which characterizes the information era, by the principle of the radically exotic. The earth has become so round that to depart from point *A* means to head for point *A*. Tourism: To travel is always to tour the globe. If the other once was the accursed part, now it is that which we are unable to retrace, because we are only looking for deviations from the familiar and can no longer see things that have fuck-all to do with it.

The absolutely exotic resides beyond all differences. It represents the "outside," which may be a temporary resident of every symbolic order, every culture, but is never on equal terms with it. Whenever the other is integrated into a culture, it is exterminated by it (Baudrillard uses the current Western absorption by Japan as an example); whereas it is exactly from outside that our thinking, our insights and seductions, derive. Free will is a second-rate affair; the foreign alone is at first hand.

What, then, exactly is the foreign? Baudrillard summarizes the dogma of the information society as: "Why talk to one another when we're communicating so well?" We have become radically exotic: total strangers. Hell (unlike in Sartre's day) no longer consists of other people, but of our inevitable communication with them. On the far side of communication, other people look each other in the eyes, revealing the secret: "that through which we escape ourselves." In the world after the media, it becomes possible to think further again. Baudrillard concludes *The Transparency of Evil* with the words "The other is that which enables me to avoid repeating myself to infinity."

Baudrillard's devotion to the radically different is not a maneuver to turn his back on the world, but a strategy to resist topicality. He keeps intervening—when the frozen freedom behind the Iron Curtain begins to melt, when the commemorative current of the fin de siècle sets in, or when Heidegger is turned on his head. These interventions culminated in his diatribe, "The Gulf War Did Not Take Place." During Desert Storm, Baudrillard, like Paul Virilio, witnessed his coming-out in the international media as the fashionable philosopher of simulation and virtuality. His success did not stop him from maintaining that "this nonwar is a continuation of the absence of politics by other means." In this virtual war without antagonists, "information" was "like an unintelligent missile; it never hits its target (nor, regretfully, its antimissile), it crashes at random or disappears into the void. . . ." Information = War. The more directly transmitted the event is, the more couched in information and inaccessible it becomes. "The only reason we watch live broadcasts is that we hope the event will turn information upside-down."

Beyond the fascination evoked by this inert spectacle, Baudrillard, with sudden concern, discerns the outlines of a conspiracy. The stiff challenge Saddam Hussein had posed to the West had all the incomprehensibility of the absolutely exotic. The Gulf Non-War was not so much designed to exterminate, but to domesticate such deviations from the rule. The other was so forcibly eradicated from the world in the name of democracy, human rights, and planetary consensus that "soon, Order will reign; a New World Order in which nothing happens, nothing exists, and nothing offers a motive or challenge." It is interesting that the last to resist this order should be Islam—"behind which, however, hide all cultural forms that still reject the West." No one can predict which side will win. But, as Baudrillard expressed his hope in March 1991, "The further the global consensus extends its hegemony, the greater the risk—or fortune—of its sudden collapse."

THE ARTIST'S MEDIA

"The ancient prophets were the television sets of their time, charged with a harsh, definite, and penetrating message."

—Boeli van Leeuwen

Now that the battle between art and technology has lost its meaning at the end of the twenty-first century, we can quietly examine what has kept the world population up in arms for so many generations. Looking back at the technological media that were installed outside of the self, we see the artists struggling with their relationship with the world of objects until recently, drawing upon the reservoir of ancient mythology to clarify the faint outlines of their predicament. With the disappearance of the separation between subject and object over the last decades, we have acquired the privilege to traverse the mythical past and supply our ancestors with the images they can elaborate on.

Keeping to conventional chronology, the late-twentieth-century impressionist media can be characterized as a system of "devices" with a secret. They derived their credibility from the fact that the users themselves were not connected, but that it was the other who looked, listened, or talked within their sensorium. At the time, this resembled a modern version of the nineteenth-century phrase "I is an other." This electronically controlled effect of alienation determined what would ultimately emerge from the artists' inner worlds and crystallize into their works. The disaffection for the media resulted from the uneasy feeling that one's authenticity was always inspired by something alien. The media had an inexhaustible reservoir of global information at their disposal. This prevented contact with the origins of the imaginary: the pictorealm of the personal unconscious almost naturally lapsed into an entropic state of disconnected items. In this eternal day of topicality, art lacked a mission of its own. Artists were driven by their lack of protection to seek maximum media market attention, an overexposure meant to safeguard their evocations of at least the shadow of a secret.

Around the year 2000, two strategies were developed which would ultimately result in the expressionist stage of the media. On the one hand, there was the flight into matter. Against the background of the highly popular antimedial mass movement, which deserted the media for reality, the socially

206

engaged artists restyled their relationship with their materials into the cult of reliability. They went back to "essentials; the perennial." They propagated their worship of substance as a reaction to the virtual, all-too-virtual of global consciousness. The artistic school of material order saw the stimulation of the memory of nature as its social responsibility. In a frenzied bid for future immortality, these ecological realists erected their monuments amid the powerful ruins of modernity. Selling their art as the ultimate chance to save humanity from the media, they engaged in a corrupt conspiracy with the World Government against the planetary population. Thus, they brought down the same fate upon themselves as had befallen folk art and social realism in the totalitarian twentieth century. With the defeat of the antimedials, even their sculptures disappeared into the dumpsters of art history.

On the other hand, the early twenty-first century witnessed the attempt of sovereign media at the dematerialization of the world. In their transnational network, the multimedial wallowed in the rush induced by short-circuiting miscellaneous media. Theirs was to be the first school to effect a direct link between the media and the sensorium. Influenced by drugs, Nietzsche, Burroughs, and Pynchon, they prepared for their ascension. Their thinkers interpreted the uneasy feeling of being visited by an Other who ignores you and imposes its world on you as white noise. Human subjectivity turned out to be a medial by-product with no further charm or danger. The sovereign artists excelled at creating artificial continents. With all their unnatural global resistance, they embarked on a journey through inner experience, from now on to be directly related to neural networks and the biosoft.

Haunted by the commercialism of psychoconsumers, the sovereign artists sought refuge in a form of medial contemplation which soon came to regard extra-laboratory experimentation as an unachievable endeavor. Threatening to succumb in their secluded world, they responded with a flight forward into research. Initially, they regarded the human brain where they had taken up residence as a model for the open architecture of their hardwares and softwares. With their neural networks and biochips, they carved a path through the think tank of Homo sapiens. Then they made an astonishing discovery: through their diligent work, they had exposed the human spirit as a timeless media matrix open for immediate exploration. But this made mere child's play of all their former tricks in VR, the cyberspace already recorded by Jules Gibson in 1985.

When art does not seek to depict its own era, it falls back on the classics. Myth is thought to contain eternal truths that can be tapped through state-of-the-art methods. Even today, mythology remains an almost inexhaustible source of forms and motifs. For centuries, the antitopical have successfully appealed to the topicality of mythology. According to them, human beings by nature imitate Oedipus or Eurydice at the most inopportune moments. They give a subtle twist to this eternal return of the same: We should not think of it as a circle, but as a spiral (Jünger) or gyre (Yeats). The unrestrained use of mythology enables the artist to present us with questionable moments that make us stop and consider the present for a moment. Even the advocates of progress are not above using myths to warn against their recurrence. After all, they're tall tales that have been around and are perfectly versatile.

The media era was a suitable age for the recovery and democratization of mythology. Having served as the legacy to the nineteenth-century poets and painters, they lost their stuffy historical connotation of traditional tales in the twentieth century. They were introduced into the narrative framework of television and computer programs as pattern recognition, which replaced the data classification of the Gutenberg universe of linear logic (McLuhan). In the twenty-first century, the authentic stories which had once united local civilizations remained universal box-office hits. Thus, they still manage to provide employment for those artists who ignore the problem of immateriality. It is precisely the physical aspect of the myths, with their candid treatment of violence, sanctity, and bestiality, which constitutes the beneficent return of a lost corporeality.

The adventurers who had set out to explore the brain of humanity and computer were uninterested in this form of mythical entertainment. When they set foot in the timeless media matrix of the mind, they gained direct access to the complex performances of the imaginary. This required no archeological excavation or prophetic gifts on their part. They found they did not have to be geniuses or chosen ones to come face-to-face with human nature and its terrors. They just happened to have the right equipment, and that in itself was shocking enough. After examining the brain's cognitive functions, they penetrated the geological strata that lay buried underneath the sensorium. In these older grounds, they encountered the grids which had inspired priests, mystics, poets, and the founders of empires and religions. The strange thing was that these heroic flagbearers of enlightenment always received fresh input from this timeless arsenal but never returned it. The only ones who could grant visions to these prophets were the ones who had access to the same strata. To their amazement, these astronauts of the brain, who were far beyond cyberspace, had to acknowledge that it was up to them to create these mental images. They accepted the invitation. After a century and a half, their science had finally found its mission. Their scientific education dictated harsh and definite messages to them. They became the artists of our present. But this also signaled the end of myth as eternal truth, and of the dialectics of art and technology.

Ever since, the task of art has been to produce the material to supply the past. After the late twenty-first century, even art will be dedicated to the pliability of the world. Artists produce images that will return forever, even in their own time. Although there exist universal works that are instant hits wherever they go, innumerable regional studios supply the local market with the future archetypes of our forebears' myths.

THE WORLD AFTER THE MEDIA

"For I am nothing, and I did not know it."
—Thomas à Kempis

The media are empty objects. Located beyond the three-dimensional, they are the mirror image of God. Just as Meister Eckhart said that loving God means loving no one, so can passion for the media only be a yearning for oblivion. Throughout history, God has always been obliged to watch over the world and to expound on meaning and future. Bombarded with prayers, sacrifices, and images, he finally died in an act of empathy with, or revenge upon, a humanity that had never accepted the fact that all he really wanted was to be no one at all.

Once God lost interest, Earth took his place as the center of the universe. When it, too, disappeared, the void at the center of the world was filled by humanity as the measure of all things. In the 1960's, after two centuries of enlightenment and industrial production, we were suddenly forced to admit that even humanity had disappeared. At that moment, the media as a whole were called in to bridge the gap and bring the ruins of history into the global picture.

Until then, the media had been innocent broadcasters of messages from transmitter to receiver. No matter how subversive or law-abiding their content, the media themselves had never defended a particular position. To rid themselves of the information they were burdened with, they had simply let it flow through. But suddenly they found themselves emancipated as the center of power in an information society advocating a belief in overall communication. Forced to be full-fledged objects, they acquired a moment of their own which would thrust them in the same direction as their predecessors.

Media became global and universal. Just as God was spread across continents by missionaries and crusades, and humans were later held responsible for all the abundance and misery in the world, so the media are now omnipresent. Every place is instantaneously represented everywhere via satellite and fiberglass; a global view is the only international perspective that remains. At the same time, every object has the capacity to become a

209

medium. Clothes, crockery, furniture, the city have become the media of a national politico-sexual identity and Zeitgeist. They are the thermometers of mental states. Trees inform us about wind force and environmental pollution. Everything transmits meaning; everything provides us with information about something other than itself. Where before there were objects, now there is information. There exists no other reality except as media. Once centralized, all things tend toward their maximum scope, only to finally disappear altogether. Even the media soon reach their omega point where spirit and matter coincide and a void is created, to be filled up by a new spirit. Whereas God needed two thousand years and humanity two centuries, the media will take two decades at the most to disappear from the stage. This megatrend is not only obvious because of the speed whereby technological systems succeed one another, but also because of the prayer-like speed of light whereby information reproduces itself. The media are already being exhibited in museums.

Film, the precursor of electronic media, was only declared the seventh art once the studio system of its industrial manufacture had collapsed. That moment, film disintegrated from an active social factor into the object of cinephilic desire. Cinephilia became the only way to view or appreciate movies. The movie industry responded by becoming mannerist and academic itself. Viewing behavior was reduced from a collective reception to an individual experience. Film, formerly a source of stories the public could easily identify with, became an art product that made you wonder what approach you yourself might have taken. Film was effortlessly absorbed by the museum as the twentieth-century art par excellence. Similar to opera as a nineteenth-century relic, film is subsidized by the public and private sectors, accompanied by the criticism and scandal that render it marketable. Cinema without media is like a fish on dry land. The same kind of conservation effort will befall the media at the beginning of the twenty-first century as the museological art of the fin de siècle. Media cannot breathe unless they are encapsulated by the digital network.

Resistance against the media's insidious self-destruction is provided by the videophile caste, who have taken to preserving the media as art in a form of protest against the threat of disappearance. These media workers have a complicated job before them. Their social position has not yet taken on a definite form. In close collaboration with the digital thinkers, they have chosen the educational task of using cable TV, the art gallery, and the museum to familiarize the backward leftist classes (who lag hopelessly behind due to their political past and are still waiting to be initiated into the medial environment) with the unprecedented possibilities of the languages and rituals of our time. On the other hand, they appear to agitate against the masses' carefree contact with the media. But their attempt to alienate or interpret television by making it appear as an object in a given environment opposes nothing, because the TV set, as a wall unit, has always been an outsider.

The World After the Media

What remains for the audiovisual avant-garde is to conduct absolutely uncommitted fundamental research into the principles of sound and image.

The isolation, aestheticization, and acceleration of images resulted in the revolutionary genre of the video clip, which immediately turned into the measure of all images and currently defines the rhythm of both feature films and news bulletins. At best, the tendency to lyophilize (scan-freeze) images and reduce television to narcissistic introspection will create a new poster culture. All the anti-techniques invented by video artists lead to an inevitable acceleration of media self-destruction. The spread of video art will contribute to the devaluation of images. In the near future, and in keeping with cinema, the public's only response to the image will be: How would I myself have produced it?

By definition, mediaphilia as a hobby is reserved for a select market segment. Passionate image collectors may be aware of the beauty of their personal preferences, yet to outsiders their collections are as meaningless as they are impressive. Indifference is the greatest threat to the still omnipresent media. The remote control, combined with the unlimited proliferation of channels, enables one to instantly eliminate uninteresting images, only to find out that none of the available images are worth watching in the first place. All-out switching between channels during commercial breaks would force even the advertisers to withdraw from the media. People will voluntarily go on a media diet out of sheer boredom, and the media addicts will be catered to by self-help groups.

Already, there are signs of a movement that, out of pure enthusiasm for an image-free society, will reintroduce socialism as a ban on images to be included in the declaration of universal human rights based on Judeo-Islamic Scripture. Just as the death of God rendered religion a private affair, so the image will become a matter of personal experience which, at best, will organize itself into secret societies of heretical mediatists. The implosion of reality in the media has been adequately recorded and proclaimed. The ban on images will cause a chain reaction: the descent of the media into reality. We will be amazed to find ourselves back in a world full of objects that no longer exude messages. Socialism, unwarranted by historical-materialist laws, will establish itself in the emptiness of the postmedial era. An object-orientated communism will reign in an image-free society.

LIFE WITHOUT CARE

The theoretical life, with all its inspirations, assumptions, dark suspicions, and far-reaching implications, becomes unbearable when the products of our pen do not result in performable tasks. Once the connections have manifested themselves, the syntaxes pose an ecological threat that requires channeling and processing. Ideas must be either safely disposed of or converted into a practicable body of thought. If they are not, the intellectual cycle becomes unsettled. Thoughts must be separated to prevent concern from accumulating. The pure thinking of yore has now become a purifying thinking, obsessed with the administration of its own mindset. This compulsive cleaning revolves around the question of disposal. Unlike before, excessive thinking no longer tends toward totalization or madness but paralyzes economic commitment. The gift of genius implies a compulsory productivity which no one in his right mind would care to accept. In the panic of being at the mercy of a processual existence full of chronic issues, it is easy to resign altogether. Urged on by the will to break out, one surrenders to the vision of a mindless nirvana. Haunted by jolts of relativism and existential doubt, we await the coming of the Spirit until all of a sudden, from an all-transcending height, we come to realize the futility of our everyday fiddlings. The cosmic perspective reveals an unburdened existence, full of clarity and simplicity. Having first glanced at this magnificence, one never wants to go back. Swept along by a rising tide of personal commitments, red tape, and inescapable dreariness, there arises an indefinable desire to be in the world, but not of it. Christian dogma suddenly sounds like a koan, lifting the veil from earthly existence.

Some stick to the daily grind; others become converts who have seen the light. But the vast majority simply gets caught up in the miasma of issues which slowly threatens to suffocate them. They are the embodiment of the demand for care. This is commonly understood as a demand for psychological advice (preferably in book form). But today, the professionals face serious competition by self-help experts, miracle workers, columnists, TV personalities, psychics, and extraordinary preachers. Any dissertation, phenomenon, or thematics may act as care. Even Madonna could help you on your way; the Adilkno agency might offer some relief; the tango could pull you out of the doldrums. Care is neither therapy nor religion. It is a practical method that alludes to the vague discontent of the multitudes. It appeals to small grievances and molds undefined self-pity into a treatable symptom in the shape of a comprehensible discourse. Care is as varied and comprehensive as life itself. It causes no harm and is obtainable without a prescription.

Apparently, care is seen as a commodity, for sale like a hotcake. Care is business, the nutrition needed to keep digestion going. Care has an aura of existential commitment lacking in everyday groceries. It frustrates any critique of consumerism. Of course there exists a flourishing market for well-being and happiness. But the genes that support our recognition of the tragic aspects of existence prevent an objectifying perspective. The economists and systematologists themselves are at a loss when it comes to current, extensive expressions of grief and despair. The sphere of care is invulnerable, and can only be understood in terms of symptoms itself. It is a different circuit. One cannot discuss care. The manual is read and never brought up again: One is ready to get back on the road. A suppression of inner confusion, it offers the comfort of a deeply involved, heartfelt pep talk. The text is mediated by a shepherd who leads his stray sheep back to the safety of the flock. It is a reassuring tale to get you back on your feet when life seems to have come to a standstill.

The crippled and maimed may proffer their severed limbs, but the psycho-prostheses readily await them. The demand for assistance has overtaken the cry of distress. Today, the genre of care functions preventatively. We are given a weekly peek at some existential abyss or other: alternative ways of mourning, divorce without stress, second-generation war criminals, gerontophilia, homeless parents, neighborhood jihads, joy without labor, bleeding for Europe. None of this bothers us, but something still just doesn't feel right. The appeal to this discomfort indicates the emptiness of being. We get a momentary glimpse of an ineffable entity rising above our daily rounds of agendas and memos. One tip of the veil of pretensions is briefly lifted, shedding light on the futility of personal encumbrances. The care managers not only have a talent for working on this state of affairs; they also possess the writing skills to express it through books, magazines, and television programs. They are the pornographers of civilized horror. Their realistic true-life tales of suffering acquaint us with the tragic turn in the lives of people like you and me.

This postmodern variation on the *ars morendi* prepares us for a meaningful chastening experience. It arms the mind against undefined threats. In place of yesterday's cod-liver oil to prevent T.B., today's pre-disabled life seeks to render us sensitive to the malady and the cure, in the secret hope that it will go away as long as you're prepared to work on it. It is all part of a process of growth, you know. Witnessing AIDS, ongoing civil wars, flesh-eating bacteria, post-Fascism, skin disease, and incontinence keeps you alert to the risky aspects of modern life. Should your time suddenly come up, then the stored info is sure to accelerate the process of acceptance. It'll give you all the time you need for a positive experience of disaster, which is beneficial for your social return. Care thus provides a sound basis for personal growth so that our human capital remains in good repair.

Panic is no longer an acute state of mind, but has become a rigid and permanent attitude. This explains the returns involved with care. It's a lot like the tabloids; even though you do not buy them, you are unconsciously being kept up to date. That is why critique of this market sector is so futile. Exposing the scam, the hypocritical pretense of commitment, the dealing in false hope, will only lead to a more carefully stylized package. At best, it will result in the dynamic revival of outdated religions or medical practices. The enlightened citizenry—the ones serial criticism is aimed at—are some of care's major customers. Doctors, teachers, managers, successful retailers, lawyers, and top officials would not be caught dead openly supporting it. Like pornography, tabloids, and entertainment programs, care is only distributed in banal editions. Easier to comment upon—besides implying that the real existential problems only affect the lower ranks of society.

A responsible and sober diet of care products enables the chosen few to plan a responsible course of life. Their prescience of maladies and diseases develops into a sense of superiority which is the real manifestation of current class-consciousness—no longer derived from income or birth, but from a ruthless sense of self-esteem that withstands everything and cannot be disturbed. They are the winners, the least needy who wallow in the consumption of lite philosophy. Instead of having to tackle terminal questions, they use care as a personal organizer to encourage functional office behavior. Like a sponge, the soft code of behavior absorbs all burning questions and renders the achievers inaccessible to human signals. After all, they themselves have noticed and explained everything in socio-technological terms at an earlier stage, so their powers of observation have grown numb and they have lost the faculty of independent interpretation. Should any problems yet arise, the only solution would be a form of metacare. But since that particular brand of wisdom is not on the market, one falls back on dishonorable self-destruction or launches an attack on the other. It is only when the conflict gets thoroughly out of hand that we really reach the peaks of human existence. Theory is not care, nor is it a substitute for forgotten services and ideologies. Now it can be dismissed of the duty to cause hope, comfort, morality, sensibility, power, salvation, and other medicinal side effects.

Self-Reception

Speculation begins beyond the zero point of meaning. When words are liberated from their burden of information, they go into ecstasy and set out exploring. Once they go their own way, they can follow any logic and anticipate any information with which they could ever possibly be saddled. Speculating with language follows the maxim "Prevention is better than deconstruction." During the working hours of the Adilkno options market, concepts, data, and unavoidable situations are short-circuited to a possible vanishing point in the future. The Adilkno speculator operates beyond the future, away from potential readers' markets. The proliferation of words evokes a chaos field through which the text determines its fatal course, leaving everybody dumbfounded, including the mixmasters themselves.

These speculative practices operate in a vacuum which the urge for text renewal has not been able to fill. The columns do not fulfill the legitimate desire for the shrieking assertion of the manifesto, nor for the careful openings of the essay. There are theories that are tired of academic discourses or journalistic impressions and simply wish to air the mind. These favorite and serene ideas soon get out of hand when they are accidentally caught up in an adilknoist line of reasoning. "Every sentence an open end" does not purify the mind, it simply makes you clam up.

The experiments with words in the twentieth century were expeditions to the center of language, and still make for neat T-shirts. Speculation, by contrast, seeks the outer edges of language, where shadows from elsewhere become legible. Here too lie the "zones of neglect" where garbage accumulates, vague rumors circulate, and the riff-raff scuttles about, hatching plots and yanking at the slot machines in the hope that the right combination of discourses will produce the winning sentence, after which the profits can immediately be put to use for new speculations. In the end, writing only costs Adilkno money, just like with the gambling addicts.

Adilkno never states its sources. This is not based on a desire for secrecy. In the media, the text needs no context, which can only increase the information load. Once the quote is pulled out of its context and perverted, magic words sprout from the textual remainder: imploded universes that do not even need to be unfolded. The magic word is not the result of reduction by data compression. It is not that which remains after all extraneous wording is deleted; the keyword simply presents itself. It does not invite to historical hermeneutics, but shifts to the future during writing.

There exists a certain pleasure in the thought of posterity who may set about deciphering it all—but that is not the issue here. The exegesis of compact text quickly reaches overload, a typical problem in contemporary text production. Speculation does not look for quality or quantity, but for amazement about the now or never of the jam session of discourses. It won't make you any richer or wiser; rather poorer, since the accidentally compiled soc/pol/cul/eco/hist ballast gets pulverized during the instant consumption of the Adilkno product. Larger connections, eras, entities, themes, moralities, and world issues disappear like a snowball in the sun. We would probably have stated the opposite tomorrow.

The unbearable lightness of the media does not have to be compensated for by diligent archivist labor. Adilkno is not expressing the fear that the text has one foot in the grave, but joyfully acknowledging the victory of the media. The old-fashioned text is thus finally relieved of its obligation to have a solid meaning, and may become impossible. The holy Script has become a toy ever since world language has consisted of images instead of words. Planetary pictoralization campaigns tread the familiar path of crisis, war, and catastrophe in order to convince the public at large of the importance of what goes on in the world. In this visual civilization, text is assigned the role of support function. As a subtitle or credit it disappears to the edge, while in the visual language of the video clip it flashes in the center as a rhythmic eye-catcher. Impossible theory does not compete with these media in a bid for popularity, but lets itself be dictated by the media it cannot do without. The world offers unlimited material, but ideas are limited and transient.

The formulation of adiltexts is drudgery compared to the dimension of data communication. Although notes are preferably made in a flush of intoxication, production time seems endless. Not because it is preceded by such thorough research, or because the final version took so long. Deleting, rewriting, improving or discussing is remarkably unpopular among adilknoists, and is done only on pain of a whole new story—"'tis only text." To us, satanic verses are not worth a war. Words are things, ways of looking at the world: and the eyes need a long time to adjust to a new view. Adilkno only works for slow media; after months of deadlines, it never sees its texts again (if at all) until six months later, by which time of course it has changed its outlook again.

The adiltext is difficult, but never causes misunderstandings regarding the permissibility of its point. Here, the dangerous text about the risky subject is played out and ruled out. Adilkno takes a warm interest in every taboo in the world, but feels no urge to break them. It is not concerned with open flirtations with (or another rehash of) the body of thought of the glorious 1920's and 1930's which examined the limits, depths, and heights of existence in the era of technology. With Adilkno, the world begins after 1945.

Self-Reception

The text has lost its deadly sting, and will never regain it. This observation lies at the basis of every adiltext.

Adilkno the author has always been a third mind: two guys and a typewriter. The acquisition of PCs has done little to change this attitude. Adiltexts cannot be produced by a single author; it takes two, four, many. The concocted text is not the sum of individuals, but something completely different, an accumulation of insights and blunders which the adilknoist alone could never have cooked up. The components of the perfect Gesamtauthor all carry their own data, stubbornly connecting them to small grievances in order to formulate adilknowledgeable patterns. The presence of the others ensures that biases and pettiness are mutually extinguished, leaving the adiltext with "observation as ideas." Adilkno is a mind-expanding substance.

The author's name is not an alias, but symbolizes a gay method, a short-circuiting, a telephone conversation. Adilkno is both cheerful theory and "happy writer." It is not a group, movement, syndicate, commune, or society, although oddly enough it is known as an agency in Greater Germany. From the beginning, it has been a foundation in formation. Adilkno has no membership or sponsors, although it does have a traveling ambassador, a special honorary member for life, and a political commissioner. Without taking the least interest in each other's particular angles, all participants just dump whatever they happen to be carrying along. It all depends on who or what drops in on an adiltext in progress.

"Sometimes a third party will call me up and say, 'Did you see or read such & such 'cos that was totally Adilknoish,' and I would have to disagree completely because it falls far below any standards of Adilknoship. Usually. Furthermore, I get the impression that Adilkno is often seen as a signal, a horn, or a guard dog; however, we may bite but we neither bark nor honk."

In dealing with the media, Adilkno does not ask itself how one may be initiated, but excommunicated. The text does not write itself out because it constantly switches from association to idea to info to deduction to the next sentence, but because it disconnects and causes breaches in thinking, theoretical casualties, and discontinuities. The rule of switching is that one thing leads to another; that of disconnecting, that one thing leads to something entirely different. The goal is not profundity, but tension. Analysis does not try to make, but to break connections. The result is textual frictions, disagreements, misunderstandings, failed or successful pranks. Concepts which once kept each other at a distance now collide. In interrupted writing, the rites of passage are reversed: from initiation to excommunication. Adilkno has achieved its goal if the general attitude becomes that of "Blah-blah-blah—oh well, it's only media." To tear and pull at the concept of "media" is a gratifying task. Media are a container with an unprecedented volume. They seem to encompass the entire world. Media theory sets out on an expedition over the edge of the medial planet, quite aware that it is round. It turns out that media omnipotence can be denied by going extraterrestrial. "We are here to go." The media are no primordial uncarved block—their surface reveals cracks and patterns, which are brought to light by the alien angle.

Media theory extracts its energy and materials from the media. It is not after symbiosis, but seeks to suck its host dry as parasitic theory. Its stake is not the revivification of connections, nor the return of the social, nor the reconstruction of the interhuman, nor the recovery of the decaying body. There are no positive goals to be discovered. Media theory is fatal to media.

AUTONOMEDIA NEW AUTONOMY SERIES
JIM FLEMING & PETER LAMBORN WILSON, EDITORS

AUTONOMEDIA CALENDARS

AUTONOMEDIA BOOK SERIES
JIM FLEMING, EDITOR

THE DAUGHTER
Roberta Allen

MARX BEYOND MARX
Lessons on the Gründrisse
Antonio Negri

MAGPIE REVERIES
James Koehnline

SCANDAL
Essays in Islamic Heresy
Peter Lamborn Wilson

TROTSKYISM AND MAOISM
Theory & Practice in France & the U.S.
A. Belden Fields

ON ANARCHY & SCHIZOANALYSIS
Rolando Perez

FILE UNDER POPULAR
Theoretical & Critical Writing on Music
Chris Cutler

RETHINKING MARXISM
Steve Resnick & Rick Wolff, eds.

THE DAMNED UNIVERSE OF CHARLES FORT
Louis Kaplan, ed.

THE TOUCH
Michael Brownstein

CLIPPED COINS, ABUSED WORDS,
CIVIL GOVERNMENT
John Locke's Philosophy of Money
Constantine George Caffentzis

HORSEXE
Essay on Transsexuality
Catherine Millot

GULLIVER
Michael Ryan

FILM & POLITICS IN THE THIRD WORLD
John Downing, ed.

AGAINST THE MEGA-MACHINE
David Watson

GOD & PLASTIC SURGERY
Marx, Nietzsche, Freud & the Obvious
Jeremy Barris

MODEL CHILDREN
Inside the Republic of Red Scarves
Paul Thorez

COLUMBUS & OTHER CANNIBALS
The Wétiko Disease & The White Man
Jack Forbes

A DAY IN THE LIFE
Tales from the Lower East Side
Alan Moore & Josh Gosniak, eds.

CASSETTE MYTHOS
The New Music Underground
Robin James, ed.

ENRAGÉS & SITUATIONISTS
The Occupation Movement, May '68
René Viénet

XEROX PIRATES
"High" Tech & the
New Collage Underground
Autonomedia Collective, eds.

MIDNIGHT OIL
Work, Energy, War, 1973–1992
Midnight Notes Collective

GONE TO CROATAN
Origins of North American
Dropout Culture
James Koehnline & Ron Sakolsky, eds.

ABOUT FACE
Race in Postmodern America
Timothy Maliqalim Simone

THE ARCANE OF REPRODUCTION
Housework, Prostitution,
Labor & Capital
Leopoldina Fortunati

BY ANY MEANS NECESSARY
Outlaw Manifestos &
Ephemera, 1965–70
Peter Stansill & David Zane Mairowitz, eds.

FORMAT AND ANXIETY
Collected Essays on the Media
Paul Goodman

THE NARRATIVE BODY
Eldon Garnet

DEMONO
(The Boxed Game)
P.M.

WILD CHILDREN
David Mandl & Peter Lamborn Wilson., eds.

¡ZAPATISTAS!
Documents of the New
Mexican Revolution
EZLN

THE OFFICIAL KGB HANDBOOK
USSR Committee for State Security

CAPITAL & COMMUNITY
Jacques Camatte

ESCAPE FROM THE NINETEENTH CENTURY
Essays on Marx, Fourier,
Proudhon & Nietzsche
Peter Lamborn Wilson

CARNIVAL OF CHAOS
On the Road with the Nomadic Festival
Sascha Altman Dubrul

AN EXISTING BETTER WORLD
A Portrait of the
Bread and Puppets Theatre
George Dennison

THE MEDIA ARCHIVE
*Foundation for the
Advancement of Illegal Knowledge*

PSYCHEDELICS REIMAGINED
Introduction by Timothy Leary,
Preface by Hakim Bey
Tom Lyttle, Editor

CRIMES OF THE BEATS
The Unbearables

PIONEER OF INNER SPACE
The Life of Fitz Hugh Ludlow,
Hasheesh Eater
Donald P. Dulchinos

DREAMER OF THE DAY
Francis Parker Yockey &
The Secret Fascist Underground
Kevin Coogan

THE ANARCHISTS
A Portrait of Civilization
at the End of the 19th Century
John Henry Mackay

BLOOD & VOLTS
Tesla, Edison, & the Birth
of the Electric Chair
Th. Metzger

ROTTING GODDESS
Origin of the Witch in Classical Antiquity
Jacob Rabinowitz

SOUNDING OFF!
Music as Resistance, Subversion, Revolution
Fred Ho & Ron Sakolsky, Editors

SEMIOTEXT(E) NATIVE AGENTS SERIES
CHRIS KRAUS, EDITOR

IF YOU'RE A GIRL
Ann Rower

THE ORIGIN OF THE SPECIES
Barbara Barg

HOW I BECAME ONE OF THE INVISIBLE
David Rattray

NOT ME
Eileen Myles

HANNIBAL LECTER, MY FATHER
Kathy Acker

SICK BURN CUT
Deran Ludd

THE MADAME REALISM COMPLEX
Lynne Tillman

I LOVE DICK
Chris Kraus

**WALKING THROUGH CLEAR WATER
IN A POOL PAINTED BLACK**
Cookie Mueller

THE NEW FUCK YOU
Adventures in Lesbian Reading
Eileen Myles & Liz Kotz, editors

READING BROOKE SHIELDS
The Garden of Failure
Eldon Garnet

AIRLESS SPACES
Shulamith Firestone

INTIMATE CORRUPTIONS
Michelle Tea

SEMIOTEXT(E), The Journal
JIM FLEMING & SYLVÈRE LOTRINGER, EDITORS

POLYSEXUALITY
François Peraldi, ed.

OASIS
Timothy Maliqalim Simone, et al., eds.

SEMIOTEXT(E) USA
Jim Fleming & Peter Lamborn Wilson, eds.

SEMIOTEXT(E) ARCHITECTURE
Hraztan Zeitlian, ed.

SEMIOTEXT(E) SF
R. Rucker, R.A. Wilson, & P.L. Wilson, eds.

RADIOTEXT(E)
Neil Strauss & Dave Mandl, eds.

SEMIOTEXT(E) CANADAS
Jordan Zinovich, ed.

IMPORTED: A READING SEMINAR
Rainer Ganahl, ed.

PLOVER PRESS

THE COURAGE TO STAND ALONE
U. G. Krishnamurti

THE MOTHER OF GOD
Luna Tarlo

AUTONOMEDIA DISTRIBUTION

DRUNKEN BOAT
An Anarchist Review
of Literature & the Arts
Max Blechman, ed.

LUSITANIA
A Journal of Reflection
& Oceanography
Martim Avillez, ed.

FELIX
The Review of Television
& Video Culture
Kathy High, ed.

RACE TRAITOR
A Journal of the New Abolitionism
John Garvey & Noel Ignatiev, eds.

XXX FRUIT
Anne D'Adesky, ed.

BENEATH THE EMPIRE OF THE BIRDS
Carl Watson

ONE NO, MANY YESES
Midnight Notes Collective

LIVING IN VOLKSWAGEN BUSES
Julian Beck

I SHOT MUSSOLINI
Elden Garnet

ANARCHY AFTER LEFTISM
Bob Black

ALL COTTON BRIEFS
M. Kasper

BELLE CATASTROPHE
Carl Watson & Shalom

SKULLS HEAD SAMBA
Eve Packer

BROKEN NOSES AND METEMPSYCHOSES
Michael Carter

WATERWORD
Star Black

RAW AIR
Cheryl Boyce-Taylor

I AM SECRETLY AN IMPORTANT MAN
Steven Jesse Bernstein

CAUGHT LOOKING
Feminist Anti-Censorship Task Force